Motherless

Motherless

A True Story of Love and Survival

KARINA SCHAAPMAN

Translated by Rosalind Buck

JOHN MURRAY

The publication of this book has been made possible with financial support from the Foundation for the Production and Translation of Dutch Literature.

English translation © Rosalind Buck 2007

First published in Great Britain in 2007 by John Murray (Publishers)
A division of Hodder Headline

1

A CIP catalogue record for this title is available from the British Library

Hardback ISBN 978-0-7195-6427-7
Trade paperback ISBN 978-0-7195-6434-5

Typeset in 11.5/14 Monotype Bembo by Servis Filmsetting Ltd, Manchester

Printed and bound by
Clays Ltd, St Ives plc

Hodder Headline policy is to use papers that are natural, renewable and recyclable products and made from wood grown in sustainable forests. The logging and manufacturing processes are expected to conform to the environmental regulations of the country of origin.

John Murray (Publishers)
338 Euston Road
London NW3 9BH

For my children.

Some things are unavoidable.

This book had to be written.

Apart from you, I dedicate this book to Eve.

Contents

I

Leiden

1968
My name is Karina and I'm eight years old. I live with my mother in a flat on the second floor of a house in Hoflaan, in Leiden. Everything is different in our home from the other children's houses in the road. There's just the two of us. My father left my mother the day I was born.

I've got a sister who's two years older than me and a brother who's three years older. They live with my father. I've never seen my father, or my brother and sister. My mother hasn't got any pictures of them. When she talks about my brother and sister it makes her cry. She misses them a lot. She always says that I ought to go and see them when I'm old enough and if I want to, but I don't want to. I think my father must be a nasty man.

My mother comes from Indonesia but most people think she's Chinese. She speaks petjo, a kind of Indonesian Dutch, but when we meet other Indonesian people she speaks Malaysian.

In the street, people often call us peanut-pooh-chinkies or rice pickers. Sometimes, when we're going up the stairs, the ladies who live in the other flats tell us to go home, back to our own bloody country. My mother looks people who say things like that right in the eye, then she just walks on without saying a word. If anybody says anything really nasty to her, she spits on the ground to show what she thinks of them. She never speaks to the neighbours.

They say we stink but I can't smell anything. My mother once told me it's because the Belandas, as she calls the Dutch people, don't use garlic or trassie shrimp paste.

We think the neighbours' cooking stinks, too, but my mother would never say anything.

★

Because my mother is divorced and doesn't work, she gets money from the Social Security. We go and collect it every Wednesday afternoon. Then we walk through town first. In the park I climb on the statue or in a tree while my mother has a rest. Then we walk past the fire station. I always hope they'll be practising because then you're allowed to hold the hose or have a ride on the fire engine. The fire station is very near the Social Security office, where we always have to queue up until it's our turn. My mother hates that. She's embarrassed. She looks at the ground all the time we're in the queue and says *adu*, so *malu*, so shameful. After she's filled in a piece of paper they give us the money.

As soon as we've got our money we go to the cafeteria in the Vroom & Dreesmann department store where I always have a chocolate cream bun. My mother has a cup of coffee. Then we go to the *toko*, the Indonesian grocer's, where we buy tofu, trassie, garlic, bean sprouts, chillies, dried fish, salted meat and rice for the whole week. The owner of the *toko* is Chinese. He always gives me a packet of dried banana as a present. And sometimes he has something special for my mother, fresh spices from Indonesia. He keeps them on one side for her. He always gives us strings of firecrackers to hang in the window on New Year's Eve. The banging chases the evil spirits away.

After the *toko* we go and see Bram, the milkman, to pay the bill. Bram comes every day with the milk and a few groceries. We buy things from him on the slate and pay him on Wednesdays. My mother never has enough money. The last couple of days in the week we usually have hardly anything left to eat. My father is supposed to pay us maintenance, which is why we get less money from the Social Security. But he's never given us a cent.

My mother's got two sisters in America, Auntie Lucia and Auntie Bea, who send us dollars at Christmas and Easter. I'm allowed to change the dollars into guilders at the bank myself and then my mother lets me go and buy myself something nice, or some sweets. Because we haven't got much money, if we need something expensive we buy it from the catalogue and pay for it in instalments. They send us a new catalogue every few months. We look through it together and make a list of all the things we would like. We don't usually get any further than making lists because the things in the catalogue are too expensive for us and you're only allowed to buy one thing at a time on hire purchase. What we would really like is a radio.

Our flat looks quite different from other children's homes. In our sitting room there's a single bed where we sleep together. Our bed is the cosiest place in the flat. We go to bed at the same time and then I always get my mother to tell me about the old days. She can tell really exciting stories.

She's superstitious so she thinks up a ritual for all the evil spirits, to keep them from the door. I found a peacock's feather the other day, a really long one, with soft, shiny little feathers. The end of the feather was fan-shaped, with a bright-blue, shiny spot in it. My mother says the spot is called the peacock's eye and it brings bad luck. I'm allowed to look at the feather and touch it but I'm not allowed to bring it home. She always burns incense to keep the spirits in a good mood. And on the wall above our bed is a *kris*, from Indonesia. It's a kind of wavy dagger. I'd really like to play with it but my mother won't let me touch it. The *kris* has to stay on the wall. If danger threatens, it will fall to the ground, all by itself. Then my mother will be warned.

My mother believes in *guna-guna*, the power of the black arts.

She likes to tell me about her life in Indonesia, where her family was rich. They had a piano and *babus* who cooked and cleaned the house. They had a tiger as well, which my grandad had found as a cub in the forest. They brought it up, but when it got big they had to let it go to a zoo. The tiger pined away in a cage there and died of loneliness.

And my mother sings Indonesian songs. *Ajun ajun ajun, high up in the coconut tree, ajun ajun masmira, djangan main gila*. We sing this song when we get together with other Indonesian people as well. It's a jolly song. She sings sad songs, too. Those are always in Malaysian. 'Jalan Kenangan' is my favourite song. She sings it in a very soft, high voice. It's about memories and tender embraces. My mother calls it a song of longing.

She can tell really exciting stories about the Japanese who committed hara-kiri after they lost the war. My mother was in a Jap camp with her mother and her sisters. And she always tells me about the long voyage to Holland, when they were sailing through the Suez Canal and they were scared they would be kidnapped by Arabs and made to serve in a harem. My mother didn't want to leave Indonesia at all but, after the capitulation of the Japanese, my grandma didn't want to stay. It was getting too dangerous. My grandad refused to go. He didn't want to eat potatoes with salt in Holland so he stayed behind in Indonesia.

I like it when my mother tells me about the old days, even though I've heard most of the stories several times before.

In our sitting room, apart from our bed, there's a little desk with two drawers in it. We use the desk as a table, too. We've got a paraffin heater but we're not sure how to use it properly; sometimes it works and sometimes it doesn't. And at the end of our bed is a cupboard. In the back room I always build huts. And then we've got the *rombeng* room, which is full of junk.

Every last Friday in the month, people put things out in the road that they want to be collected by the dustbin men. Before school I look around the streets for things I can play with or make something out of. Sometimes my mother helps if I've seen something I want that's too heavy for me to carry. She always makes jokes when I come home with my arms full of stuff. She laughs and says, 'You look like a real *tukang rombeng*, a rag-and-bone man.' I keep everything I drag home off the street in the box-room.

What we haven't got is a radio or a television. When I sit by the window in the evening I can look through the window of the neighbours' across the road. I can always see their television, a blue, flickering light, but it's just too far away to see what's on. In the summer, when the windows are open, I can hear the sound of televisions and radios.

Our kitchen is a bit empty. We haven't got a fridge or a washing machine or a gas cooker. My mother cooks on a paraffin stove. The rice steamer is on all day because we eat rice for breakfast and lunch, too. I know the other children eat bread then. Actually, I think bread is nicer. Sometimes, my mother buys bread for me, as a surprise.

The other mothers in the road all look a bit the same. Most of them have blond hair and they wear aprons all the time. They do the washing on Mondays and they all speak with a thick Leiden accent. My mother says they are common. She thinks the people in our road have big mouths. She keeps saying she doesn't want me to grow up like them.

My mother wears completely different clothes. She makes most of them herself, by hand. She buys material at the market. Sometimes she wears a sarong, but other times she wears trousers. The other mothers never do. My mother always wears makeup. She uses eyebrow pencil, draws black lines under her eyes and puts on lipstick. When we walk past workmen, they whistle and call things after her. My mother's got really long, black hair, which I like playing with. I give her a bun, or plaits, and sometimes we both make our hair curly.

I think my mother is pretty, but I still wish she looked like the other mothers.

Sometimes we go and see Mrs Dezentjé. She comes from Indonesia, too. My mother speaks Malaysian with her. Mrs Dezentjé cooks a lot and she makes nice food. She nearly always gives us something to take home. Sometimes we help her with the cooking, making *lempers* or spring rolls. Her children are already grown up, but they still come round to dinner a lot. Mrs Dezentje smokes *kreteks*, clove cigarettes. My mother smokes them with her. When we get home after visiting her, my clothes smell of *kretek*, nice and sweet. I keep smelling them. Now and again she gives us a bag of second-hand clothes.

A few times a year, we go to The Hague for a *kumpulan*, a meeting of Indonesian people. I really like that. Everybody takes something to eat and they all talk and sing about Indonesia. My mother knows loads of people there. She talks and laughs a lot; she never does that in Leiden. She always finds it really difficult to say goodbye when it's time to go home. Whenever we've been to the *kumpulan* she gets homesick for Indonesia. Then she can't help crying, it's so *kassian*, so sad. Sometimes we even stay the night with friends of hers from a long time ago.

Sometimes we have to go to court. That's in The Hague, too. Then my mother is always scared they'll make me go and live with my father. He wants custody.

★

There's a playground on the corner of our road where I go after school every day. There's a little wooden hut in the playground. That's where the caretaker sits. He's really old and nice. He sorts out the old newspapers every week. I usually help him because there are always a couple of *Donald Ducks* in with them and he lets me take them home. I think he's the only person in the road who ever says anything nice about my mother.

I don't like it at school. I get bullied so I always have to be on my guard. Sometimes the children let me play with them but that usually means they need me for something. Sometimes they start bullying another girl and they tell me to go and hit her. I think that's nasty but I do what they say because they let me play with them as a reward. Then I'm one of them for a little while. When we have gym and we have to be in two teams, I'm always the last one to be chosen. I can tell nobody wants me in their team, except when we have dodgeball. I'm really good at that. I get everybody out and then I'm the last one in.

The children in my class say I stink. When we're getting dressed after gym, they deliberately go and stand a long way away from me. Sometimes someone pushes another girl against me and then she brushes herself off really hard. As if you can catch something off me. I think they're horrid children but I'd like to be friends with them, all the same.

My mother fetches me from school every day. In the summer, we walk home through the rose garden. My mother likes flowers and she picks rose petals to put in our bed. Sometimes we go to the Leidsevaart Canal and she throws flowers in the water in memory of her brother who died at sea in the war. When she does that I always hope none of the children from our road will see us. I get embarrassed when she does Indonesian things in the street.

After school I sometimes play with Sandra. She lives a bit further up the road in a house with her parents, her auntie, her uncle, her cousin and her nan and grandpa. Their house has got two floors and they've got nine rooms. It's full of furniture, lamps and ornaments. It looks really cosy. All the furniture and curtains are pink or red.

Everyone in the road is a bit scared of San's family. They talk really roughly and don't mind getting into arguments. My mother always ignores them because she's scared they might suddenly shout at her. She says San's mother uses a lot of bad language. I like San's mother, though. You can have a laugh with her. San's grandpa's got a beer belly. He sits by the window all day with her nan. They've got mirrors on the outside of the window, too, so they can look back down the street from where they're sitting.

San's got a lot of clothes and toys.

November 1968
Late in the afternoon, we're on our way to buy a can of paraffin for the heater when San's mother speaks to us. She hangs out of the window and asks my mother if she wants a puppy. The mother dog hasn't got any milk left and it's too much work for them to have to feed all those puppies themselves. My mother, who would rather have walked straight past San's mother, politely answers that she'll think about it.

We go and buy the paraffin at the chemist's. On the way back I keeping saying 'Please can we have that puppy' and then, all of a sudden, to my surprise my mother says, 'Okay, Karina, you can have the puppy.'

I'm so pleased when we ring the bell at San's. We wait in the hall and after a while San's mother comes back with a tiny little Alsatian. It just fits in my mother's hand. San's mother gives us a bottle with a pipette which we can use as a teat. The puppy can't eat by itself and has to be fed several times a day. She tells my mother what kind of food she should give it.

My mother carries the puppy home under her coat. When we get home we put it on the bed. It looks as if it can't walk yet. My mother says the puppy is actually much too small to be taken away from its mother. We'll have to take really good care of it. I make it a cosy little nest out of a blanket. The puppy starts whining. My mother goes and mixes some food for it.

Once the puppy has been fed and is sleeping happily, we think of a name. It's a little girl dog and it's black and brown. I want to give it my mother's name. She doesn't mind. So now the puppy is called Nita. Nitadog.

The next day, at school, I can hardly wait until the bell goes. I keep thinking about Nitadog. When school is finally over, I run ahead of my mother, home to Nitadog. I've never run so fast.

January 1969

It's been snowing. There's a thick layer on the street. The cars and bushes are all white. On the grass behind our house, some children are making great big snowballs to build a snowman.

I go out on the balcony with my mother. There's lots of snow on the edge of the balcony. We make snowballs and throw them down. There are some big boys on the grass further up. When they see us throwing snowballs, they come and stand under our balcony and throw snowballs back. At first it's fun, but we soon realise they don't mean it as fun. They're throwing them really hard and starting to swear, too.

Some fathers come out and join in. My mother pulls me inside, into the kitchen. We can hear them calling us, daring us to come out again. My mother tries to ignore it. But when they start shouting at us to go home, back to our own country, filthy whore, peanut-pooh chinky, then she can't stand it any longer. She runs out on to the balcony and furiously starts throwing snowballs back. I help her.

The neighbours are squeezing the snow tight into ice balls now. An ice ball hits my mother hard in the eye. I want them to stop. Then the kitchen window breaks behind me. My mother drags me inside. Her eye is all red and swollen. She bursts into tears. I start crying with her. What happened? We can still hear them shouting outside and snowballs keep thudding against the windows.

My mother goes and lies on the bed with a damp cloth over her eye. I think it's so *kassian*. I feel so sorry for her. She warns me not to go too near the windows in case they break another one. Together, we wait for the shouting to stop. I'm frightened.

In the afternoon, when things have quietened down, we go to the shop to buy some nails. My mother's wearing a headscarf. She keeps her head right down, as if she's afraid people will see she's got a black eye. It's all watery and swollen shut. We walk quickly. I don't dare to look around. I'm scared the neighbours will start throwing snowballs at us again if they see us.

When we get back, I help my mother nail a board across the broken window. When we've finished, she draws the curtains in the sitting room.

She says she's never going to open them again. She doesn't want to have anything to do with anybody any more.

February 1969

We keep a folder in our desk. All the important papers are in the folder.

There are thin sheets of old paper from Indonesia. There's a form that says my grandad acknowledged my mother as his child when she was six years old. There's a paper that says she behaved herself properly in Indonesia. Without that, she wouldn't have been able to come on the boat to Holland. There are also letters and papers from my mother's divorce in there.

We look in the folder quite often. There's a story to go with each paper. I know them all.

A little while ago, my mother found a newspaper on a bench in the park and brought it home. There was an important article in it. She cut it out and put it in the folder. She told me to keep it always. It's about fathers who are divorced from their wives and children and don't pay any maintenance, or mistreat them. In the past, when these children wanted to get married, they had to ask their fathers for permission, even if those fathers didn't live at home any more and they didn't know them. The article says there is going to be a new law. My mother says that when I'm grown up and want to get married, I won't need my father's permission. Permission from the court is enough. The newspaper article has gone all brown. My mother looks at it a lot.

Spring 1969

There's a coal box on the balcony. It's got a little door at the bottom and a pair of pigeons recently started using it as their house. The pigeons are used to me. If I stand really still, holding out some rice, then they land on my arm and peck the grains from my hand.

They've built a nest in the coal box. If I lift the little door, the pigeons just sit there on their nest and don't move. They've laid some eggs and I'm hoping that babies will come out of them. Then, one day, it finally happens. My mother fetches me from school and tells me the eggs have hatched. We carefully peep in. There are two ugly little baby pigeons in the nest. They're bald, with bulgy, closed eyes and red beaks with a thick yellow edge. They sit chirping away with their beaks wide open. The mother pigeon sticks her head right down inside their open beaks. That's how she feeds her chicks. My mother explains exactly how it works. I could watch the pigeons all day long. The babies are growing very quickly and are really tame. They sometimes eat out of my hand, now, too.

One day, the doorbell rings and a boy we don't know comes upstairs. He's holding a wounded pigeon. The poor bird is bleeding. He found it in the road and someone told him we kept pigeons. Perhaps we could look after it?

My mother takes the pigeon from the boy and thanks him. She puts it on the counter in the kitchen. Its breast is torn and its wings are all limp. I can hardly bear to look at it, it's so *kassian*. My mother washes the wound with cotton wool and wraps little strips of sheet around the pigeon. She puts it in a little basket and gives it a few grains of cooked rice. She's afraid it won't survive, but maybe the pigeon will be lucky.

We haven't had any money for a few days now. There's nothing left to eat in the house. My mother is worried. Just a bit longer and then we can go to the Social Security, but today I'm hungry. My mother suggests going for a good, long walk with Nitadog; it will help me stop thinking about food all the time. When we get back from the walk, I feel sick. We're already nearly home but I think I'm going to faint. I grab hold of a lamppost.

My mother begins to cry. She picks me up and carries me home, where she lays me on the bed and promises to make me something nice to eat. She starts talking about the injured pigeon. She tells me it has got worse and it would be better to put it out of its misery. At first I don't want to hear about it, but she assures me it's better for the pigeon; it won't suffer any more and she can cook the pigeon with spices, so we'll have something to eat. I never knew people ate pigeons but my mother says it's actually quite posh, because only rich people eat pigeons. In Indonesia rich people eat frogs' legs, as well; the Belandas don't eat them but they taste really nice.

She manages to convince me. When I ask how she's going to kill the pigeon, she says she'll chop its head off in one go, so it won't feel a thing. But she wants me to stay in the sitting room so I won't see. I agree. While she's in the kitchen I go and sit at the desk and press my hands tight over my ears. I'm so scared I'll hear the chop. I must have fallen asleep while I was waiting. Now my mother is waking me up: 'Dinner's ready. *Selamat makan!*'

I can smell something delicious. My mother puts a dish on the table. I can't recognise the pigeon. It looks just like a little *ajam*, a chicken, on my plate. I start eating and it actually tastes rather nice. My mother takes a very small piece for herself. While I'm chewing the meat off the bones, I remember the wounded pigeon. I hope it died straight away but I don't dare ask about it.

In the evening, we drink the stock it was cooked in. My mother says it makes you as strong as a lion.

June 1969
My mother can draw and paint beautifully. Mostly she does Madonnas in watercolour, or lilies, which are her favourite flowers. I always make paper dollies, then cut them out to play with. I usually make a family with twelve children, including a brother, an ugly mean sister, a nice fat sister, a really pretty sister and a little baby. Then there's a father and mother, a grandad and grandma and a couple of uncles and aunts. My mother helps me make a house for them out of cardboard boxes. She makes glue from the water she's cooked rice in. It gets really thick and sticks paper well. Sometimes she uses it to stiffen the collars of her blouses, too.

We chose a radio from the catalogue and we've ordered it. I hope it comes quickly. Around dinnertime I can always hear the neighbours' radio playing. There's a man with a really nice voice who does a request programme and plays records for people's birthdays. I love the man's voice; I could listen to it all the time.

When I get home from school a couple of days later, there's a parcel on the table. My mother asks me if I'd like to open it. It's the radio. It's even nicer than in the catalogue. It's got two round knobs and a glass plate with numbers behind it. You can move a little red line over the numbers if you turn the knobs.

First, my mother reads the instructions. Then she takes the lead out of a little bag and plugs it into the radio. Then she puts the plug in the socket. She waits for a moment, to make it even more exciting, and then she switches it on. The room fills with music. It's so lovely. It sounds funny now when we talk to each other.

We try all the different stations that belong to the numbers. Sometimes it just crackles, or you can hear someone talking. We put the line on a number where music comes out. I keep stroking the radio. The front is cream and the sides are mint green. Now I can listen to the request programme every day.

Summer 1969
On the corner of the street, next to the playground, is a big field where a circus comes every year. There are posters up everywhere now. The day the circus arrives I get up early. When I stick my head out of the window, I can already see the big lorries in the distance. I go over for a minute with Nitadog before school. They're busy putting up the tent. A lady comes out of a caravan and calls me over. She asks if I'd like to fetch two buckets of water for her.

Luckily it's Wednesday and I only have to go to school in the morning. That afternoon, when I go to look at the circus again, the tent is up. There's a barrier and circus lorries and vans all around it in a big circle. I can see the performers behind the barrier. They're busy dressing up the animals. The woman I fetched the water for waves at me. She asks if I could hold a horse for a minute. I clamber over the barrier and go and stand where she shows me. There I am, with a dressed-up horse. The lady explains to me that someone else will come and fetch the horse in a minute. In the meantime, she goes off to change for the show.

There are artistes dashing up and down all around me. Music is coming from the tent and I can hear children shouting. The ringmaster welcomes the audience. Each time they clap, the curtain flies open and the artistes go on one after another. The horse lady is wearing a sparkly dress now. She is performing with dogs. Then a man takes the horse from me and disappears into the tent. Just for a moment, I don't know what to do, but then a clown calls me over. He shows me a place where I can watch the show through a split in the curtain.

The next day, my mother comes with me to look at the animals. There are lions and panthers. I want to show her the horse, too, but all the animals are still in their trailers. We're just about to go, when a man comes up to us. I recognise him; it's the ringmaster. He recognises me, too, and asks if I'm going to come and hold the horse again today.

That afternoon, after school, I walk along the barrier. The ringmaster calls to me. He asks me if I've come by myself. When I nod, he gives me two tickets for the show. One for me and one for my mother. I run home as fast as I can. My mother doesn't want to take the ticket – she never likes to accept things from people. She tells me to go to the show with one of the children in our street.

I go with Sandra. When the show is over, the ringmaster says the circus is leaving that night. He asks if there any children who would like to help take the tent down. I put my hand up and he chooses me and a couple of others. We stay behind in the empty tent. A man comes up and asks us to help carry planks from the stands to a lorry outside the tent. When the tent is completely empty, it is taken down.

It's late by now, and starting to get dark. My mother comes to see where I've got to. I want to stay and help for a bit longer. Then the ringmaster goes over to my mother and shakes her hand. While they're talking to each other, I take advantage of the situation to help with the carrying.

All the lorries and vans are ready to leave now. The field is empty again. I can see my mother still talking to the ringmaster. They're standing next to the lions. She's accepted something to drink and is holding a cup. She calls me over and tells the ringmaster my name. He ruffles my hair. Then we go home. My mother shakes hands with him. She looks happy and a bit naughty and says goodbye to him in a funny way. Walking home, we both think it's a shame the circus is moving on.

A week later, there's a letter in the postbox. A letter from the circus with a red and green circus stamp. As soon as my mother opens it, her face is suddenly all smiles. When she's finished reading it, she takes me in her arms and we dance around. The ringmaster from the circus wants to come and visit us. He asks if that's all right. My mother writes back straight away. A week later we get his reply. He's coming on Friday night.

My mother is really nervous. She laughs, talks and sings and the whole flat gets a spring-clean.

Finally it's Friday night. My mother has made herself look really beautiful. Nitadog is just as nervous as we are. My mother has made up a bed for me in the back room from one of the mattresses I usually use for building dens. She thinks the ringmaster might want to stay the night and we won't all fit in the single bed in the front room. We agree that I'll go to the back room like a good girl when she tells me.

The doorbell rings. My mother opens the door. I hear her saying softly, '*Selamat datang.*' Welcome. She comes back into the front room, followed by the ringmaster.

He's wearing a smart suit and smells of cologne. He gives her a bunch of flowers and me a big bag of sweets. He says the sweets were left over from what they sell in the interval. I've never had so many sweets at one time before. I go and sit on the bed with Nitadog to sort them out. My mother has specially bought a jar of Nescafé and makes a cup of coffee for the ringmaster. They talk and laugh. And then my mother says, '*Ajo, tidur*. Okay, time for bed.' I go to the back room as we agreed. First I shake hands with the ringmaster and say goodnight. My mother promises to come and give me a kiss. I take my sweets to bed with me.

Nitadog and I lie listening to them. I can hear their voices but I can't understand what they're saying. I can't sleep. When my mother comes to kiss me goodnight, I ask when the ringmaster's going home. I want to get in her bed as usual. I can't sleep by myself. She says he's going to stay the night and I must to try and get to sleep by myself. If I need her I can call. Nitadog gets under the blanket with me.

They're laughing; it sounds as if they're playing around. I can see a strip of light between the curtains in front of the sliding doors. If I look through the gap perhaps I'll be able to see what they're doing. Quietly, I slip out of bed. I can see my mother sitting on the ringmaster's lap. He's pushed her dress up and he's holding her bare bottom.

I'm shocked. I hear my mother laughing loudly again. I don't want to see them or hear them any more. I go and lie down next to Nitadog with my hands over my ears, as far under the covers as possible.

When I wake up in the morning I go into the front room. The ringmaster's still asleep. My mother puts a finger to her lips. I lift the blanket and snuggle up next to her. She takes me in her arms. But she stinks. I get out of bed. She smells quite different.

I go into the kitchen. When my mother comes over to me, I can smell that smell again. I push her away and tell her she stinks. It makes her laugh. I want the ringmaster to go. She tells me he's leaving in a minute because he has to take care of the animals. I can see him in the front room putting on his pants. I get a shock when I see his willy; I've never seen anything like that before. Once the ringmaster has got his shirt on he puts on some cologne. At least that smells nice and fresh. He doesn't want anything to eat; he's in a hurry. He'll come again next week, he says. In the hallway, he hugs my mother and kisses her. I can see them putting their tongues in each other's mouths when they're kissing. He shakes my hand.

My mother is in a good mood after he's left, but I'm really cross with her. I don't like them doing things like that. She says she's in love. His name is Rob Roberti and from now on I should just call him Rob. But I mustn't tell anyone she's in love or that he stayed the night. If the Social Security hears that, maybe we won't get any more money.

I promise her I won't tell anyone.

Autumn 1969

Now Rob the ringmaster comes every weekend. He's staying in Aalsmeer, the place where the animal stalls and the caravans are parked for the winter. I've been there with him a couple of times. His parents live there, too, in a wooden house with an orchard. Behind the orchard is a large greenhouse, which is where the stalls are, and there is a big workshop where the props are done up for the new season. Outside the greenhouse is what looks like a junkyard. It's full of old cars and stuff that's not used any more. Rob's caravan is right in the middle of it. He lives there by himself.

Spring 1970

Rob comes round a lot and we often go to Aalsmeer, as well. He's worked hard on a new programme all winter but he still hasn't managed to find enough artistes to make a really good show of it. Performers cost him a lot of money. And it's difficult to find lorry drivers who want to help put up the tent and take it down.

He's decided to stay at home this season and do up the circus. He might even buy a new tent when he's saved enough money. Rob wants to go for the next season in a big way. He's bought two new horses. They're called Hassan and Macness. They still have to be trained. The circus is getting a new colour scheme, too. The circus's colours used to be red and yellow and now all the vehicles, the barriers and the props are is going to be painted blue and yellow. Rob's father is painting horses and elephants on the entrance. We help as much as we can.

We visit other circuses and talk to the performers; maybe they'd like to come and work with us. I'm allowed to do tightrope walking; I've already started practising an act. Actually, I prefer the trapeze but my mother is afraid I'll fall. Not so much can happen on the tightrope. The rope won't be put up high until I'm good at it. Right now, I can't fall more than a few feet.

July 1970

We've had a telegram from Rob's mother. He's been attacked by the lions and he's in hospital. My mother rang his mother straight away from a telephone box. She came back crying. Rob is in the teaching hospital in Amsterdam. He's badly injured. His father is hurt, too, but less badly than Rob. My mother wants to go and see him but she hasn't got enough money for the train fare.

She doesn't want to wait for the Social Security, so she decides to borrow the money from Mrs Dezentjé. Once she's been to fetch it, she goes to visit Rob. I'm not allowed to go with her.

I wait all afternoon and all evening. It is dark by the time my mother gets back.

I can see she's been crying. Her makeup is all smudged on her cheeks. Rob has got wounds all over his body. His arm was almost torn off and he's got scratches from lions' claws and deep bites everywhere. He's had an operation and is covered in bandages except for his face. He's in a lot of pain and will have to stay in hospital for at least a couple of weeks. His father has already gone home; he only needed stitches.

My mother tells me that the accident happened when Rob was just going to rehearse with the lions. He'd forgotten to take his pistol into the cage with him. The animals probably sensed something was wrong and then they attacked him. Rob's father heard him screaming and tried to pull the lions off but then they attacked him, too. It was only when Rob's mother sprayed the lions with a fire extinguisher that they left Rob alone and his father was able to drag him away. His whole body was torn open.

He's afraid he won't be able to perform any more. He might never be able to move his arm again. Rob's not allowed to keep the lions now they've attacked him so they have been taken to a zoo.

September 1970
Rob is back out of hospital. He's got thick red scars all over his body. You can clearly see where his right arm was almost pulled off. He practises with it every day. It's getting better all the time; he can already lift things. He's lucky he can still move his hand.

His mother is glad the lions have gone. She doesn't ever want Rob to have big cats again. Rob disagrees.

Now that he doesn't have to travel with the circus, he can stay with us longer. His father looks after the animals when he's at our house. So now he comes every Saturday evening and stays until Sunday afternoon. He brings his portable television with him. I watch telly until late on Saturday evening.

Rob always parks his car a couple of streets away so no one can see that he sleeps at our house.

October 1970
We've had a letter from the Social Security. We don't have to go and collect the money every Wednesday any more. From now on, they will send it to the bank on the corner of our street.

Now we can go and get money out of the bank every week with a deposit book. My mother is really pleased about that because she won't have to stand in the queue any longer. You never get used to it, she says. I think it's a shame, really, because we never go to Vroom & Dreesmann any more on Wednesday afternoons to have a bun. We still go to the *toko*, though. Rob gives my mother some extra money when he's with us; he loves Indonesian food. My mother doesn't really want to take it to begin with, but it does mean she can make extra-nice things for him. So she accepts it after all.

December 1970

We celebrated Saint Nicholas for the first time. I got some presents from Rob, a packet of plasticine and a box of coloured pencils. My mother doesn't know how to celebrate Saint Nicholas; they never did it in Indonesia. She feels embarrassed when she gets presents from Rob. She would really like to put them on one side; in Indonesia you never open presents in front of other people. It's really difficult for her to do it.

Spring 1971

It seems like my mother is getting more scared of the people in the street now that Rob comes round so often. She keeps warning me that nobody must know he sleeps at our house. She thinks she won't get any more money from the Social Security if they find out and she's afraid the Child Welfare will take me away from her.

Summer 1971

At last it's the summer holidays. I'm allowed to go on tour with the circus. The last few days I could hardly stop myself telling Sandra and the other children in the playground. Instead I told them I'm going to stay with my uncle. My mother is staying at home and will only come to the circus at weekends with Nitadog.

There are some new performers this season but I already know everybody. When I arrive in the circus grounds, Francien takes me straight to the kitchen wagon. In the back, next to Hans the clown's room, they've made a little room for me. A tiny space with a really narrow bed. You can hardly stand up in there. In the corner there's a pee bucket.

Everyone is sitting in the kitchen wagon, ready for coffee. They're glad I'm travelling with them for the whole of the holidays. They make jokes, saying I'll have to work really hard. As soon as they've drunk their coffee everyone gets to work; there's a performance this afternoon.

The show goes smoothly. Now I know exactly which number follows which and what has to be got ready for each one. Rob has had a jacket made for me, with the circus's name on it. The stable boys and the props managers wear jackets like that, too, and he's asked me to put the jacket on when the show starts.

When we move on to another town we always have to get up early. Rob wakes everybody up in the morning by banging on their doors. He bangs on Hans's door until he answers. It's still only six o'clock by then. One by one everybody comes to get a cup of coffee. Rob is the first one to set off. He has to drive up and down twice, sometimes three times, with the lorries, because there aren't enough lorry drivers.

When we arrive in the town we park the vans in a circle round the place where the big top will be. Everyone lends a hand putting up the tent. I fetch buckets of water for the animals.

While the tent is going up I help lace the canvas sheets together. I'm really quick at that. Then the men get on and put up the stands and the ring while the women go and do the shopping. Once the ring is ready, I can scatter the sawdust and rake it smooth. The sawdust smells of resin.

Once most of the work has been done and the barriers are set up, the newly painted entrance is put in place. It's a kind of gateway the audience will be going through in a while. Putting up the barriers is a job I enjoy; usually some children come along to watch. Sometimes I have to ask the people to move back so I can put up a barrier. They do just as I say.

After lunch, the animals are fed and watered and the preparations for the performance begin. Rob is usually in the ticket wagon, selling tickets.

If we're staying longer than one day then people rehearse in the tent in the evening. Everyone works hard. Sometimes I'm allowed to go and help put up the posters in the town where we'll be the next week. Rob has had photo cards advertising the circus printed, too. I stamp the name and address of the circus on the back and give them out to curious children who come and watch us fixing the posters to the lampposts.

I'm always proud to be with the circus.

Winter 1971

Now we are spending a lot of time with Rob in the winter quarters at Aelsmeer.

The circus did well last summer so Rob wants a larger tent and more artistes. He wants it to get bigger every year. He always says, 'We don't perform in the circus to earn money; we earn money so we can perform.' My mother teases him about it. She says he doesn't know when to stop and he's *bingoeng*, a bit loopy. When she says that they always start messing around.

Rob thinks it's a shame he still hasn't got a licence for big cats. He says he'll just have to tame my mother, then. Her Indonesian expressions always make him laugh. They kiss and cuddle a lot, too.

Rob is going to buy us a gas cooker. He loves Indonesian food and he says you can cook it better that way. My mother doesn't really want him to buy it, but I mustn't tell Rob. She says you shouldn't look a gift horse in the mouth. I'd rather have a television; I think it's a waste of all that money.

Spring 1972

Rob has bought a new tent, one with two poles. It can seat a thousand people. We set up the tent in Delft and then the photos are taken for the new posters and the photo cards, which we don't give away free any more. Rob is worried that the new season might not make enough money. The tent was terribly expensive.

It's only been standing two days when there is a heavy storm. The roof is torn to shreds. Rob has to take it to Germany to get it mended. He sends the artistes home. They can't perform as long as there's no tent.

Summer 1972

My mother's got some sexy magazines. Sometimes I get them out to look at the pictures. I want to have breasts, too. Some of the girls in my class have already got them. My mother gave me a bra, which I stuff with bits of cloth.

Since the boys in my class found out I've got those magazines, they don't bully me any more. I sneakily take them to school and let the boys look at them. They go to the bike sheds with me and I play the boss and tell them who's allowed to look and for how long. The girls don't know anything about it; it's our secret.

Next term I'm going to the domestic science school in Leiden but first I'm going away with the circus for the whole of the summer holidays.

The tent has been mended and the circus is back on the road. There is a goat and dog act and an artiste called Corry is performing with her white doves. Apart from that, Hans is doing a clown's act, together with Rob. And there's a horse act. We've got a conjurer, too, who performs every day but isn't travelling with us. He drives home from wherever we are. Every day Rob worries that he won't turn up. He doesn't want him next year. The most beautiful number this year, I think, is the French lady, who has a really dangerous trapeze act. She can swing through the air, hanging on to the trapeze bar by her heels. She wears soft ballet shoes and net tights you can see her bottom through. She wears a really tiny, glittery gold leotard. When she comes on, she has a shiny cape around her, which she removes with an elegant gesture. Then she takes hold of a rope and they hoist her up into the trapeze. She does her act without a safety net. Every time I'm scared she'll fall. She's got strong arms and legs and only speaks French. She never comes into the kitchen wagon.

Theo, the stable boy, is always drunk but you can have a good laugh with him. He's really good at carrying things. Rob still wants a big cat act with panthers and lions. Even though he was almost killed by the lions, a big cat number is what he wants most of all. Now and again he applies for a new licence but he keeps getting turned down. You can see his scars quite clearly still, but they are less thick and red. I counted them; there's ninety-two.

Rob wants me to have my own act soon, but I'm not sure what I'm good at yet. Every evening after the show I practise on the tightrope.

Sometimes, when the French lady is in a good mood, I'm allowed to go up in the trapeze. Then we hang it lower than usual; otherwise my mother wouldn't let me. I can climb up really quickly. I want my arms and legs to be just as strong as the French lady's.

The circus has moved to the Rekreade in The Hague, where it will stay for two weeks now. The Rekreade is a big fairground on the Malieveld. It's nice to be in the same place for so long. That way you really get to know the others working at the fair. There are lots of kids my age. We play with each other. Everyone thinks I'm Rob's daughter so I get to go on the rides for free, except when it's crowded.

Behind us is the roller-coaster. It gets inspected every morning. Once it's been checked over, they test it out a couple of times and then I can have a ride. The roller-coaster is what I like best in the whole fair. It doesn't matter how often I go on it, I still find it a bit scary when the car slowly takes me up and then thunders back down.

Rob is grumpy. Now we give two performances a day and that's really tiring for him. But the tent is nice and full every time. It's getting more and more difficult to attract a large audience when we travel around. Rob often worries about it.

Autumn 1972
The holidays are over. I'm going to the domestic science school and so are some of the other girls from my class. It's an old building and a good half-hour's walk from home. The headmistress is a nun. We have a lot of different teachers.

The very first day we learn how to cook potatoes and make hot chocolate. The cookery mistress, Mrs Kneppers, has got a little dimple in the end of her nose and wears a snow-white apron. We have to eat everything we make ourselves, even if it's burnt. First we learn how to peel potatoes. I can tell I'm the only one who doesn't know how to. The mistress comes and helps me. She says I'm holding the knife wrong. She peels towards herself. My mother always peels apples or vegetables the opposite way. I don't dare admit that it's the first time I've done it. I bet Mrs Kneppers doesn't realise we never eat potatoes. But I like learning to cook, then I can do it at home sometimes.

We also have Dutch and maths, sewing, ironing, silver polishing and swimming. I'm glad I've left that other school. The mistresses here are quite strict, they really want to us to be brought up properly. Now my mother gives me sandwiches for lunch. Bread and *gula jawa*, palm sugar, which she crushes first. Sometimes she melts the sugar and lays the bread in it to soak it up. I sometimes get a sandwich from other girls if it's something they don't like. White bread with smoked sausage is what I really like best.

There's another Indonesian girl in my class. She talks just like my mother and is really shy. I don't want the others to know my mother comes from Indonesia. Luckily she never comes to fetch me.

Winter 1972
The bigger tent didn't attract any bigger audiences in the end. Apart from which, a lot of councils have raised the fees and that costs Rob so much money that he can't afford to pay his performers enough any more. He's written a letter, which he's sending to the towns he wants to visit with the circus. It hasn't done much good yet, though. My mother spoils him with nice things to eat and we're helping as much as possible to get everything ready for next season.

Spring 1973
Rob hasn't managed to find enough performers and now he's signed a contract with the Beekse Bergen attraction park in Hilvarenbeek. He's not taking the tent; we'll be performing all season in a hall. That's much less work for Rob. Now he doesn't have to keep putting the tent up and taking it down. And we only need one stable boy.

During the week I'm with Nitadog and my mother in Leiden and I go to school as usual. At the weekends and in the holidays we go to Beekse Bergen. Rob gives my mother money for the train and to buy clothes. Now she accepts it without any fuss.

Summer 1973
They've predicted a heatwave. That means no one will come to watch the performances. You can see already how hard it is to get people into the hall on a hot day. Rob says the circus will go bankrupt if it goes on like this.

For the rest of us, this summer is a bit like a holiday, now we're not travelling around. The animals have got permanent stables in a corner of the hall. In another part of the hall the seats are set up round the ring, just as they were in the tent, actually. But we don't have to keep putting everything up and taking it down again and there are only performances in the afternoon. The vans are parked at the back of the hall.

Rob has had lovely red leather harnesses made for the horses, Hassan and Macness; they look gorgeous in these and with plumes on their heads. Macness is pure white. When the circus tours, his body keeps scraping against the side of the horse box. Sometimes he's covered in manure and mud, too. Rob and I used to whitewash him before every performance. We don't have to do that now. With Hassan that doesn't matter; he's brown and white, so you don't see the marks.

This year, Rob's just doing a clown's act and he's ringmaster. That's because Andreas and Olga Schelfhout are working with us now. Andreas used to work at Circus Boltini and Circus Sarrasani as a horse trainer. Now he performs with Hassan and Macness. He's trained them really well recently; he's better at it than Rob. Now they can do all kinds of tricks.

Andreas and Olga have also trained six Vietnamese pot-bellied pigs. They make a terrible noise grunting and squealing when they don't want to do something. Olga and I have to make sure we get the leather harnesses on then in plenty of time for the show. At first we used to do it just before they had to go on, but the pigs made such a row that they startled the horses that were in the ring at the time.

Every evening, Olga helps me find my balance on the tightrope. Now I have to learn to walk without a balance pole. Sometimes I manage it just for a moment, but I prefer to walk with the pole. Now I can get halfway across without falling, and bend my knees until I'm sitting on the rope. With the pole I can get up again, but I can't do it without. I'm going to start performing as soon as I can. My mother has made a leotard for me and sewn shiny sequins all over it.

The hall is next to a big lake. On the other side there's a safari park. Every evening you can hear the lions roaring. You can swim in the lake. The water is as smooth as a mirror early in the morning. I'm usually the first in. It seems as if the water loses its smoothness after that. As if the ripples you make stay visible the rest of the day. If I stand really still in the water, little fishes come and nibble at my legs.

There's a jetty in the lake. Rob's taught me how to dive off it. He can do somersaults, too; I'm going to learn that as well.

On the other side of the hall, the grounds border on a pony camp. I often go there after swimming. There are some older children working there. They're mad about ponies and if they look after them they're allowed to ride every day for free. The ponies get trained, too. I help out now and again.

In the evening, when everyone's gone home, I hold a kind of rodeo. I pick out a pony and run up to it. Usually they all start trotting. The trick is to get on the back of the chosen pony. It's a wonderful feeling, riding bareback, holding your body tight against the animal while it trots. You can feel its strong muscles moving under the musty, greasy coat. You have to hold on tight to its mane so as not to fall off.

Later in the evening, we all go and sit in the hall. The performers use that time to repair their props or rehearse new numbers. Andreas has built a model of Circus Sarrasani from wood and cloth, with a real tent and wagons, and even tiny little animals and people. He works on it every evening with a pair of tweezers. When it gets dark, he puts on the lights in his miniature circus. It's really beautiful and seems almost real. I'm not allowed to touch anything. I can only look.

During the afternoon performance I stand at the edge of the ring and help by passing the props or holding the animals back. Macness has a habit of walking out of the ring in the middle of a number. Luckily, Andreas has trained him to run in a circle first before leaving the ring. During the performance, he keeps an eye out to see if the horse is starting to go round in a circle. Usually there's just enough time to correct him. But he's still a stubborn animal. The other day, Andreas whipped him as hard as anything. I couldn't watch and ran off until I was far enough away not to be able to hear the lashes any more. I only went back when I was sure that Andreas was no longer in the stable. Macness had thick weals on his flanks. I think it's horrible of Andreas. Macness is my friend.

This year, Tony Wilson is working with us; he's the new conjurer and he's a great laugh. We have a cup of coffee with him in front of his caravan every day. At the weekends, his wife and two-year-old daughter come over, too. The other day it was Tony's birthday and a few of us put an act together which we surprised him with during the show. Rob announced me as Karina Roberti, and I was allowed to give him the presents on behalf of the performers. I was really nervous.

I sleep in the back of the cabin of one of the trucks. It's boiling hot there day and night. I keep forgetting to empty the pee bucket, too, so it stinks as well.

August 1973
My mother's here this summer, too, for the whole of the holidays, together with Nitadog. But she's had stomachache for the past few days. She stays in bed in the caravan; I hardly see her.

After a week, the pain is so bad she wants to go back to Leiden to see the doctor. At first I don't want to go with her, but Rob doesn't want my mother going alone. I think it's a pity to leave the circus; I'd like to stay here for ever.

We go home by train. Nitadog is under the seat, panting and shivering; she's not used to trains. My mother is in so much pain that she keeps groaning. I feel really sorry for her. Now I feel bad that I didn't want to go with her. She's afraid she's got appendicitis.

We go straight to the doctor when we get to Leiden. I sit in the waiting room while my mother goes into the surgery. It seems like ages before she comes out again and when she does I can see she's been crying. She's holding an envelope. On the way home she tells me that the doctor thinks she's got a gall bladder infection. He's not sure, so she has to go into hospital for tests this afternoon. The letter he gave her says exactly what she has to take with her.

When we get home my mother lies down on the bed. I open the envelope for her. It says she needs to take a dressing gown, a nightie and slippers. She hasn't got any of those; she always sleeps with nothing on. I go and buy them for her. Plastic flip-flops from the chemist's and a pink dressing gown and a nightie with roses on it from the shopping precinct at the end of our road. She wants me to ask the neighbours if I can use their phone to ring for a taxi. The lady downstairs rings the taxi for me when I tell her my mother has to go to hospital.

It's quite a way to the Diaconessen Hospital. When we arrive, someone shows us to the ward where my mother has been admitted.

We walk down a long corridor which smells like the doctor's waiting room. When we reach my mother's ward, the nurse asks me to wait in the corridor for a minute while my mother gets changed but my mother says I can go in with her.

We go into a big room with four beds on each side. The ladies in the beds nod at us. The eighth bed, by the window, is for my mother. The nurse pulls a curtain around us and goes away. My mother gets undressed. The nightie looks really nice with her black hair. It fits perfectly. She gets into bed. What a funny sight, my mother in a nightie in such a stiffly-made-up bed. It makes us both laugh. Then the nurse comes back with information about visiting times. She says it would be better if I came back this evening, because they're coming to fetch my mother for an examination.

My mother tells me to phone Rob later this evening. She writes down his telephone number on a piece of paper for me. Then she asks me to go to the bank and get an authorisation form so that I can take money out for her. She gives me a few guilders for the bus fare and to buy something to eat for me and Nitadog.

October 1973
I can hear Nitadog howling from halfway down the street. She can't stand being alone.

Sandra and her cousin Rita have been coming over in the evenings recently. They know my mother's not at home. We keep really quiet because if the woman downstairs hears us, she'll come and complain. Rita has got some cigarettes, which we smoke. We talk about the girls in our street who've already had it off with boys. Then Rita comes up with a plan: she thinks I should do it with a boy. I think it's mean of her; she always has rotten ideas like that. And San eggs her on, too. Rita insists I do it with a boy while they both watch. That's what happened when she did it for the first time and now she's acting as if that's how you're supposed to do it. She goes out to look for a boy. I'm cross and I don't understand why Sandra doesn't help me. I'm sure she wouldn't dare do it, either.

After a while, Rita comes back, making a lot of noise, with a couple of boys trailing behind her. And after them comes the woman from downstairs who is really furious, snapping that this has got to stop. Everyone has to leave. She threatens to go and tell my mother. San, Rita and the others go off, swearing at the neighbour. I don't go with them. I'm relieved the woman sent them away because now I don't have to do anything with a boy. As long as she doesn't go and tell on me to my mother.

The next day all the kids are swearing in the street at my neighbour. Luckily they've stopped talking about what they were planning to do with me. I don't dare tell my mother.

November 1973

My mother's been ill for months, now. I go and visit her every day. If I've got enough money I take the bus to the hospitals, but I have to walk there more and more often.

Every time I get money out of the bank with the authorisation form, I have to take it to her. Then she divides it into portions. She gives me some every other day; otherwise I'll spend it all at once. But even now it goes too quickly. She tells me not to spend it on anything extravagant, just food for me and Nitadog and bus fares. But actually I buy the same thing every day. A carton of caramel blancmange, a tin of Pal for Nitadog and a Mars bar. Except on Sundays, when the shops are closed.

My mother asks me how things are going at school, and I always lie about it. I pretend things are going really well, but I find it so boring. Actually, I don't really want to go any more. But my mother wants me to.

The hospital is quite a long way from our house. Visiting hours start at seven o'clock, but I'm usually early and wait downstairs in the hall. Now my mother has got a room to herself. From time to time I take her a little present. I bought her a stone horse. It looks like Macness.

I haven't seen Rob since the summer. My mother thinks the circus is doing badly, which is why he hasn't got time to come over.

The flat is in a real mess. I just can't get round to clearing it up. The annoying thing is that everything keeps going mouldy. When something really smells awful I throw it in the bathroom. That's where all the rubbish is that I don't dare touch any more. When my mother comes home again I'll clean it all up.

My mother's really scared that the Child Welfare will come and take me away if they find out I'm living on my own. She keeps on nagging at me to comb my hair. And to look after Nitadog properly.

Now that it's winter, it's cold in the flat. The heater doesn't work. It's warm in bed; Nitadog always snuggles up to me like a hot-water bottle.

These past few weeks it really hurts when I go for a wee. The skin between my legs is all raw. When the wee touches it, it stings. My pants rub against it, particularly if I've been sitting still for a while. Then they get warm and it hurts even more. I'm afraid the teachers and the other children can smell me. I can smell myself really strongly.

One day when I get home the women from below stops me on the stairs when I get home. She asks me which hospital my mother's in. She wants to tell her the flat is in a mess. She says everybody in the building is bothered by the smell. It's a scandal, she says angrily. I beg her not to go and see my mother. I tell her she's coming home soon and I'm going to clean everything up. She goes back down, muttering. Hopefully that will satisfy her.

San and her cousin offer to help me clean the place so I let them come in. Rita takes charge. She decides what everyone has to do. But it seems like the mess is only getting worse. San has thrown a couple of buckets of water over the floor. Now it's running all over the living room. I'm sorry I let them in again now.

Then the girls can't be bothered any more. All of a sudden they've legged it. I go and look for them in the playground but they're not there. Disappointed, I go back home. I think it's rotten of them. Nitadog starts wagging her tail as soon as I come into the living room. I want to go and buy something nice for us to eat, but when I go to take the money from the mantelpiece, there's nothing there. I look on the floor. Maybe it's fallen off. I'm sure that's where I put it.

Then suddenly it dawns on me why they went off. They've pinched my money. Furiously, I go back to the playground but they're nowhere to be seen. What's the good, anyway? They're bound to say they don't know anything about it and then they'll blame me for suspecting them, the rotten cows. I swear never to let them in again and walk back home to dry everything up.

When I get home, my mother is there, just like that. Nitadog is lying in bed with her. How awful for her to come home right when, now everything is soaking wet. If I'd known she was coming, I really would have cleaned the whole flat properly. I tell her what happened. She says it's a good lesson for me for next time.

It's great having her back home! My mother tells me she walked out of the hospital. She wanted to be home again. She's worried about me. She had to sign a form in the hospital saying that she was leaving at her own risk.

She asks me to make up a bed for her in the back room, she's in so much pain and she wants to lie down quietly. Straight away I make a bed on the floor with the mattress and it's dry and cosy. I'm so glad she's back. When she gets up to go to the bed in the back room I can see how difficult it is for her to walk. My mother says she's worn out from the journey and wants to sleep. She asks me to go and get some more money out of the bank and do some shopping. I want Nitadog to go with me but I can hardly get her away from my mother. She's missed her, too.

When I get back, it's as if something has changed in the flat, as if the silence has gone. I sit beside my mother's bed the whole evening. She can't stand me sitting on the bed. She groans now and again and then, suddenly, I hear a terribly loud noise coming from her tummy; it sounds like it's bubbling. She asks me to lay warm, wet cloths on her tummy to take away some of the pain. Holding towels under the hot tap in the kitchen I can still hear her tummy. She calls, telling me to make the cloths as hot as possible. Her voice sounds high and shrill; now she's asking for something to drink, too.

When I'm standing by her again, she turns down the covers and asks me to lay the cloths on her tummy. I hardly dare. The bubbling in her stomach sounds so loud. As soon as the cloths have cooled down I make new ones. My mother drinks little sips of water. She's in so much pain she can hardly speak, she wants to be alone.

In the living room, I try to get to sleep, deep under the covers, with Nitadog right up against me. At least that way I can't hear the bubbling.

★

The next day I don't want to go to school. My mother says I have to. I'd rather stay with her and chat. But she says I'll get bored, she's too tired for chatting.

When I come home from school in the afternoon, I find her lying in the bed in the front room. I hope that means she's feeling better. But that evening she tells me she hasn't got long to live. She thinks that by Christmas she won't be here any more.

I think it's crazy for her to talk like that. I don't want to hear it. But she won't stop going on about it.

She says she doesn't want me to come and look at her when she's dead.

She says I would always have a dead image of her and she doesn't want that. She would rather I remember her alive.

I promise her. I want her to stop talking like that; of course she's not going to die.

My mother doesn't eat much. She prefers to drink soup. I've bought packets in different flavours at the supermarket. Late in the evening, her tummy starts bubbling again. She wants the wet cloths.

When I get home the next day, my mother is all worked up. She tells me the doctor came round but she didn't open the door. She says I mustn't open the door, not to anyone. They want to take her back to the hospital and she doesn't want to go. She tells me to take the key on the string out of the letterbox. She's scared the doctor will get in.

A little while later the doorbell goes. I crawl into bed next to my mother. But nothing happens.

It's a bit scary being so sneaky. I don't dare go out and play; I'm afraid I'll bump into the doctor.

During the day I go to school and then quickly run back home. I find it so cosy at home. Now I can tell her lots more things than I could during visiting hours at the hospital. My mother's in a lot of pain. She can't even change beds any more.

Then my mother calls me. I can hear by the tone of her voice that it's something serious. She wants to talk to me. As long as she doesn't start talking about dying again.

She tells me that in the afternoon, while I was at school, she talked to the doctor. He didn't come in. She didn't open the door when he rang the bell, but he talked to her through the letterbox.

He said it couldn't go on like this any longer. He said it wouldn't be good for me to find her dead if she died.

I get a shock when I hear that the doctor thinks she's going to die, too.

My mother asks if I understand.

I can quite understand that they don't want me to find her dead, but she's not going to die, is she?

My mother says it might be better if she went back to the hospital after all.

I don't want her to. But she's arranged with the doctor that an ambulance will come and pick her up tomorrow. Then I don't have to go to school. I can go with her to the hospital.

Two ambulancemen carry my mother down the stairs on a stretcher.

The neighbours are standing out on the street by the ambulance, watching us. They don't say anything.

I'm allowed to sit in the back, next to my mother. They've wrapped her up warm in a blanket. Over the blanket is a grey canvas cloth, held in place with belts and buckled underneath. She is very quiet. When she saw the neighbours looking, she closed her eyes. I don't think she likes them seeing her like that without makeup. She has got terribly thin.

She gets a room to herself in the hospital.

December 1973
Seven o'clock. *This is the* ANP *radio news service*, I hear the newscaster on the radio say.

As soon as I turn over in bed, I can feel the soggy, wet patch in the mattress again. I was trying to avoid that patch all night.

My wet clothes are sticking to my back. Nitadog has found a better place to sleep. She's lying on the floor under the blanket, which she has pulled halfway off the bed. Her paws are moving in her sleep. A whining bark comes from her muzzle, she's dreaming.

The edge of the iron bed seems frozen, it's so cold. I peel off my sticky clothes and hastily rummage through the pile of clothes next to the bed to see if there's anything dry left.

Quickly to the loo. An icy wind blasts through the corridor from the broken pane in the front door. I just hope I'm not dreaming. I often dream I'm sitting on the loo and have to pee, and then I wake up in bed, soaking wet.

As soon as I sit down on the loo I shut my eyes tight to relieve the stabbing pain. Now it's really raw between my legs. I squeeze my wee out as hard as I can, waiting for the last drops; those are the worst. It doesn't hurt as much if I clamp my jaws together and suck the cold air in between my teeth with a hissing noise. I say *Ow, ow, ow*, out loud; that helps to relieve the pain, too. I listen to the sound of my voice. It seems to roll up along the walls, echoing a bit, then bounces off the ceiling. The silence that follows sounds muffled.

My mother always told me that in Indonesia there were *tokehs*, geckos, in the loo. They went in there to cool off against the ceiling. They made a tock-tock noise and sometimes dropped on you when you were on the loo. I'm glad there aren't any *tokehs* here. That must be creepy, having an animal like that falling on you.

Sometimes I talk out loud and listen to the sound of my own voice. I have the radio on at night, too. Then it's not so quiet.

There hasn't been any toilet paper left for months now. I use old newspapers and bits of paper, but now it's so sore between my legs that the paper is too rough. I can only bear to wipe myself with soft cloth now.

There are all kinds of old clothes lying around the loo that I've been using to wipe myself with recently. I can't flush them down the loo because it would get blocked. There's pooh on everything; I can't find a single clean piece of material.

Legs wide apart, I shuffle off to the living room, looking for something soft to dry myself with. Nitadog can see I'm in pain. As soon as I sit down on the bed after going for a wee she puts her head between my legs and carefully licks my sore crotch clean.

Every day it gets more difficult to find a decent pair of pants. All my pants are wet or stiff from being worn so often. First I always rub over the stiff gusset of the pants with a piece of Sunlight soap. That makes it softer. And it smells soapier. But now I'm so sore down there, the soap stings too much. Now I bend the hard gussets backwards and forwards a few times until they get soft.

When I pull a jumper over my head, I can smell what I'm afraid the others can smell, but now I like it myself. It's a mixture of Nitadog and me.

A little bit of light finds its way in through the closed curtains. I can see by the colour whether the sun is shining, or if it's raining or snowing. It's been really dark in the mornings recently. They've forecast snow. My favourite song is playing on the radio, 'Ben' by Michael Jackson. Nitadog snuggles up against me; as always, she feels nice and warm.

Lying on the last dry bit of the bed we listen under the covers, through the music, to the sounds of the neighbours. I can tell what day it is by the noises. Luckily it's not a Saturday or Sunday.

The man downstairs always leaves for work first. Every morning he slams the street door with a bang. Then I hear him starting his car. After that comes the man upstairs. First he flushes the loo; I can hear the water clattering through the pipes alongside our room. When he closes the street door I can count to eight, sometimes nine, before he starts his moped. Then the kids next door run stamping down the stairs, with their mother shouting after them.

And that's the sign for me to go to school, too. I cover up Nitadog. She watches me put my coat on. It's terribly cold out. Going down the stairs I can see that the window of the porch is covered in frost flowers.

I get something to eat at school.

One girl always has sandwiches with *speculaas* biscuits in. Her father is a baker. She doesn't like them and if I'm lucky I get her sandwiches. In cookery, we're not allowed to throw anything away. We have to eat what we make or give it away. A lot of the girls in my class don't like what they've cooked. We often have to cook milk puddings and hardly anyone can do that without making it lumpy. I like all kinds of milk pudding, with or without lumps. Sometimes my whole table is full of pudding bowls. I eat everything.

Christmas holidays 1973

The clubhouse in the playground is closed, as it's the Christmas holidays. Every day I sit with San at the top of the slide, in a kind of little hut. It's pretty cold out. In the evening some boys who are a bit older come from another area. We mess around with them. They try and get us to go off with them. San has already kissed one of them.

One day I'm walking home with her from the playground when her mother comes running towards us. The Child Welfare have been round to our flat, she gasps. They want to put me in a home. But San's mother has promised I can stay with them for a while.

Now I sleep in San's room with her; our beds are almost right up against each other. Nitadog sleeps downstairs with her mother, on the sofa.

Every night before we go to bed, San's father brings us sausage and chips with onions. He always pops round to the snack bar when he walks the dogs.

I'm a bit scared of San's nan and grandpa. I really have to behave myself with them. You have to knock before going into their room. You have to take your shoes off and you're not allowed to eat anything on the sofa; they're afraid of you making stains. They've got a dog, too, Nitadog's brother.

San's father never says much. He works in a slaughterhouse. On Saturdays, he listens to sport on the radio. San's mother's funny. She talks in a really rough way. She often walks around the house without her false teeth in and pulls funny faces. She's very easy going. She even lets us smoke with her. She says we can smoke in the house on New Year's Eve, too. San's mother always has the radio on loud, particularly when there's a Demis Roussos record on. Then she sings along at the top of her voice. San likes the Jackson Five and I like Donny Osmond and Michael Jackson.

It doesn't hurt between my legs any more since San's mother gave me some clean pants. But when I went to the loo just now, I suddenly saw a whole lot of blood in the water. It was all over my pants, too. I've started my periods and I'm dead scared someone will see it. I don't dare tell San's mother. I took a flannel from the bathroom and folded it up in my pants, but it keeps leaking.

*

My mother's got even worse. She is terribly thin. When she lifts her arm, there's loose skin flapping where it used to be nice and round. You can see the veins on her hands; they are almost transparent. Her face is so sunken that her hair is like an odd, thick mass around her head. It looks so strange, it's not right. But she's not in pain any more.

I feel less and less like visiting her. I don't really know what to say and the way she looks now frightens me. It seems as if some new part of her body has fallen in every time I see her. When she hugs me, it feels like being grabbed by a skeleton.

Sometimes she asks how things are going at San's, but I don't want to tell her anything. I'm sure my mother thinks I've changed since I've been staying with San. She's given me some clothes. She's got cupboards full. My mother would never have bought these clothes for me. But she hasn't said anything.

It's as if we both know, without having to mention it, that she would have liked things to have been different.

San's parents have never visited her. Rob comes to the hospital occasionally. The circus is bankrupt. My mother is being brave but I can tell she feels awful about it.

New Year's Eve 1973
There are fireworks going off all over town. Nitadog is panting, scared to death of the bangs. As it's New Year's Eve, I go and visit my mother in the afternoon. It's best not to be out on the streets in the evening with all those explosions.

When I go into my mother's room, I see a drip standing next to the bed, full of blood. It's not a pretty sight, that dark red bag of blood. But I can't stop looking at it.

My mother wants me to come and sit next to her. She wants to talk to me. She tells me they're going to operate on her today.

Why? I ask. I don't want them to. I don't want them cutting her up. I suddenly start crying, I find it so scary.

When I've stopped crying, my mother tells me there's no other way. She pulls the blanket aside. She's wearing a hospital gown that does up at the back and she's half naked. There's nothing left of her breasts but two flaps of wrinkly skin. Her tummy is enormous. It's so swollen it looks as if it might burst at any moment.

36

She tells me they're going to operate on her tummy. Then it won't be so fat any more. She shows me where they've drawn eight lines on her tummy. The doctor did it, so he'll know later on exactly where he has to cut.

I don't want to look at it. I don't want them cutting her open. She tries to reassure me by saying she won't feel it and it will be a relief when her tummy is thin again. *Betoel*, she says. Really and truly.

The blood drip catches my eye again. She tells me the blood is for later on, after the operation. Next time I come and visit she'll have the drip in her arm. I burst into tears again. I would really like to get into bed with her for a minute but I don't dare to because of that swollen, scary tummy. My mother tells me I'd better go. She says the operation will soon be over and it should be fun this evening, with the fireworks.

1 *January 1974*
I have to go back to the hospital again today, but I don't really want to. I'm scared of seeing her. I hope they've taken the blood drip away.

San's mother has given me a big basket of fruit to take with me and San's father drives me to the entrance of the hospital. He doesn't go in with me.

My mother isn't in her room. A nurse takes me to another ward. She tells me my mother will be in here for a few days. Then she'll go back to her own room again.

We walk down a quiet corridor closed off with double swing doors. Then we come to a place with doctors and nurses sitting behind a desk. When I say who I've come to see, a nurse tells me my mother is still a bit drowsy from the anaesthetic. I'm not allowed to take the fruit basket in with me. She points through a window. I can see four beds, surrounded by equipment. You can hardly see the people lying in them.

When I open the door, I can hear the beeping and humming of machines. In the bed the nurse pointed out I can see my mother's black hair. Her body is covered in tubes and drips. I bend over her, but don't dare touch her.

37

She raises her eyes to me. In a low, cracked voice she says I don't have to come if I don't really want to.

That really gives me a shock. How does she know? I fib. I tell her I did want to come.

It doesn't matter, she says. It's a lot of effort for her to talk. Her lips are very dry and scaly. 'Happy New Year, Mama,' I whisper. And she wishes me the same.

Then she wants to rest again. She says she will feel better tomorrow.

Standing outside once more, I'm relieved to be out of the hospital.

5 January 1974

Today my mother is back in her own room. It suddenly looks really big and sunny. She's cheerful and sitting up in bed. There are two plastic bags hanging next to the bed, attached to her tummy by tubes. One bag is for wee, the other for pooh. My mother explains that from now on she doesn't have to go to the loo anymore. She jokes about it.

She makes me laugh. I'm glad she's not in pain any more. But when I'm sitting next to her, all of a sudden I feel my leg getting warm. The bag is filling with wee. I quickly pull my leg away.

I tell her it's San's cousin's birthday tomorrow and I've been invited to her party. The party is in the evening. If I go, I can't come and visit my mother. She says I should definitely go to the party. She hopes I have a good time.

Before I leave, she asks if I will go and lie down next to her for a moment. I don't dare to; I'm scared I might lean on the tubes. She lifts the blanket and says, *'Ajoen, ajoen.'* I creep in next to her. She holds me tight for a long time, rocking me in her arms. *Ajoen, ajoen.*

As I leave, I kiss her. See you the day after tomorrow.

6 January 1974

It's San's cousin's birthday party tonight. We put on some makeup; we've got lipstick and eyeshadow. Then the doorbell goes and a little while later San's mother comes into the room with a dead straight face, followed by a woman. She's come to see me.

She introduces herself as the hospital social worker. Right away I know there's something wrong with my mother.

She takes a book out of her bag. Then she tells me that my mother died about an hour ago, at around six o'clock.

San's mother starts sobbing. The woman opens the book. It's a Bible. She's written something in the front. It's the passage a priest read to my mother just before she died. She gives me the Bible as a present. San's mother takes it.

The woman asks if I want to go with her to the hospital to see my mother. I'm startled. My mother made me promise I wouldn't go and look at her when she was dead. So I say no. On the woman's insistence, San's father agrees to go with her and bring back my mother's things.

They go. I look at Sandra and suddenly we get the giggles. Then we go to see San's nan. This time we don't knock. When I go into the room, San's nan hugs me. She presses me tight against her. It feels really odd; I don't know if I should let her. I stand stock-still. She's crying. Finally, she lets me go.

I pretend I'm crying, too, but I can't. Actually, I can't understand why San's nan's crying. She doesn't even know my mother.

An hour later, San's father comes back with a plastic bag with the nightie, the slippers and a couple of papers of my mother's. He'll look after them for me.

I ask if we're still going to Rita's party.

San's mother hesitates but as San really wants to go she says it's okay. San's father takes us in the car. At the party, San tells everyone the big news. She sits next to me all evening and I deliberately stare into the distance, looking sad. We sit and look sad together. After the party, San's father comes to fetch us and we pop into the snack bar on the way home for sausage and chips.

That night, lying in bed, we fantasise about how we might become real sisters, now.

The next day, we're woken up by the doorbell. San's mother says there's an uncle of mine at the door. I quickly get dressed and go to the front door. Rob's in the hall. I haven't seen him since Beekse Bergen.

He doesn't want to come in; he wants to go to our flat. On the way, he tells me he went to see my mother yesterday evening. But he was just too late. It was one of the Sundays when you aren't allowed to drive the car, so he couldn't get there quickly enough from Aalsmeer. By the time he got to the hospital she was already dead.

I feel sorry for him, but even sorrier for my mother. So *kassian*.

At home it's dark and silent. It stinks of rubbish. Rob walks straight over to our little desk and starts searching through the drawers. I ask him what he's looking for. He wants their love letters. I find the pile straight away and can see he thinks it's a bit strange that I know exactly which letters they are. As soon as he's got them, he leaves. He says he'll see me at the funeral.

I go back to San's house. I don't like the fact that Rob's taken the letters. They're ours. And it gave me a shock when he mentioned the funeral. I hadn't thought about that at all. When will it be?

San's mother is already looking out for me. There is another visitor for me. It's the priest. He tells me that my mother passed away peacefully. She died with a smile on her face, he says. When he says that, I can't listen properly any more.

I don't believe him. Why did he say that? I bet it was to comfort me, but I don't feel sad. Apart from that, I'm certain she didn't die peacefully. I wasn't there, Rob wasn't there; it can't be true. He's says he'll be at the cemetery the day after tomorrow for the funeral. He thinks it would be better if I simply go to school in the meantime. Then at least I will be distracted. He'll inform the school.

As he's leaving, I hear him telling San's mother in the corridor that my mother had cancer of the colon. I didn't know that. I'm relieved when he's gone. Died smiling? I don't believe a word of it.

8 January 1974
Today I go to school as normal. I've already got used to the idea that my mother is dead.

The teacher is really nice to me. He tells the children in the class what's happened. Everyone looks at me and I put on an extra-sad face. After sitting there with a faraway look in my eyes for a long time, I glance at the teacher, who winks at me. A really nice wink. And usually I could never get on with him.

After school I go to the clubhouse with Sandra. Everyone in the street knows about it by now. Women who never speak to us pull their curtains aside and wave. Sandra and I walk around arm in arm being sad. In the clubhouse we stuff ourselves with crisps and cola.

Tomorrow's the funeral; we're pretty nervous about that.

9 January 1974

Today my mother is being buried. San and her mother are going with me; the others are staying at home. We wait for the car from the funeral parlour. We've got new clothes on.

When the car finally arrives, we get in the back. The car is big and black. It's got black curtains at the windows. We draw them aside. In the front is a chauffeur with a cap. He looks so serious that Sandra and I get the giggles.

San's mother tells us to be quiet. We want to, but can't because of the giggles. Then San's mother gets the giggles, too. We keep telling each other we can't behave like this. But every time we look at each other, we burst out laughing.

The car drives slowly out of the street. All the curtains in the street are twitching; it seems as if everybody is watching us. After driving for a little while, the car stops. Another car moves in front of us. That's the hearse.

I feel myself stiffen. Through the window I can see a bit of the coffin. So my mother's lying in there. I can hardly bear the idea. She's lying there, under the lid.

The car stops. We've arrived at the cemetery. When we get out, I can see Rob's car but I can't see him anywhere.

We go into a hall full of chairs and sit down. The priest comes in and goes and stands behind a table. He starts to talk.

Behind him is the coffin. That must be my mother's coffin. It's creepy. Supposing the lid opens up and she comes back from the dead. My mother used to tell me about people who came back to life.

I daren't look at the coffin any more.

When the priest has finished talking, we go outside. The cemetery is like a big park. We have to walk quite a long way before we get to the place where she's going to be buried.

We stop by a freshly dug hole with the coffin next to it. The priest starts talking again. Then some men lower the coffin into the hole on ropes.

I can see Rob over in the distance. It's as if he doesn't dare come any closer. We exchange a glance.

The priest asks if I would like to throw a trowel-full of sand on to the coffin. Someone puts a trowel in my hand. The sand thumps on to the coffin. Now the others can do the same.

I don't really want to do this at all; I don't want to bury my mother.

I give the trowel to San, but she doesn't dare. San's mother is crying.

I do my best to cry, too, but I haven't got any tears, I can't. I want to get out of here.

At the exit, Rob comes up to me. He promises to write soon.

January 1974

There's a funny atmosphere at Sandra's. It's as if no one knows exactly what's supposed to happen to me. Next week someone from the Child Welfare is coming to talk to me about where I'm going to live. No one in the house mentions it. We're waiting to see what happens.

A woman from the Child Welfare has already been round. San's mother told me they've tracked down my father and he says I can go and live with him, my brother and my sister. I can tell that San's mother is relieved when I say I'm okay with that.

I'm really curious about my family. My father's coming to meet me next week. I can hardly wait. I'm even more curious about my brother and sister. I wonder if I look like them.

This week I have to get anything I want to keep out of our flat, as the council is going to empty it soon. I go over there with San. I'm not sure what to choose. I'll take the folder with the papers from Indonesia, in any case.

There are two of my mother's dresses in the wardrobe. They smell of her. I sniff them again and resolve never to wash these dresses or throw them away.

I ask if San wants anything. She chooses the mirror in the hall. Her nan will like that, she thinks.

We go. Just in case, I take the box with the bills from the catalogue and our bank book.

End of January 1974

The council has emptied our flat. There was a van in front of the house and they threw everything into it.

My father's coming today. I could hardly sleep last night I was so nervous. I went out with Sandra to buy a new pair of trousers yesterday, real soul trousers, like the ones the Jackson Five wear. Tight at the top and then flaring out wide from the knee. They're bright green and black. We put on some bright blue eyeshadow.

San's mother's nervous, too. We're waiting for a lady from the Child Welfare. She'll arrive first and be there when my father comes to meet me.

The bell goes. Sandra is sitting stiffly on the sofa next to me. Nitadog climbs up in between us. Nitadog, I only hope Nitadog can come, too.

A woman comes into the living room. She shakes hands with me. She's from the Child Welfare and is called Mrs Jansen.

She asks if I'm nervous. She says it's important for me to ask lots of questions about my father's house. She'll help me. I ask if Nitadog can come with me. She suggests I ask my father when he arrives. If Nitadog's not allowed to come, then I'm not going either, flashes through my mind.

The bell.

The living-room door opens and there he is, my father, a middle-aged man with glasses. He's wearing a suit. He comes up to me, smiling. I don't really know what I should do. He shakes my hand.

There's someone else behind him, my sister; she shakes hands with me, too. She's called Diana. She's got really long hair, lighter than mine, and blue eyes. She's wearing jeans and no makeup. I'm immediately sorry I put on so much makeup. I hope she doesn't think I'm stupid.

My father says my brother couldn't come.

I don't dare ask anything. Mrs Jansen asks my father all kinds of questions about where he lives and how he lives.

They live in a house with a garden where grapes grow in the summer. My sister goes to a domestic science school, too, and my brother Johan goes to the Junior Technical School. My father talks about his work and about Zaltbommel, the town where they live.

My sister is looking at me in an investigative way the whole time. I can see we're different kinds of people. I just hope she likes me.

Mrs Jansen wants to know if there's anything else I'd like to ask. I pluck up the courage to ask whether I can bring Nitadog if I go and live with them. My father says that's fine.

They agree that he will organise things with the Child Welfare so that I can go as quickly as possible. Then they leave. I shake hands with my father and sister. Mrs Jansen stays and talks for a little while longer.

San thinks I really look like my sister, only darker. She thinks my father is very smart.

9 February 1974

Today I'm going to move to Zaltbommel. I'm happy and sad at the same time. Yesterday I said goodbye to everyone at school and all the children in the street. San's mother's got tears in her eyes all the time. We keep laughing about it and saying she has got to stop, otherwise we'll all be crying in a minute. San's father has already got my stuff ready in two bin bags upstairs. One bag with my clothes and school things and one with my mother's stuff.

Nitadog can feel we're nervous. She keeps coming and sitting on me. Finally, a car stops outside. It's my father. He doesn't come in.

We say goodbye. We promise to write. I thank them; it was really nice of them to let me stay with them.

I can't get Nitadog in to the car. It takes a lot of pushing and pulling before she's finally sitting on the back seat and then she starts panting and trembling terribly. I get in the front, next to my father. It's silly really; I've never said Papa before in my life. I don't know if I dare.

We wave, toot the horn and drive off. Driving past our house, I look up. The flat is empty, just the curtains are still hanging there. I wouldn't mind getting out for a minute to look round one last time. But the car is already turning the corner, on the way to Zaltbommel.

Nitadog's dribbling down my neck, she's still trembling. I apologise for her and tell my father that she's not used to being in a car.

My father wants to talk to me about something he didn't mention last time. His girlfriend lives in their house, too. She's called Auntie Wilma. I'll get to meet an aunt and uncle of mine, too, his sister and her husband. She's called Auntie Katrina and he's Uncle Dirk. I suddenly remember my mother talking about them once. Didn't they live with them for a while, just after they came over from Indonesia? I ask my father. I say my mother told me that.

My father doesn't answer. I have to forget my mother, he says in a harsh voice. It's best for everyone if I don't talk about her any more. He wants me to agree that I'll never, never talk about my mother to Diana or Johan. Shocked by his tone, I promise.

We're nearly there, just another half-hour, says my father. Now I'm really getting curious.

Nitadog is asleep. I'm just going to stroke her when my father says it would be better if we took her to a dogs' home.

I can't believe my ears, it's such a shock. But he's serious. It's better for everyone, he says.

I'm so shocked I don't dare say anything else. I feel numb.

We drive over a long bridge.

Look, there on the right is the tower of Bommel, says my father. I see a stumpy tower. I don't want to go to Zaltbommel any more. He had promised I could take Nitadog with me, hadn't he?

A few minutes later, we stop outside an animal refuge. My father gets out. He goes to ask if they can take Nitadog.

Nitadog, my lovely Nitadog. This is really mean.

Nitadog can feel something's wrong and starts licking me. What should I do? This can't be happening. If I'd known this was planned, I'd never have come.

My father comes back. He opens the door on my side and says he's arranged it. We have to get her into a cage ourselves.

I get out.

It's as if Nitadog can sense what's going to happen. We can't get her out of the car. She refuses to budge and stands there with her tail between her legs. I have to drag her into the refuge.

Inside, we go down a path surrounded by cages full of barking dogs. Nitadog's dead scared. The man from the refuge holds a cage open for me. Nitadog tries to get away. With a lot of pushing and shoving, I manage to get her into the cage. Then the door shuts. Nitadog starts to whine.

I run away, my hands pressed hard against my ears. I can't bear to hear it. My sweet Nitadog, what am I doing to you?

We drive off. I can still hear the howling in the car. I'm so upset; I didn't even get the chance to stroke her again.

I don't want to be here any more. I just want Nitadog.

2

Zaltbommel

This is the street where we live, I hear my father say. His voice seems to be coming from miles away. I see a wide street of houses. They're all the same. All built in a row, with little gardens in front. Strange, I thought their house was white, with a sloping roof, surrounded by a big garden with grapes in it. These are ordinary terraced houses.

We stop. I see a door open. A small blond woman comes out to meet us. Behind her is my sister. The woman shakes my hand. Auntie Wilma, I hear her say. My sister shakes my hand, too, and then we go in.

We enter a little hall. My coat goes on the hallstand. I see stairs going up. We go through a door and find ourselves in the sitting room.

It's a big room. There's a three-piece suite with a coffee table in front and, in a corner, a television. In the room at the back I can see a dining table. Behind that is another room which looks out on the garden. The furniture is brown, the wallpaper brown, orange and beige. Everything looks bare and polished. I sit down on the sofa.

Auntie Wilma comes in with coffee. I light a cigarette. Diana says she wasn't allowed to smoke when she was my age. I can't tell if she means I shouldn't do it now. I don't really dare ask her. Then Auntie Wilma slides an ashtray over to me. Luckily it looks as if it is allowed.

My father says we've got some things to discuss.

He thinks it's better for everyone if I'm introduced to other people as Diana and Johan's cousin. Zaltbommel is a village where there is a lot of gossip and it would only raise awkward questions if a sister just appeared out of nowhere. For that reason I won't be going to the same school as Diana, in Zaltbommel, but to a school in Den Bosch.

I listen to what he is saying but Nitadog's howling still resounds in my ears.

Diana shows me round the house. Upstairs, a room has been got ready for me. She opens the door. The room is big. There's a bed, a cupboard and a little desk. It looks out over the garden. Next to my room is the room where my father and Auntie Wilma sleep and then, next to that, Diana's room. Johan sleeps in the attic.

Once I've seen everything, we go back down again. I thank Auntie Wilma and my father for my room. I try to be nice even though I know for certain I'll never forgive my father for what he's done to Nitadog.

Ah, there's your brother, I hear Auntie Wilma say, just as I sit back down on the sofa. A tall guy with coal-black hair is standing in the doorway. He startles me a bit. This is the first time I've seen a guy with such long hair. He looks like an Indian.

Johan mumbles something and goes off again. He doesn't come in and shake hands with me. Don't take any notice, says Auntie Wilma. He's always like that.

Then the back door opens and a plump older woman comes into the room. It's Auntie Katrina, followed by her limping husband, Uncle Dirk. They saw me as a baby, they say, and what a big girl I am now.

Luckily, Diana asks if I want to go back upstairs with her; I wouldn't know what to say to Auntie Katrina and Uncle Dirk.

Diana's room is painted dark blue. She's got cushions on the floor and there are bottles all over the place, with dripping candles in them. The ceiling is hung with fishing nets and on the wall there's a cloth made from knotted rope with beads woven into it.

Diana lights a couple of candles. It looks really cosy. She says she's got some other clothes for me. What I'm wearing are soul clothes. Most of her friends are hippies. I quite like her denim clothes. No one wore jeans in our street and they thought hippies were dirty, but Diana's really smart. She gives me a dark blue T-shirt and a pair of old, worn-out jeans. I change into them. I can't quite manage to do the jeans up. Diana says it will work if I lie down on the ground and hold my tummy in; that's what she always does. They're supposed to be tight. I try it and it works.

Diana's got a record player in her room and a whole row of LPs. She shows me a couple of albums, but I don't know any of them. She says it's progressive music. I don't know what she means but when she turns the sound up really loud I can hear a lot of electric guitars. She sits cross-legged on the floor and shakes her head from side to side to the music. Diana's a real hippie. When the record's finished, she tells me the band is called Deep Purple. She thinks they're really great.

I make a mental note of the name. I want to be a hippie, too. Diana thinks I should take the makeup off my eyes. Hippies don't wear makeup. But they do pluck their eyebrows.

She'll pluck mine if I want. I wash my face in the bathroom. In the meantime, Diana has got a pair of tweezers. I have to lie with my head in her lap so she can get at them easily. When my head touches her lap, I suddenly feel happy. I like her. How nice it is to have a sister like this.

Diana pulls out one of my eyebrow hairs and I jolt upright from the pain. We both get the giggles. You don't feel it after a while, she says. But it goes on hurting. When she's finished, I look in the mirror and see that my eyebrows have almost disappeared. My skin is bright red. Diana reassures me that the redness will go away in a minute. I feel bare without makeup.

Diana draws her curtains. She tells me she always goes to a café called De Boemel, where you can dance, too. She'll ask if I can go with her some time. She lights a joss stick and a penetrating scent spreads through the room.

I'd like to tell her my mother always burned incense, too, but little stones, on All Saints Day, to chase away the spirits. But I don't; I've promised my father not to talk about my mother.

Diana says one of her friends will be coming round in a minute. She says please don't ever let on that I'm her sister. I swear I'll never tell anyone. Relieved, she puts on a record and we listen to the music together.

Late that evening, when I get into bed, the sheets feel cold and stiff. The mattress is soft, outside it's really quiet, downstairs they're still watching television and I'm so tired. The bin bag with my clothes and school stuff from Leiden is in my room. At the bottom is my folder with the papers from Indonesia. I put it under my pillow.

I can't see the bag with my mother's clothes in; I'll have to ask where it is tomorrow.

This morning, when I woke up, I couldn't remember where I was for a minute. Everything sounds so different in this house. No Nitadog. I wonder how she's getting on? I hope she isn't scared. I miss her terribly.

After I've been to the loo, I go back to my room. I don't dare go downstairs. Then I hear Diana. She asks me if I slept well. She takes me downstairs, where she gets things to eat out of the cupboards and shows me where everything's kept. Today she's going out with a whole bunch of people to the De Kroon café, in Kerkdriel. You can go dancing there on Sunday afternoons, she says. They have bands performing there, too, now and again.

Then my father and Auntie Wilma come into the kitchen. When I see my father it makes me think about Nitadog again. I don't feel like speaking to him. Auntie Wilma is friendly towards me.

We have a big breakfast, with all kinds of nice things on bread, quite different from at San's. Diana does the washing-up after breakfast and I help her. She complains about Auntie Wilma and says she thinks she's incredibly stupid.

When Diana has gone to the café in the afternoon I sit in my room. I look out at the shed in the garden, where my brother is taking a moped apart with a friend. He still hasn't said a word to me; he just keeps looking crossly at me.

It's a nuisance I still haven't found the bag with my mother's stuff in. I decide to ask Auntie Wilma about it. She thinks my father knows where it is. When I go up to my father, I wonder what to call him. I don't really want to say Papa. Actually, I'd rather not talk to him at all. I can't stop thinking about Nitadog.

I ask him about the bag.

He says he's thrown the bag away.

Shocked, I tell him there were some of my mother's things in it.

He says he saw that, but I have to forget her. It's best for everybody.

I go back to my room. I can't believe it. That bag had my mother's favourite dresses in it, and the bills from the catalogue. How could he just throw it away?

I quickly get my folder out from under my pillow. Supposing he got hold of that? I must find a good hiding place for it because otherwise he'll take the folder away. Good thing it was in with my school things.

18 February 1974

Today is my first day of school in Den Bosch. My father takes me to the railway station and tells me to take note of the route. Tomorrow I'll have to go by myself on the bike.

Luckily the way to the station isn't difficult. It's about five minutes by bike. At the station my father buys me a monthly season ticket. The journey takes us exactly seven minutes. The school is right opposite the station in Den Bosch. I can see the building from the platform.

We report to the headmaster, who is expecting us. He discusses with my father what I'll need for the coming year. Books, an apron and a gym kit. The headmaster has got a school diary and the lesson timetable for me.

When my father leaves, the headmaster takes me to my new class. Walking along the corridors, I make up my mind that I'm not going to be bullied at this school. We go into the classroom. Thirty girls look at me. The headmaster talks to the teacher for a moment and then leaves me.

The teacher asks my name and where I come from. Karina, I say, from Zaltbommel. He has a little chat with me. The girls are laughing. Shocked, I look at the teacher. He immediately reassures me and explains that the girls are laughing because of my accent. He asks if I've ever lived anywhere else, because of my pronunciation. I nod. Leiden, I reply quietly, scared they'll laugh at me again.

He tells me to go and sit at a desk. As soon as I've sat down, I resolve to learn to speak like the other girls as quickly as possible. I'd never imagined you could hear from my voice that I came from somewhere else. I'm the only one in denim, too. I just hope they're not going to tease me about that.

March 1974

My father is an inspector for a housing association. He works every day and often in the evenings, too. Auntie Wilma is always complaining that he considers his work more important than her. When he's home in the evening, my father always falls asleep in front of the television. When he starts snoring, Auntie Wilma gives him a shove to wake him up. She can't stand it.

My father takes medicine every day; he's got an artificial heart valve. Diana told me he almost died a couple of years ago. He had another girlfriend at the time, a woman who was really mean to her and Johan. Diana's always arguing with Auntie Wilma, too, and Johan never says anything to her. Auntie Wilma complains to me that they act as if she was their servant. I quite like her. She can cook well; there's always bread and ham and stuff and meat with gravy. The thing that does bother me is that she's quite often drunk and then she has terrible rows with Diana or my father. Every day she starts drinking sherry early in the afternoon and asks me if I'd like to have a glass with her. Then she tells me about The Hague, the city she comes from. I don't like sherry but Diana always has a glass with her after school.

I think my father's horrible. I hate him because he got rid of Nitadog. He never asks us to do anything; he just orders us around. If he doesn't like the way something is done, then he gets bad-tempered. He can get furious without any warning and then he shakes me violently. If I don't do something quickly enough, then he hits me.

The first time it came as an awful shock. He hit my ear hard with the flat of his hand. It was glowing and, for a long time afterwards, I could hear a loud ringing noise. When he hits me, he hits my head. When he's in a really bad mood, he punches me, usually on my upper arms, but sometimes in the tummy.

Sometimes I refuse to do as he tells me. When he sees that slapping or thumping doesn't help, then I have to go and kneel with my bare knees on the coconut mat in front of the door for punishment until it hurts so much I ask if I can please get up.

I don't want to use his surname. At school I change my name on every test paper to my mother's surname.

I've written a letter to Rob and one to San. I miss her, and the playground. I hope they write back.

During the week I go to school on the train every day. There are always the same people on the train. I like it at school. We've got a gym teacher we're allowed to call by his first name. He's called Evert and he likes the same kind of music as Diana. He likes Santana. The other girls in the class don't know that band. We're allowed to call the Dutch teacher by her first name, too; she's called Ans.

I recently made a friend. She always takes the same train to school as me. She lives in Culemborg where her father is the mayor. He thinks she ought to go to the ordinary secondary school instead of the domestic science school, but she's not a good learner so now she has to go all the way to Den Bosch because he's ashamed of her. She's going out with a Moluccan boy. Her parents have forbidden it but she does it sneakily anyway. We're always getting the giggles. Her name's Janine.

Even though we tell each other everything, I don't dare say anything about Leiden. And I don't say a word about the circus. I'm scared she'll think I'm weird. I don't dare ask Janine over to my house, either. She knows me as Karina, but in Zaltbommel they call me Karin. I wouldn't have a clue how to explain why I'm the cousin there.

End of March 1974
I've had a letter from San's mother. She asks how Nitadog is and if I'm starting to get used to everything yet and if I'm still eating as much as I did at their house. At the end of the letter, she writes, 'Karina, I hope you won't forget about us. Even though you will soon get to know other children. There aren't many people who would have taken you in just like that, the way we did, don't forget that.'

The letter makes me start missing Leiden again. I miss the playground and Sandra and the other children in the street terribly. I wish I could be with them, just for a little while.

April 1974
There's no school today. It's dead quiet in the house; luckily my father's at work. I hear the post falling on to the mat in the hallway. I pick it up and see an envelope addressed to me.

I recognise Rob's handwriting straight away. I quickly stuff it into the pocket of my jeans and put the post back on the mat. That way, my father won't notice I've touched it. Lucky I'm on my own in the house now.

Up in my room, I shove the bed against the door so no one can come in. With shaking fingers I open the letter. I have to read it a couple of times before I understand what it says.

Rob is working for another circus.

He misses my mother, too. I write back to him, saying things are going well at school but that I don't get on with my father or my brother. I say that I hope I can come and see him some time, secretly, because I'm sure my father won't approve of anything to do with Leiden. Maybe I can come to the circus when it's in our area. I ask him if he's still got any pictures of my mother. I remember someone was taking photographs a week or so before she got ill. I miss her so much.

I'm glad Rob hasn't forgotten me. I put his letter in my folder like a precious treasure. I don't suppose it was his fault that he didn't visit my mother very often. I have to stop thinking about it. I get my bike out and ride into town, buy an envelope and stamps and post my letter.

It's a pity I never mentioned the circus to Janine because Rob was performing near her in Culemborg. I'd love to show her the letter but it would look as if I hadn't trusted her enough to talk about the circus.

That night, in bed, I read the letter a hundred times over.

Dear Karina,

I got your letter from my parents last week. Sorry I haven't had time to reply recently, but I'm on tour again. Not with my own circus this season, but with Circus Mariska. I perform with the horses, Hassan and Macness, and with a clown entrée.

Andreas and Olga are here, too. We play a different town or village every day, which is quite a job. Sometimes we have to drive a long way through the night. This week we're going from Oudewater (near Gouda) to Monnickendam in North Holland.

It's already eleven o'clock at night when I'm writing this letter. We've just finished the show. There weren't that many people, about

55 or 60, I'd say. But that's not my concern any longer, because here at Circus Mariska I get a fixed weekly wage. I've got the Bijenkorf van with me, with Hassan and Macness in and, behind that, the little caravan Corry was living in last year. So I only have to make the trip once a night and I don't have to put the tent up or take it down, either. The luxury Mercedes is in Aalsmeer.

I don't know yet whether we'll be coming to Zaltbommel with the circus, but if we're in the area I'll write and let you know. Then maybe your father will let you come over for an afternoon, okay??? The programme is really good and completely different from last year.

I miss your mum, too. Especially now I'm here on my own. I think about her a lot. She was sweet and very understanding, despite the fact she had plenty of her own problems, which she was really good at hiding.

Well, Karina, I'll finish off for now.

Lots of love,

Rob Roberti

I miss him so much. I miss the circus, the animals, Nitadog.

I miss my mother.

Suddenly, I can't help crying and it seems as if I'll never be able to stop. I have to make an effort to cry quietly. Sometimes a loud sob escapes and I'm scared my father will hear me.

It's like I have to talk to her for a moment. I whisper very quietly to her.

'Oh, my dear Mama, where are you now, where have you got to? I can't stay here, all alone like this. Please come back, even if it's just for a moment. I want to be with you just for a moment, and then you can go again. But then you have to come back again and never go away again. If only I'd been able to say goodbye to you, if only I'd comforted you, held you in my arms. I love you so much. Why did you go away and abandon me? I didn't want it to happen. So why did you do it? Would you have let me go if you'd known I would come and live with my father? He is so nasty. I wish I'd taken something of yours, a lock of hair. Then I could have held it now. Oh, dear, dear Mama, where are you now? Are you floating around somewhere? Or are you lying rotting away in the dark ground. I can't bear the fact that you are lying there under the ground, I can't bear the fact that you're gone, without a kiss, without anything, without me.

'Dearest, dearest Mama, come back to me.'

I cry and cry, I cry my eyes out, but I do it quietly.

When the crying finally subsides, I feel miserable and worn out. My pillow is all wet.

I put the letter from Rob back in my folder. My father must never find it.

May 1974

A woman from the Child Welfare came round. First she talked to my father, then to me. She told me the juvenile court is going to place me here officially. Custody will soon be arranged.

She asked me how I'm getting on and I didn't dare say I'm home-sick for Leiden, for San, for my old school and the playground and the street, that I miss my mother and Nitadog. I'm so ashamed of being the cousin here. Everyone in Zaltbommel thinks I'm called Karin, and Johan still hasn't spoken to me.

I tell her I am trying to get used to it, in the hope that she'll understand what I mean, but she just says it may take a while to settle down.

I'd love to tell her my father got rid of Nitadog after he'd promised I could keep her, but I don't dare. Maybe I'll have to go into a home if they think I don't like it here.

She asks me about school. It's going well; I like it at school.

I ask her if she can ask my father whether I can go and stay with Sandra some time. Maybe my father will let me if she asks him.

The woman leaves. When she's gone, Auntie Wilma wants to know what she asked me. I tell her she just asked about school. I don't think it's fair to tell Auntie Wilma that I don't like it here. She's always nice to me. I wonder if she knows anything about Nitadog or my mother. I don't like to ask in case my father hasn't said anything about them and it might lead to another row.

What I do like about it here is that there's always enough money and food. I regularly get given money to buy clothes. Then I go to Den Bosch with Diana and we buy jeans and T-shirts, always black or dark blue. We wash new jeans a couple of times so they look used.

Sometimes we rub a stone over them in places, to add to the worn effect.

Diana's got a great pair of light-blue jeans with patches on. She always knows where to find terrific boutiques where they sell Indian clothes and joss sticks and little bottles of perfume. She likes patchouli. It smells really strong and musty; it gives me a headache. She's bought an Afghan coat, too, which stinks of wet dog. But it looks great.

I wear exactly the same kind of clothes as Diana. At school, they've accepted the fact that I'm a hippie. I've got Russian army boots with steel toecaps and a barracks bag for my school stuff. I've written all over my bag in felt pen, peace symbols and the names of bands, Deep Purple, Lou Reed, Pink Floyd. I feel pretty tough because the other girls' parents won't let them draw all over their bags. And they're not allowed to wear hippie clothes, either.

6 June 1974
Today's my fourteenth birthday. When Auntie Wilma found out she gave me ten guilders. Diana doesn't know it's my birthday and my father's at work.

There's a song playing on the radio.

Ah Margerita, the roses will bloom
Though you will see me no more
And through your tears you'll smile again
Just like you did before

I go cold. It could have been written for my mother, for me. She loved flowers. It makes me think about the rose petals she used to pick and put in our bed.

When the song finishes, I run up to my room. It goes on playing round and round in my head. I wish I could switch it off. I get confused for a minute; of course I know my mother's dead and it seems like I've forgotten about her most of the time. Except when I got that letter from Rob. And sometimes when I hear music, or hear someone singing, then it reminds me of her.

I think about Nitadog all day long. Actually, I miss her far more than my mother. I hope she's still alive, hope they didn't put her down at the dogs' home. I keep a good look-out on the street in case I happen to see her walking past. The other day, I thought I saw her. I yelled out her name but the dog didn't react. When I realised it wasn't her I burst out crying in the middle of the street. Luckily nobody saw me.

How come I miss Nitadog more than my mother? I can't stop thinking about Nitadog all day long.

June 1974

Johan has joined up early to do his national service. Just the kind of thing he would do. He always wants to fight with everybody; well, now he can do it for a living. He still hasn't said a word to me. Luckily he won't be coming home at the beginning.

Now I go out with Diana every Friday and Saturday night. I have to be home by eleven and not a second later. My father's always waiting up to make sure that I am. Diana's allowed to stay out later than me. The annoying thing is that I have to bike home through the dark on my own. I get scared because I have to pass a cemetery. As soon as I get near it, I start pedalling like mad. I hold my breath until I'm past. I don't dare look at the cemetery. I expect to see ghosts or moving gravestones at any moment.

Diana's really popular with the boys. She's always got a new boyfriend and she stands snogging with them for hours. She drinks a lot of beer. Now and again a boy will try chatting me up, but usually I don't dare talk to them. Mostly I dance on my own all evening, until exactly ten to eleven.

Diana always keeps an eye on me, even when she's snogging. She's afraid I'll open my mouth and tell someone I'm actually her sister.

29 June 1974

I got another letter from San's mum. She wrote that she's sorry she forgot my birthday. There are three fivers in the envelope. San is going up to the next year at school. They're going camping in the holidays.

It makes me laugh when I think about San's mum. She always pulled funny faces when she took her false teeth out. Everybody's got false teeth at San's. Her nan prefers not to wear them. She could laugh really loud without her teeth in and you could see her gums, with a ridged edge at the top and bottom.

Everyone was cheerful at San's house. They sometimes had rows, but not like the kind I have with my father. San's mother could really swear, too. If something upset her, she would say after every sentence: 'Sod it'. She called San's father a dickhead, but then she would say, 'Dickhead, dickhead, eat it on a piece of bread, bye-bye dickhead' and she couldn't help laughing. She never stayed cross for long.

With my father you never know when or why he's going to get angry, or how long it'll last.

July 1974

I'm in love with a boy in De Boemel. His name is Bart van Dam, and he's in love with me, too. We meet up secretly so Diana doesn't see us. We snog in alleyways, in the park or under the big bridge over the Waal. We make a date every day, before or after school.

Bart van Dam wants to have it off with me and so do I, really, but it's difficult to find a place to do it. Now we've discovered an old shed at the strawberry auction. We've agreed that we'll go and have it off there tomorrow. I'm really nervous because I'm scared it'll hurt. I've felt Bart's willy when we were snogging and it feels so big; it'll never fit in.

I tried with a pencil at home to see if I was actually deep enough. I managed all right with the pencil, but Bart's willy is much fatter. I tried stretching my fanny open with my fingers, but I'm sure it's not wide enough.

Bart's done it a few times before. He's nicked a Durex from his dad. He didn't dare buy them.

It's draughty in the shed and everything's wet. There isn't a clean spot anywhere to lie down. In the end, we find a dry patch under an old boat that's being stored there. We giggle nervously as we go and lie down under the boat.

I pull my trousers down and Bart tries to stick his willy in. I can feel it won't fit. It hurts. Bart says it always hurts the first time. I'll wait and see; maybe it would be better if he shoved it in all at once.

He pushes and I let out a cry of pain. He slides it gently in and out and after a couple of times it doesn't hurt any more. Then I remember we've forgotten the Durex. He quickly puts it on. He thrusts hard a couple more times and then he comes. When he pulls off the Durex it's full of sperm. He throws it away.

I look down at myself. It feels like I've been stretched, but there's nothing to be seen, no blood, either. Well, now I've lost my virginity.

Bart wants to go home.

We agree to meet under the bridge tomorrow. I didn't like it that much. His willy is too big. But maybe I'll stretch if we practise more often.

Maybe it'll feel as nice as it says in the sex books.

August 1974
The last few days there's been a row every time my father comes home. Nobody in the house can do anything right. I creep quietly upstairs when they're arguing and put my head under the pillow. I can't stand all that yelling.

One morning, after yet another row, I come across Diana and my father in the sitting room. Auntie Wilma has walked out of the house. Diana's glad but my father's furious. He blames us. I get the full blast. I think that's unfair, seeing as I was the only one who got on well with Auntie Wilma.

From now on, Diana and I have to do the housework. I have to do the cleaning and the washing; Diana has to do the cooking. My father will do the shopping for the whole week on Saturdays.

In the evening, while Diana and I are doing the washing-up, she is cheerful and clearly relieved that Auntie Wilma has left. But I think it's awful. Particularly as she didn't say goodbye to me. We actually had quite a nice time when there were just the two of us but she didn't even leave me a note.

24 October 1974
I've had another letter from Rob. They're travelling from one place to another every day, now, he writes, and that's really tiring for him. Every night, he has to drive one of the circus lorries up and down

twice, so he always gets to bed late. Andreas and Olga are working at Boltini now; Andreas looks after the horses. Hassan and Macness are doing well, Rob says. The only problem is they've turned out to be little devils. They bite and kick. The whole circus is scared of them. Next week they're going back to the winter quarters and he'll send me the pictures with my mother in.

I hope he does. Then I can look at my mother again.

If Circus Boltini comes round, then I'll go and see them. Won't Andreas and Olga be surprised?

November 1974

I've just spent a week in hospital, having my tonsils out. I kept being ill and the doctor could see that my tonsils were really swollen. He thinks I will be better off without them.

My father didn't visit me once in the hospital and neither did Diana. When I was allowed out, he came to fetch me. I sat next to him in the car but he said nothing all the way home.

I think we hate each other; him as much as me.

I can't imagine why he wanted me to come and live with him.

Since Auntie Wilma left, I have to do almost everything in the house. Hoovering, washing, ironing. Every day when I come home from school there's a note on the kitchen table with jobs for me to do. At five o'clock, my father comes home and checks to see if everything's been done.

He often makes unreasonable demands. I have to get the dust out from under the radiators, for instance. Then he feels with his fingers for any dust I've missed. He keeps thinking of things I can't do properly even though I really do my best.

He's never satisfied. He seems to enjoy it when I haven't done something right. Then he makes me do it all over again while he watches. And while he's watching, he waits for me to do something else wrong. Then he says, in a sneering tone of voice, 'Oh, did your mother teach you to do it like that?'

I hate that. He won't let me talk about my mother, but he does, and then like that.

Then he loses his temper and orders me to it differently, exactly the way he wants it.

When I see the bare skin of his hands, it disgusts me. I can't stand the way he runs his fingers through his hair. The little bit of skin between his socks and his trouser legs makes me feel sick.

I've recently found a way of making him less furious. He hopes I'm going to answer him back but I don't any longer. At first I did. That gave him a reason to get angry and an excuse to hit me. He slaps really hard. Sometimes I can still feel the place where he hit me glowing an hour after the blow. Sometimes he punches me, too. The bruises I get last for ages. First they're red, then blue, and then slowly they go brown.

In the beginning, I objected to what he said about my mother. I don't any more because it only leads to a far worse punishment. Once I told him my mother did know better, that she would never have given such stupid orders. Then he dragged me so roughly up the stairs by my hair that my head was covered in bumps.

He doesn't need a reason to pick on me and, since I know that, I try and do my best. It's not him hitting me that's the worst thing, incidentally. I know exactly when the blow's coming, so I hold my breath and it doesn't land so hard. The thing that bothers me far more is the horrible things he says about my mother. And I can't stand it when he gives Diana hell, either. He's even tougher on her than he is with me. The other day, he was squeezing her throat for ages. I thought she was going to suffocate but I didn't dare do anything.

Sometimes I think he's mad. As far as I know, nobody realises how badly he treats us; he's extremely polite to the outside world. I can't understand why my mother ever married him.

I hope he gets a heart attack. Sometimes I fantasise about punching him in the heart, against his artificial valve. Maybe it'll stop working.

End of November 1974
My father's got a new girlfriend. She's coming to meet us today. Diana and Johan don't want to see her, to my father's great annoyance. If she likes the house, she'll come and live here. She's got a son of twenty and a little boy of five.

I think Auntie Agnes, as we're supposed to call her, is about the same age as my father. She's got short, blond, curly hair, blue eyes, and doesn't wear any makeup. She looks a bit dull. I can see she's nervous. I think it's a bit hard on her that Johan and Diana don't want to meet her.

My father keeps joking with me during her visit. It makes me want to puke. The hypocrite. I wonder if she realises just how stupid he is. Maybe I'll tell her.

At school I've been chosen as form captain. I get along well with the girls and most of the teachers. If I like a teacher, then I try that bit harder. I'd really like to tell them about my mother. They've got no idea that she's dead or that I've only just met my father. And that in Zaltbommel I pass for a cousin. But I just wouldn't know where to begin.

I make up my mind to put a photograph of my mother next to my book in maths. It's the only picture I've got of her, from when she was still a young girl. I hope Henk, the teacher, will see the picture when he walks past my table and ask me about it. Just to be sure, I write MAMA in big letters on the photo.

I can't concentrate during the lesson. I keep thinking about the moment when Henk will pass my desk and notice the photo. I really hope he asks if it's my mother; then I'll say yes. Yes, but she's dead.

But Henk has already been past a couple of times and hasn't asked anything. Surely he must have seen it. When the bell goes, I put the picture away safely in my folder, disappointed that Henk didn't ask about it.

I'd like to tell Evert, the gym teacher, that my mother's dead, too. I can't use the photo with him. But if I sit and stare into space and don't want to join in, he's bound to ask me why I'm acting so strangely. Then I'll say it's because my mother's dead. I hope he takes me on one side to do it. If I have to say it in front of the other girls, then I won't dare.

I sit out on the side during gym, staring into the distance. Evert notices but doesn't ask me why. It just makes him increasingly impatient and grumpy. Who knows; maybe he'll have a word with me after the lesson. But no, after the lesson we have to take a shower and change.

Evert didn't ask me anything, either. The only other teacher I can try it with is Ans Buis, our Dutch teacher.

December 1974

Diana's got a steady boyfriend, Paul. She's introduced him to my father. He comes from Kerkdriel and now she's arranged it so I can go with her to the De Kroon café there.

The café is a bit like De Boemel, but much bigger. There's a hall where bands play occasionally. I saw Kayak perform there and Margriet Eshuijs, and a disc jockey from Radio Veronica's coming soon. A lot of young people from the surrounding villages go to De Kroon, all of them hippies. Most of them have got a moped, a Puch with high handlebars and a fox tail attached to the back. Diana's got a moped too. Actually, it's a boys' moped, but that makes it all the more glamorous if you're a girl.

I hope I get a moped as well because now I have to go all the way to Kerkdriel by bike. Diana often gives me a tow; I ride next to her, holding her shoulder; that goes really fast. She seems not to keep such a close eye on me now she's with Paul. Maybe it's because she's realised I can keep our secret.

I get to know a lot of new guys in Kerkdriel but I never have anything to do with the girls who go there. Most of the guys are already in their twenties. Sometimes I get off with them. I'm scared Diana won't approve, but she hasn't said anything up till now. Sometimes Johan comes, too, and then I keep a low profile.

Everyone keeps their head down when Johan is there. He's got a reputation for being a bruiser. I think he's proud of that because he walks around with his chest stuck out and his fists clenched, looking provocative and aggressive.

It's dark in De Kroon. They project liquid slides on to the walls and that makes a lovely effect. You can look at it for ages because the shapes and colours on the wall change continually.

Diana drinks a lot of beer. I don't. I've recently started smoking joints with a couple of guys I've got to know. Diana doesn't mix with them; she thinks they're filthy drug addicts, but I think they're nice. Diana has never smoked dope. She gets all nervous about it. She says you get addicted straight away once you've done it.

One of the guys lives in Zaltbommel, too, in a big detached house. His name is Kees. He's a bit slow, skinny and has a little goatee beard. He always wears a crocheted hat and a long, blue-and-white-striped

Indian shirt with white embroidery and usually goes around barefoot. He likes calm music. I get the giggles from dope but Kees never does. He's a really serious person and thinks deeply about everything.

It was Kees who showed me how to roll a joint. He does it with great ceremony. He pays a lot of attention to smoking, too. He inhales with a hissing sound, then holds the smoke in for a long time and blows it out gradually. Then he passes the joint on to someone else, who proceeds to smoke with equal ceremony. When I get passed a joint, I do exactly the same. But I don't actually like it that much. Sometimes the smoke is so hot or the taste so strong that it takes a lot of effort to hold it in. It gives you a nice dreamy feeling, though.

Christmas holidays 1974
My father's been staying at Auntie Agnes's in Boxtel the past few weeks. He comes to visit now and again. She doesn't want to come and live with us, I think because Johan and Diana refuse to talk to her. At first, my father was really cross about it but now he acts as if there's nothing wrong.

Actually, I quite like Auntie Agnes. She helps me clean the house and I babysit for her little boy sometimes. He's terribly difficult. I don't think he's completely normal. I usually draw with him, which he likes. Her other son is already twenty. He lives in a bedsit in Nijmegen and comes round now and again. He's a hippie, too. I get along with him okay.

Last week Auntie Agnes had a stomach operation. Now my father wants me to go and stay with her, so I can look after her and her little boy. I don't mind. It's the Christmas holidays and I'm bored stiff all day, anyway.

In Boxtel I play with Auntie Agnes's little boy during the day. In the evening, when he's asleep, the two of us sit and chat. Luckily, now I'm here my father is staying in Zaltbommel. Auntie Agnes tells me she had another child, who died a couple of years ago. She's really sad about it. I feel sorry for her. I would like to tell her about my mother, that I know what it's like when someone dies, but I don't dare.

After a couple of days, I decide to tell her about my father. I want to warn her that he can be nasty. I want her to know that he's quite different with us from the way she thinks.

But Auntie Agnes won't hear a word of it. It's as if she suddenly can't stand the sight of me, when I've hardly told her anything. Of course she thinks I'm making it up, or that I'm jealous of her. She thinks Diana's jealous of her, too.

She wants me to go back to Zaltbommel the following day.

Well, that's fine by me. I warned her. It's up to her.

New Year's Eve 1974
My father's not surprised I've come back early from Auntie Agnes's. I ask him if I can go and celebrate New Year's Eve at Janine's, in Culemborg, and he says it's okay.

Janine lives in a big house with a big garden. Her parents are strict but not unfriendly. They talk and eat posh. Janine has had to promise she won't see her Moluccan boyfriend again, otherwise she'll be sent to a boarding school. We're not allowed to go to Stoned Hill any more, either. That's a farm in Culemborg where hippies live who always have plenty of dope. Janine's parents found out we went there once. She was grounded, but now she's allowed to go into town with me for a while.

As her father's the mayor, everyone knows Janine. He's scared she'll give him a bad name.

There's a coffee shop in the centre of Culemborg where we go and drink hot chocolate and smoke roll-ups. Two older guys are sitting smiling at us. When we get up to go one of them asks if we'd like to go round to their house for a cup of tea. They give us their address.

Janine wants to go and so do I. We promise we'll go round that afternoon. It's a bit scary, though. At her house we make ourselves up identically. We don't dare tell her parents what we're planning to do.

When we ring the bell at the address they gave us, one of the guys sticks his head out of the window. He calls down and tells us to hang on a minute. The other guy opens the door. We go into an old, bare house. They introduce themselves. The tall guy is called Rutger and the short one Dave. We don't really know what to say but the boys make jokes. In the meantime, Rutger rolls a huge joint. They pass it to us while we listen to Roxy Music. I like Rutger; I wouldn't mind getting off with him.

When the joint is finished and we've had a cup of tea, we go home. Janine is scared we'll be late for dinner. The guys ask if we'll come back again that evening; they'll be at home. We're not sure. We're celebrating New Year's Eve at Janine's house. We don't know if we'll be allowed out, but we'll do our best.

When we get outside, I squeeze Janine tightly. I fancy Rutger. I could shout it out. And Janine fancies Dave. We skip back to her house together.

There, we're on our best behaviour, in the hope that we'll be allowed out for a while. But Janine's parents won't let us go. We try not to make it obvious that we mind so much. Fed up, we sit in Janine's room and decide to try again the following day.

At midnight, everyone wishes each other a happy new year. Janine is allowed to light sparklers outside. Apart from that, things are quiet in the street. Now and again we see a rocket explode in the distance. I can't help thinking of Leiden. New Year's Eve was always really exciting there. Loads of fireworks were let off in our street. I always had long strings of bangers, which the Chinese man in the *toko* gave me.

New Year's Day 1975
Today we go and wish Rutger and Dave a happy new year. They're at home and they're glad we've come. Like yesterday, we listen to music and smoke a joint. It's as if we've known each other for ages. It's all really relaxed.

I notice the guys fancy us, too, but exactly the other way round. Dave fancies me and Rutger fancies Janine. It doesn't really matter. Janine's noticed, too. I answer her enquiring look with a shrug, to show I don't mind.

We get the giggles. The guys ask if we're going to stay until the evening. I'd like to, but I'm sure Janine's parents wouldn't let us. She says stuff her parents.

We stay. Dave makes another pot of tea and now he comes and sits down close to me. Janine goes off to another room with Rutger. She waves to me and we burst out laughing. She finds the situation funny, too; how typical that it hasn't turned out the way we wanted.

Dave puts his arm around me. I lean back and let him do what he wants. The joint has made me feel nice and warm and dopey. He kisses me gently on my face and neck. It feels nice. He asks if I'll go with him to his bedroom. I follow him and notice, when I stand up, that I'm a head taller than he is.

On the bed, he slowly undresses me. He does everything slowly and gently. He whispers that he thinks I'm sweet. I lie on my back, with my eyes closed, and feel his hands stroking me. It makes me feel a bit sad. I wish I could lie like this for ever.

When I open my eyes again, I see he's undressed himself. Now he's undoing my jeans. He asks if I'm cold or if I'm scared. I just lie there, only feeling his hands and his lips. He licks my tummy and legs with his tongue. It makes me think of the sexy magazines I've read.

This is one of those nice love-making sessions they describe. Dave turns me over and kisses my back and my bottom. Everything is soft, wet and warm. I feel like I could fall asleep any moment.

I'm startled awake by Rutger's voice. He's asking for tobacco and it flashes through my head that he can see me lying there naked. But then I hear the door close again.

Dave keeps on stroking and kissing me. He turns me over again. I let him move me into any position he wants. I keep my eyes shut. I'm scared it'll be over if I open them.

Dave's going to screw me. I open my legs wide for him. It only takes a couple of thrusts before he comes on my belly. He massages his sperm into my skin until it disappears entirely. I'm still feeling dopey and enjoying his kisses. Then he rolls off me to go to the loo. I pull the covers up over me.

I seem to be slowly waking up. I'm cold and thirsty and wonder what Janine's doing. I quickly get dressed. I just lay there; I didn't touch Dave or kiss him once. I just let it all happen to me without doing a thing. When he comes back again I don't dare look at him. I'm ashamed that I just lay there like a limp rag doll.

Janine comes to get me; she's alone. We have to go home. I say goodbye to Dave as if nothing's happened. I hope I never see him again.

Outside, Janine asks if I had it off with Dave. I nod. Rutger and she talked the whole evening about her old boyfriend and her parents, she says.

On the way home, we get more and more worried about what we're going to say to them. We didn't go back for dinner and it's already almost midnight. We agree not to say where we've been. We swear it. We'll just say we've been to the De Piep-In café.

Janine's house is in darkness. Everyone's asleep. Janine quietly opens the door. We creep up the stairs. But as soon as we're at the top, we hear Janine's mother calling out to us. She's really cross. She doesn't want to hear our excuses. I have to go home in the morning and I won't be allowed to go to Janine's any more. Feeling guilty, we go to Janine's room.

As soon as we're in bed, Janine falls asleep. I think about Dave. It was the first time I've enjoyed making love.

February 1975

Since I warned Auntie Agnes about my father she has stopped coming to our house. I haven't seen Johan for ages either. He got into some kind of trouble at the barracks where he's doing his national service and now he's in a military detention centre. My father's at Auntie Agnes's most of the time and Diana's at Paul's.

Now that I hardly ever see Diana I start making new friends. I'm not going out with Bart van Dam any more, but we get off with each other now and again, when we're bored. We don't screw any more though. It still doesn't fit properly and Bart's scared I'll get pregnant.

I wouldn't mind having a baby, all to myself. A sweet little baby I can look after and love. A little baby that loves me. I'm probably much too young but I know I'd make a good mother. If I get pregnant I'll run away. Then I want to have my baby all by myself, because nobody's going to take it away from me.

March 1975

I saw my mother again today. I got another letter from Rob. There were eight photos with it.

They were taken on Tony Wilson's birthday, the magician. I remember it just like yesterday. It was a week before my mother got ill. She looks healthy and happy in the pictures. You can see she's laughing at Tony. He used to make jokes all the time. Rob and his parents are in them, too, and Tony's wife and their daughter, a cute little girl of two. I used to play with her a lot, she was my living doll. In the background you can see the lake I used to swim in every morning and evening. The jetty where I learned to dive is there too.

Rob writes:

Dear Karina!!
I got a letter from Andreas and Olga this week with a few photos in, which I asked them to send me for you last time. Your mum's in all of them and most of them were taken on Tony Wilson's birthday. Looking at the photos again like this brings back old memories and I have to admit it was a nice time.

The dove act has been sold. A Swiss lady came here for five days this week to learn the act and went back to Switzerland with the birds and the props on Tuesday.

The geese have been rented to Circus Piste, like last year. The horses are still here and I haven't got anything for them, but you never know, maybe they'll get hired out, too. I haven't got an engagement for myself yet for next season, but it could still happen. Don't forget to thank Olga and Andreas for the pictures.

Well, Karina, until the next letter, or when I see you again,
Lots of love,
Rob Roberti

I'm so pleased with the photos. I take them to my secret place at the end of a breakwater in the Waal. There's a pole there I sit with my back against. It's lovely and quiet, so far out into the river. Now and again a big boat sails by. When it's very windy, the waves smack up high against the breakwater, sometimes so high I get wet.

Sometimes I talk to the waves. It's as if the water understands me. Talking out loud helps me sort my thoughts out. I often feel so confused.

I just can't understand how my mother could ever have married my father. I don't understand him at all. I can't do anything right. I wonder if he was like that with my mother, too. How could she ever have made love with him? But they must have done it, otherwise we wouldn't have been born. Maybe he forced her. I can't imagine he made us out of love. But I know for certain my mother wanted us. How could she have married him?

April 1975

I've had another row with my father. I'm going to murder him tonight, the bastard. I can't stand the sight of him any more. I wonder what the best way of killing him would be. I think I should hit him as hard as I can in the heart.

The scary thing is that he'll see me coming and maybe it won't work. His heart is definitely the weakest spot, but he's stronger than me. Maybe I'd better get him from behind.

I'll hit him on the head tonight. I'm going to bash his head in.

I get an empty Coke bottle from the kitchen. It's easy to hold and the bottom of the bottle seems hard enough. I practise with the bottle in my room, working out the best way to use it. I wait for him to come home.

He's late this evening, typical. The bastard. Now it'll take even longer.

Then I hear him opening the front door and going into the kitchen. I creep quietly down the stairs. I can hear the tap running. I've got the bottle behind my back. I hope I'm strong enough to kill him with one blow.

Softly, I walk down the hall to the kitchen. He hasn't heard me. He's standing with his back to me, in just the right position. The sound of the running water is loud. There's a bald patch on the top of his head. That's the spot where I want to hit him.

I try to aim the bottle as well as possible. I have to do it now. Quickly.

But my arm refuses. I can't lift it high enough. My knees start shaking. It's no good. I can see every pore in the bald patch on his head. Right there, that's where I have to hit him. But I can't get my arm to move.

I turn round and walk out of the kitchen, away, as quickly as possible. He didn't even notice me. I run upstairs.

I sit on my bed for a long time, trembling. I'm angry with myself that I didn't succeed. How come? Normally I've got really strong arms and I can manage to do anything I want.

I hate him from the depths of my heart. I'm staying in my room this evening. I can pee in the basin. I never want to see him again.

The next morning he's already gone to work when I come out of my room. Luckily it's not the weekend, so I can go to school. I'd rather stay at school all the time; if needs be I'll sleep on the mats in the gym.

I make up my mind that as from today I'm not going to do anything my father wants, even if he beats me to death. From now on I'm not going to speak to him. He can't stand that. Then if he gets mad I'll threaten to tell everyone he's been in prison in Indonesia. I'm sure he doesn't know I know. I heard my mother talking about it once with an old Indonesian woman who had been in the Japanese camp with her. They didn't realise I was listening. They were talking about the fact that, during the war, he covered someone in tar and threw him in the sea. That's why he went to prison. After that I never heard my mother talk about my father again. She never wanted to tell me anything about him, but I always remembered that.

If he does anything mean to me again I'll tell him I know.

June 1975
Now I'm really in the shit. I screwed this guy.

It wasn't even a guy I really liked: I'd never want a baby by him, but I was bored. Now I'm scared I'm pregnant anyway.

He was really rough and the Durex tore. I had loads of sperm inside me. I've tried rinsing it out with water, but every time I go to the loo I can see it's still coming out. I'm not sure what to do. Janine thinks we ought to tell Miss Jansen. Maybe she can help.

Ans Buis, the Dutch teacher, says I need to get the morning-after pill from the doctor, but she can't take me without getting permission from my father. Well, there's nothing else for it. The headmaster calls my father. Now I'm in real trouble.

The thought crosses my mind that I should tell Ans my father will beat me up now. But maybe she won't believe me; my father's always so polite to other people and everyone thinks he's really nice.

The doctor doesn't make any fuss about it. He writes out a prescription and tells me I'll feel sick for a couple of days because of the pill. Then I'll get my period. I have to make sure I finish the course. Ans goes with me to the chemist's and then drops me off at the station.

When I get home, there's a note listing all the things I have to do, as usual. I can tell by the handwriting that my father was cross when he wrote it.

For the first time I refuse to do anything. I take my first pill and go and lie down on the sofa in the sitting room. I'll say I feel too ill to do the cleaning.

Then the door bursts open. My father storms into the room. He's furious. He calls me a slut and a whore. He wants to know the boy's name.

I hadn't expected that. What's the point in that?

He asks me again who it was.

I don't answer.

He slaps me hard across the head; the back of my head slams against the wall.

But I still say nothing. I feel ice cold inside. Secretly, I cherish the words my mother so often said to me. One of her rules was that you should never betray anybody.

My father shakes me and yanks at my hair. I can see he realises I won't say anything. I couldn't care less about his rage. The only reason I'm a bit scared is because I know he'll stop at nothing to find out the boy's name. He walks out of the room and says he'll find out for himself. He doesn't come back all evening.

The next day I feel pretty sick. But I go to school anyway because I'm dead scared I'll run into my father.

Ans Buis asks how I am. I tell her my father's furious, that he hit me and now he's trying to discover the boy's name. She's shocked. I'd love to tell her what a bastard my father is, but I don't dare.

Now my father knows who did it. He's spoken to the boy's parents and he's going to talk to him, too. I can't see what there is to be gained from this so I lie to him. I say it was another boy. But my father is sure of his information.

From now on I refuse to say another word in this house. I won't go down to watch telly any more, either. From now on, I'll just stay in my room. I don't want to go to De Boemel or De Kroon. I only want to go to school.

I'm doing just what my mother did. I can quite understand why she drew the curtains when we were attacked with snowballs. She must have felt just like I feel now.

I don't want anything to do with anyone in this house any longer.

It's like living in a loony bin.

March 1976

I'm at school early again today. I've got the first couple of periods free; it's another two hours until my first lesson.

There's a bench in the corridor, opposite the headmaster's office, next to the chocolate milk dispenser. That's gradually become my regular place. I wait there until the girls from my class come in. It's still early. They're probably all fast asleep. It's dead quiet in the corridor; all the lessons have started.

The headmaster comes up to me. He sits down next to me and asks why I'm at school so early. Suddenly, I can't help bursting into tears.

He takes me into his office and gives me a glass of water.

I don't seem to be able to stop crying. When I finally manage to say something, I tell him I'd much rather be at school than at home. The headmaster asks me why. He asks all kinds of questions and finally asks me if I might like to go and live somewhere else.

It's as if something just clicked in my head. Why didn't I think of that myself? That's exactly what I'd like to do; I'd love to go and live somewhere else, but where and who with?

He asks about my family.

I haven't got any family, I reply. I tell him I'm scared I'll have to go into a home. I don't like the idea of that, although I wouldn't mind it so much as I would have done before. Suddenly I'm sure I don't want to live with my father any longer.

He tells me to stay where I am, while he pops over to see Marian Engel. She teaches social studies and knows a lot about the social services.

When he's gone, I feel so happy. Just imagine. Imagine I could go and live somewhere else. Imagine I could get away from that bastard.

After quite a while the headmaster comes back, with Marian Engel. She says I can go and live with her for a bit, until they can find a good solution. I'm amazed it's so easy to organise. I wish I'd known this earlier.

Then she says my father has to agree to the arrangement.

I start crying again. You can't talk to him. I know he'll never agree. But Marian Engel says she'll sort it out with him. I'm allowed to stay in the headmaster's office until I've calmed down a bit, but I've lost all hope. I'm absolutely certain he'll never agree. They don't know how nasty he is.

After another long wait, the headmaster comes back. They've spoken to my father on the phone and made an appointment to see him.

That afternoon, the headmaster comes into the classroom and asks me to come into the corridor for a moment. He's spoken to my father and my father has given his consent. I can't believe it. But the headmaster says it was a good conversation and my father realised this is the best solution for us both for the moment. I still can't believe it. I hope they don't think I'm making a fuss about nothing.

That same afternoon, after school, I'm allowed to go and meet Marian Engel's family. Ans Buis will take me in her car. She is my favourite teacher and I like the idea of going to live with Marian for a while.

Marian's got three young children aged seven, five and three, who look at me shyly with big eyes. She lives in a huge house. The living room is big, with sliding doors and high ceilings. It's decorated in a really unusual style, not as brown and bare as at my father's. The walls are lined with high shelf units, full of books. Part of the back room has been made into a play area for the children.

The house is a bit messy.

Marian pours out some tea, then she starts telling me about her family. She's married to Bram, who works in Eindhoven and does something with computers. He gets home late every day. Bram's sister and her husband live in the house, too. They're called Els and Walter. Together, they form a sort of commune. Upstairs, everyone has their own room, but apart from that they share everything.

Marian shows me the house. On the first floor are the bathroom, Marian and Bram's room, a study and what will be my room. On the next floor are Els and Walter's room and the children's rooms and above that an attic. I'm totally amazed at the size of the house.

When we get back down again, the table in the kitchen has been set. Dinner's ready. Els is home, now; she's fat with curly hair. She looks friendly. Walter's got a beard and is wearing a checked flannel shirt, corduroy trousers and sandals. My sister will be really jealous; she loves these arty kind of places.

We sit down at the table without waiting for Bram; he always comes in later. The children want to sit next to me. Els tells me Marian called her that morning to ask if it was okay for me to come and stay with them for a while. I tell her I still can't believe I'm here.

Then Bram comes in. He's got a beard, too, and wears the same kind of clothes as Walter. He shakes hands with me and we start eating. Bram doesn't say much but the others do. There's a really nice atmosphere at dinner. We agree that I should go home after dinner and come and live with them the following day. Marian takes me to the station. On the way home in the train I get more and more scared of what my father's going to say. I still think it's really strange that he seemed to be okay about it. Has he changed in some way? Well, even if he has, I don't want to stay with him. And if he's horrible to me, then at least I'll be rid of him tomorrow.

As soon as I go into the house, I can tell there's something up with my father. He's pacing backwards and forwards in the sitting room. When he sees me, he storms up, furious. He yells at me to go and pack my things right away.

He drags me up the stairs and screams that no one is going to tell him what to do. He'll decide what's good for me. He gives me five minutes to get my things together.

I can only think about one thing. Getting away.

I can't get out of the window. It's too high to jump out of, but not far enough for the fall to kill me. And I want to die; I'd rather be dead than live with that madman.

I smash the mirror. I'll cut my wrists with the pieces. I stick a piece of broken glass into my wrist. It hurts. I'll have to press harder to make a cut. I don't dare to.

I pack my clothes. I pack my school things. I pack my folder. My folder, the only thing I won't let him take away from me. Then my father's already in my room and dragging me downstairs.

He shoves me roughly into the car. I struggle, but he's stronger and I give up. He drives like a madman out of Zaltbommel, on to the motorway. If he goes on driving like this, he's going to kill us both.

After half an hour, I pluck up the courage to ask where we're going.

To Zundert, he says. To his sister's. We'll soon see who's the boss here.

I say nothing. I hate him. How stupid of me. How could I believe he'd be okay about Marian? Of course he said he agreed, the shit. His sister. I remember my mother saying she was a narrow-minded old frump.

I see the signposts to Breda-Zundert shoot past me on the motorway. When we arrive at Auntie Katrina's house in Zundert I'm told to go straight upstairs. My father comes after me. He shoves me forward and I fall into the bedroom. He doesn't bother holding back in front of his sister.

I'm not allowed out of the room and I'm instructed that if I need to go to the toilet I have to call her.

A wooden wardrobe with a mirror fills the room. There's a mattress on the ground. It smells musty in here, as if the room hasn't been used for some time. I can hear their voices downstairs. Then the front door slams. A car starts and screeches off. As far as I'm concerned my father can crash and kill himself stone dead.

Auntie Katrina comes into the room. She gives me a lecture. It's not nice what I've been doing to my father. I'm not to be allowed out of this room for the time being. She gives me some bedclothes. I can put my things in the cupboard.

She goes back downstairs. I hang my clothes in the empty wardrobe. I hang my bag, with the folder in it, between my clothes, afraid of it being found. Then I make up the mattress with the sheets she gave me; they're ironed stiff.

I'm tired. Before I go to sleep, I call as I'm supposed to and say I want to go to the toilet. Auntie Katrina goes with me. She stands guard outside the loo. On my way back to the room I see Uncle Dirk sitting in the kitchen. Out of the corner of my eye, I see him give me a friendly nod, which it looks as if he's trying to hide from his own wife. Uncle Dirk. That gives me a bit of hope.

Next morning, Auntie Katrina wakes me up bringing me breakfast in my room. It's quite a luxurious prison, here, getting breakfast in bed. Now she's less strict with me. She says I will have to stay in this room for the time being, as my father has ordered, but if I calm down, then later on in the week I'll be able to go downstairs.

I ask how long I'll be staying with them. She shrugs. She doesn't know. My father's coming back at the end of the week.

It's Saturday now. I ask if I can use the phone.

No, is the answer, that's what she's agreed with my father. Auntie Katrina starts getting strict again because of all my questions. She leaves me.

How awful for Marian. Now she's waiting for me for nothing.

Half the week has gone by. I'm allowed to go downstairs now and again and in the evening we watch television. Uncle Dirk is nice to me and it seems that Auntie Katrina would actually like to be nicer to me than she is. She's obviously keeping to the agreement she made with my father.

I act really nice towards them because I've got a plan. I'm going to run away.

Maybe I'll be able to sneakily phone Ans Buis and ask her to pick me up somewhere in the car. Auntie Katrina goes out for a while every evening to deliver the curtains she's been making during the day. While she's away, Uncle Dirk always starts a chat with me. I hope he'll let me call Diana.

If he gives me permission, then I'll call Ans instead of Diana. I write Ans's number on my arm. As soon as Auntie Katrina has gone out, I ask Uncle Dirk if I can phone Diana. I tell him I need some more clothes, which my father can bring when he comes at the end of the week. Uncle Dirk says it's okay.

The telephone is in the hall; luckily he stays in the kitchen. I dial Ans's number. I just hope she's at home.

Ans answers and I quickly and quietly ask if she will please pick me up on the edge of the motorway. I explain that I can't talk for long because I'm being held prisoner.

Obviously shocked, Ans asks how I am.

Okay, I say. I'm pretending to call my sister. Ans understands.

She can't just come and get me, she says, I have to run away myself. If she helps, she may be guilty of kidnapping.

Okay, I say, 'bye. As I put the phone down, I hear her asking where I am. But I've already hung up. Now I've got to think of something else.

Next day, I'm told that Auntie Agnes is coming round. I hear the doorbell and then for a long time the buzz of voices downstairs. I hope I can go home with Auntie Agnes but as soon as she comes into my room I'm startled. I've never seen her like this.

She starts shrieking a fire-and-brimstone sermon at me. How could I think of breaking my father's heart like this? She never would have expected it of me. And him such a nice, hard-working man. They've decided I should stay in Zundert. They've found a school for me, too; I can start on Monday.

When she says this, something snaps inside me. I want her out of here but she keeps on talking. She's trying to intimidate me but I'm not standing for it. If she doesn't go now I'll kick her out the door.

Furious, I stand up and start pushing her out of the room. Auntie Katrina comes running up the stairs and throws me to the ground. I just manage to give Auntie Agnes a good kick in the shin before she leaves the room screaming and yelling. She sounds like a Vietnamese pot-bellied pig.

The door of my room slams shut. For the first time since I've been here, I almost start crying. Stay here? Never. Go to school here? Forget it. I'll show them.

Now it's been decided I have to stay and live here, Auntie Katrina says I don't have to stay in my room all day any more. I can come down and join them. On Monday I'll go to my new school. It's some way outside the village. Auntie Katrina will take me and pick me up in the car every day.

Tomorrow is Saturday and they want me to go with them to Breda to buy some clothes for the new school. Auntie Katrina thinks I dress too sloppily. Submissively I agree with everything. The sooner I gain their confidence, the quicker I can make my escape. The incident with Auntie Agnes hasn't been mentioned again.

It feels funny, doing the shopping next day in Breda. If only people knew that I'm actually a prisoner.

Auntie Katrina picks out a frumpy blouse and some frumpy trousers for me. I try them on willingly. I get new shoes, too, just as frumpy as the clothes. I pretend I'm pleased with them. To Auntie Katrina's great delight I keep them on. She asks me if there's anything I'd like to buy for myself.

I'd like a sketchbook; then I can draw at home.

In the car on the way home she gives me some pocket money. I thank her and pretend I'm happy with the idea of living with her and Uncle Dirk. I talk sensibly. I tell them my hobby is drawing and that what I like to draw best is animals. I ask if I can go and draw the deer in the park opposite the house some time. Auntie Katrina says it would be okay.

It's working. My plan's working. That evening, after watching telly I quickly go upstairs. I've got it all thought out how I should run away. Once I'm sure they're in bed, I get out my sketchbook. I'm going to make a hitchhiking sign. I haven't got any felt pens but I've still got my eyebrow pencil in my old jeans. That'll do fine.

I write BREDA in really big letters on a page of my sketchbook. Then I get my schoolbag and put the sketchbook in and my folder inside the sketchbook. The spiral binding of the book sticks out of my bag but luckily you can't see the folder.

I can hardly sleep for nerves. Next morning I'm awake really early. I put on my old clothes and wait on the bed until Auntie Katrina and Uncle Dirk wake up. Finally I can hear them moving around. When I'm sure they're both downstairs I go down too. Breakfast is calm. Auntie Katrina announces she's going to see her son that morning. Uncle Dirk will stay with me.

As soon as Auntie Katrina has gone, I ask if I can go and draw the deer. Uncle Dirk says it's okay. He'll come over in a minute, too.

I feel like punching the air as I go upstairs to fetch my sketchbook. It's going to work. Just a little bit longer. Back downstairs again, I ask Uncle Dirk if I can borrow a pencil. It has to look genuine. He finds a pencil for me. See you in a minute, he says.

I cross the road and go into the park. As soon as I'm out of sight, I start running. I run through the park as fast as I can. I've got to come out at the beginning of their street. That's where the road to Breda is. Once I'm outside the park I keep running, even when I'm long past the sign to Breda, to be on the safe side. When I can't run any more, I get out my hitchhiking sign. Now I notice there are hardly any cars on the road. It's Sunday morning. Everybody must be having a lie-in.

Then I see a bus coming in the distance. I put my hand out. The bus stops. It's going to Breda. Thank goodness Auntie Katrina gave me that pocket money; now I can pay for the ticket.

In the bus, I don't dare sit next to the window. I'm dead scared someone will see me. I get off at the station and buy a single to Den Bosch. I've still got enough money. Will Uncle Dirk have already noticed that I've run away? I hope my father isn't waiting for me at the station when I get to Den Bosch.

In Den Bosch I run out of the station hall, on my way to Marian. The only thing is, I don't remember where she lives. More by luck than judgement I run in the direction Ans Buis took when she drove me to Marian's. I come to a wide road. Marian lives in this kind of road, I seem to remember. A few moments later, I see the same kind of houses. It has to be here somewhere. Then I recognise the park she lives opposite. I peer cautiously into the houses. After a couple of houses, I've found it. That's it. Through the bay window I can see Marian and the children inside. They've got visitors. Marian sees me, too, and jumps up. I hear her crying out my name behind the window.

I walk up to the front door. Marian almost drags me into the hall-way and then into the kitchen. Els comes in, too. The only words I can get out are, please can they help me.

Els asks me if I'd like some coffee and Marian says she just has to say goodbye to the visitors. I sit on a stool in the kitchen. Els puts a cup of coffee in front of me, which I down in one. It's the best coffee I've ever tasted.

When Marian comes back into the kitchen a little while later, she's carrying a diary. She asks me if I've run away and I tell her everything that's happened over the past week.

Marian goes and calls the Child Welfare office. I'm scared they'll take me back to my father, but she assures me that won't happen.

When she's made the call, I start to feel hopeful again. I have to get away from here as quickly as possible, though, Marian says, because if my father comes to the door with the police, then I will have to go back with him. They can't keep me with them without permission. Luckily she knows a lot about the social services. She goes and calls Ans, to ask if she can come and fetch me. Now I'm really getting scared in case my father arrives first.

When the bell goes, it's Ans. I run with her to the car. Marian calls after me that everything will be all right.

In the car with Ans I hide on the floor. I'm so scared. Ans keeps reassuring me. She's taking me to Henk, the maths teacher, she says. He lives in Rosmalen. They won't find me there.

When I tell her what's happened, Ans says she's so sorry she didn't help me when I called. If she'd known what was going on she would have done. Now my anxious behaviour is making Ans nervous, too. She keeps looking in her rear-view mirror to see if we're being followed.

We're relieved when we get to Henk's house. He's surprised to see us. Ans explains the situation and luckily he doesn't mind us staying there for a while. His wife makes some coffee. No matter how often Ans and Henk say they'll never find me here, I'm still scared. I don't dare go too near the window. Actually, what I'd really like to do is lie down on the floor under the windowsill, then at least I can be sure they can't see me.

Ans calls Marian, who tells her I'm expected at the Youth Advisory Centre in Eindhoven at the end of the afternoon. They'll find a safe house for me where I'll have to stay for a couple of months. In the meantime, the Child Welfare office will find out exactly what's going on. Then there will be a court hearing, after which, if everything goes well, I'll be put in the custody of a foster family. Ans says we left Marian's just in time because my father turned up and was causing problems on the doorstep. She had to call the police to have him removed from her garden.

★

It's already almost dark when we arrive at the YAC in Eindhoven. The building looks closed. Ans reassures me; the social worker we've got an appointment with has to come from home, as the centre is closed on Sundays. He should arrive any minute now. I get cross and rebellious. Don't they understand the danger I'm in?

Then a man with a red beard comes walking towards us. He shakes hands with us and apologises for being late. Once inside, he asks me what's happened. For a moment, I'm scared my story won't be enough of a reason to place me in a safe house. But then he starts to explain the YAC's procedure and picks up a card file of addresses from his desk.

After a couple of calls, he finds a safe house for me. Ans goes home. There's nothing more she can do now, and in any case she isn't allowed to know the address. Before she leaves, she gives me a piece of paper with her telephone number on and Marian's. I can call them any time.

The social worker drives me to Son, a village near Eindhoven, where he introduces me to a man and a woman. They regard me distrustfully, examining me from head to toe with their eyes. The social worker recounts my story. Then the people ask to speak to him in private. A while later he comes back with the news that they have decided against taking me in. It's too risky.

He says it's not a problem; he'll find me something else. Actually, I'm relieved; those people looked at me in such a strange way. We leave. In the car, he decides to stop looking for that day and suggests driving to his place so we can get something to eat and have some sleep.

He lives in a flat in Eindhoven. We take the lift up. He gets some things out of the fridge and, after we've eaten, shows me to the spare room, where he folds out a bed for me. He tells me to call him if I need anything.

I can hear him getting undressed in the other room. One by one his shoes fall to the floor and, suddenly, I get scared that he might want something from me. I don't dare get undressed but get into bed with my clothes on and lie there listening. I make up my mind to stay awake whatever happens.

Next morning I hear him calling me to say breakfast is ready. I'm amazed that I've slept after all. I was so determined to stay awake. I go into the living room. He's dressed. I'm scared of him but he's really nice to me. While we're having breakfast, he tells me we're going back to the YAC in a minute. Then, if everything goes right, he'll find an address we can visit this afternoon.

Everything doesn't go right. There is no family that can take me in that quickly. But the social worker doesn't give up. I thumb through one magazine after another. Finally, he's got good news. He's called Marian and a friend of hers is willing to have me. She's not registered with the YAC but that doesn't really matter, according to the social worker.

He's asked Ans to come and take me to buy some clothes before dropping me off. I need a change of clothes. I ask him if it's risky. He explains that, officially, I'm on the police's missing persons list so if they do find me, they can take me away with them. According to him, though, they would never return me to my father if they know the YAC is involved. It doesn't reassure me an awful lot.

We buy another pair of trousers, a shirt and some underwear. I keep looking round to make sure we are not being followed by the police. Then we set off for Marian's friend's house. She lives in Valkenswaard. Ans doesn't know her.

After driving around a bit, searching, we stop in front of a big house. A man and a woman with a little girl in her arms come out to meet us. They look friendly. They introduce themselves as Sonia and Rick. Like Marian's, the house is very modern inside. They've cleared out a room for me upstairs. Sonia thinks I'll be staying for about six weeks. That's how long the Child Welfare procedure takes.

Sonia and Rick are really nice to me. I can tell they're being careful what they say. It's nice that they don't have to know what happened to me. It's as if it's simply okay for me to be there.

Now and again we go and have a cup of coffee with their friends further up the street. Marian has brought some homework from school so I can keep up a bit. She said all the teachers said hello and that everyone hopes I'll be back soon.

The Child Welfare wants me to write down why I ran away. I wrote that my father hits me and there's nothing but arguments at home. I just hope it's enough. I don't know what you need to have suffered to be able to go to a foster home for good, and I'm really scared they'll send me back to Zaltbommel.

One day, a lady from the Child Welfare comes round to talk to me. She tells me there's going to be a court hearing shortly, because they want to question my father. She notices that this gives me a shock and tries to reassure me. She promises I'll never have to see him again if I don't want to.

I can hardly believe what she's saying, but she says it sincerely. How can she be sure? The judge hasn't even heard my father's side of the story yet. Maybe the school was asked for some information about me. But they don't know about everything that happened in his house. And they don't know anything about my mother's death, either.

The lady tells me the investigation procedure normally takes a minimum of six weeks. But she thinks that in my case it can be completed in three. She explains how a juvenile court works and reassures me once more that I need not be scared. They are busy looking for the best solution for me.

If all goes well, I'll be sent to a foster family.

April 1976

The days are passing quickly now. Since the lady from the Child Welfare came, I've been feeling nervous. The idea of going to court scares me and so does the thought that I'll have to leave here afterwards. I like it here.

I got a really sweet letter from Marian. She's coming to see me today in her new car and she'll bring some homework for me.

That afternoon, a little bright-green car stops in front of the house. It's Marian. I can see she's excited and it's not just because of her new car. She's got a surprise for me, she says, taking my arm and leading me into the sitting room.

There she tells me that the judge has already questioned my father. He kicked up such a commotion they had to remove him from the court. She heard all this from a social worker she's in contact with. Elated, she tells me they have registered as a foster family because she would like me to live with them. The Child Welfare says it's okay. At least if that's what I want.

Of course it's what I want. Now everything will be all right after all.

Marian gives me two big kisses and hugs me tight when she sees I'm so pleased. I do have to go to court next week, though, but nothing can go wrong, according to Marian. She'll go with me because my father will probably be there, too.

Marian stays all day. She goes through the homework with me. Now I'm allowed to go and live with her, I can stay at the school, too. Won't the girls be surprised when I go back?

Now the days are going really slowly. Sonia does her best to fill the time so I don't get bored. We go and buy some new clothes and shoes for the hearing. I'm allowed to choose them myself which I find terribly difficult, as I'm not sure what I want and I don't know Marian well enough to know what she would like, either.

Finally, the day of the hearing arrives. Marian comes to pick me up. She's nervous, too, I can tell. We have to go all the way to Arnhem. On the journey, she tells me they have decided to question my father separately from me, as it's better for me not to be confronted with him.

Thank goodness. I don't want to see him. I feel really scared of him. I know he'll attack me if he sees me, wanting to have his revenge.

Marian explains that he's somewhere in the building but he can't do anything to me because there are guards everywhere. It doesn't reassure me entirely but I try not to think about it. I feel happier that the judge is going to see me separately; at least that means the case is being taken seriously.

At the court we have to wait in a little room for ages before somebody comes to fetch me. Marian wishes me good luck.

The judge's room is quite different from the place where my mother and I had to go in The Hague. It's not a big hall but a cosy little study with a desk, behind which the judge is sitting. There's a chair in front of it for me. The judge is a woman; I always thought only men could be judges.

She's really friendly. She asks me if I know why I'm here. She asks me to explain what I hope will be decided in this discussion. She tells me she read my letter and she's discussed what would be best for me with the Child Welfare officer. She hardly asks anything about my father but says she agrees with me going to live with the Engel family. She also tells me that my father can never demand to have me back again and he's not allowed to bother me, as he's been bothering the Engel family recently.

The judge asks if there is anything else I'd like to know. I ask her what I should do if my father goes on bothering us.

She reassures me, saying Marian or I can always go to the police because he no longer has custody of me. She also says a social worker will be coming to visit us in the near future. She will be coming on a regular basis to make sure everything is going all right and help us with any problems. Then the judge shakes my hand and shows me to the door.

3

Den Bosch

April 1976

I'm going to Marian's today. My stuff's standing ready in the hallway. Sonia and I are waiting for Rick, who's going to take me to Den Bosch. I'm sad that I won't be seeing Sonia and her little girl for a while. They're so nice.

Sonia kisses me when I leave. I thank her for everything she's done for me, but Sonia says that's nonsense.

I don't think she realises the half of what it meant to me that she was willing to take me in.

At Marian's house, there's a festive atmosphere. There's coffee and an enormous slice of flan because Marian feels we've got a lot to celebrate. The children can't wait to take me upstairs to the room they've done up for me.

It's bright and cosy. There's a big wardrobe where Marian puts my clothes straight away. And there's a desk. I get my folder out and tell Marian that I never want to lose this and no one is allowed to touch it. The children look at it curiously but Marian explains to them that they must do as I say and not touch anything in my room. Then they want to show me their room and a little while later we're all playing together.

At lunchtime, we're all sitting in the kitchen. Walter and Els are there, too. Marian takes grilled pineapple and cheese sandwiches out of the oven. She explains that Bram goes and buys white bread every Saturday and then they eat hot sandwiches. How nice it is, all of us together, just like a big family.

After lunch, Marian wants to speak to me alone for a minute. We go and sit in my room. She's obviously got something difficult to tell me; all kinds of nervous expressions pass over her face, as if she doesn't know where to start. Then she says that my father has been constantly bothering them for the past few weeks. The police have been round a couple more times to remove him from the garden. They think it's better for me not to go out by myself for the time being. The school knows all about it and will intervene if my father turns up there. The judge has ordered him to deliver the rest of my things to them but she thinks there's not much chance of him actually doing so. We'll just have to wait and see.

Well, I'm not bothered about my stuff. I've got my folder. And I can always buy more clothes.

I apologise for having caused them so much trouble but Marian won't hear a word of it. She obviously wants to put me at my ease because she starts explaining that the Child Welfare Service has organised everything. They get a fixed sum per day for me so I don't need to worry about costing them anything. She will give me pocket money every week and a clothing allowance and if I need anything for school, I can always ask her for it. Once I've been here for a while I'll be given a job to do in the house, too, but first they think I should just get used to my new home.

When Marian has gone back down again and I'm sitting on the bed, looking around me, I make up my mind to do my very best so they never find me a burden. I'm so looking forward to going back to school. Won't they be surprised?

20 April 1976
Back to school today. Walter's taking me. I'm grateful to him for that, because all the way there I'm getting more and more scared. I'm relieved to find myself safe and sound in school.

The head comes and puts an arm around me. Welcome back, he says. The girls crowd around and teachers wink as they walk past. In the classroom, the teacher asks me to tell everyone briefly why I've been away so long. I don't have to tell them everything, she adds. I'm allowed to go and sit on her desk. Everyone is quiet.

I'm not sure where to begin. Actually, I haven't really thought about what's happened since I was last at school. It all just happened.

I start by saying that there was so much arguing at home it was better for me to go and live somewhere else. That Marian wanted to have me, but my father wouldn't agree. That he took me to my auntie's. That I ran away and that now I'm living at Marian's after all. Yes, I think that's just about how it was.

Back in my seat, the events of the past few weeks flash through my head. How could I tell them what really happened? I didn't say anything about the safe house or the court. Or that my father might still cause trouble. Actually, it's only now that I realise I might never see Diana again.

At the end of the lesson, it's as if I've never been away. Nothing has changed at school. Well, I have, because I've resolved to do the very best I can. I think my school has really helped me a lot; I want the teachers to know I'm grateful to them.

I'm starting to get quite used to things at Marian's. I get on well with the children. When they're home, we spend all the time playing together. Bram works hard and has a headache most evenings. Els and Walter work long hours, too. They're only at home in the evening. Marian works three days a week and does most of the housework. Everyone takes a turn at doing the cooking. I tell Marian that I'm settled in now and would really like to help around the house. She feels I already do my bit by playing so nicely with the children. She's more than satisfied if I keep my room tidy.

22 April 1976
I've got no lessons for the first three hours of the day. I'm doing my homework in the sitting room when, suddenly, I see my brother standing in front of the window. I immediately duck down and wriggle on my tummy to the back room. Marian's standing in the kitchen. I want to call her but the shock has paralysed my voice. I can't utter a word.

Cautiously, I check to see if he's still standing there. And, sure enough, there he is, legs apart, arms folded across his chest. He looks really furious. I'm sure he's seen me.

I crawl into the kitchen. Marian can see straight away there's something wrong.

My brother, I say. I can't say any more.

She walks into the living room. When she comes back, she tells me he's gone. When she went to look out of the window, he was just getting into his car and driving off.

I'm still sitting on the floor. She tells me to sit on a chair but I can't. I feel like I'll never be able to stand up again. I'm so frightened. Just when everything was going so well, he has to come along.

Marian gives me a glass of water. Shaking, I take it. My stomach feels clenched, as if the water is getting stuck in my throat. It almost chokes me. Marian strokes my head. She says she would have called the police if he had still been there. She tries to reassure me. But I can still see him in front of me, so scary, that big body and that evil expression.

In the evening, when everybody in the house has been told about it, I can see how shocked they are, too. They try to make light of it but I can see they're behaving differently from usual. When I'm in bed, Marian comes to kiss me goodnight. She asks if I'm still scared.

I pretend I've got over it because I don't want to worry her. It's not necessary for her to know that my brother is really dangerous.

May 1976
I've been here a couple of weeks now. Things are going well at school. Marian and Walter often help me with my homework because I've still got a lot to catch up on. My father has definitely lost custody of me.

When I'm at home, I play with the children. We build big houses out of Lego and paint and draw. I like sitting in the kitchen with Marian when she's cooking, too. Although she's completely different from my mother, she really does remind me of her.

I hope she'll become a second mother to me.

Every night, before I go to sleep, she always comes to say goodnight.

Twice a week, she brings me two clean flannels and two towels. One for the top half and one for the bottom, she always says. That makes me feel embarrassed. I only wash my face. I wet the flannels and dampen the towels to make it look as if I've used them. I find it terribly difficult to put my underwear in the laundry basket like the other do. I'm embarrassed about my pants, particularly if I've had my period. But I don't dare stuff them away somewhere. Marian would notice that. Then I'd have to admit I'm embarrassed. That would be even sillier.

★

The nights are bad. I keep having nightmares and I start dreading going to sleep hours before bedtime.

As soon as I'm lying in bed and turn the light off, I can't help thinking about my mother. I just can't manage to think about anything else, and it seems to be getting worse. The past few days it's been happening more and more often during the day. Then I start wondering if she's really dead. Maybe she's living somewhere else, but they're pretending she's dead. Maybe it's a conspiracy, or a mean trick of my father's. If that's true, then I'll find her again, or she'll find me. Just imagine if she walked into my room one day.

1 May 1976

Last night I had a nightmare I just can't get out of my head. I dreamed I was in the cemetery, standing on top of my mother's grave. From deep down under my feet I could hear her voice. She was calling, screaming at me to help her. I started digging as hard as I could. I dug and I dug, until I got to her.

Her body was completely rotted away. Her head was attached to her torso by just a little piece of skin. There were creatures swarming all over her body. They looked like eels. She was screaming that there was one in her intestines and telling me to pull it out. I tore open her intestines with my nails. I slid my hand into her innards, right through the eels which were as thick as my wrist, but no matter how deep I stuck my arm in I couldn't get hold of the creature. I just couldn't. Get it, get it, she screamed at me. I could see the creature. Deeper and deeper it squirmed into her intestines. By this time, my whole arm was in her innards but I still couldn't get at the creature. I started screaming back at her that I couldn't do it. Then I woke up with a jolt.

The nightmares haunt me for days, even during the daytime. Sometimes I think I'm going mad. I'm afraid of the dark and afraid of falling asleep. I don't want these dreams. Now I'm convinced that anyone who believes in God is stupid. If there was a God, why would He have let my mother die?

I've never been to visit her grave. And since my nightmares I'll never dare to now. The idea that she'd be lying there rotting away, so close, just terrifies me.

I read an article about near-death experiences in *Panorama* magazine. People who've had them all say the same. The moment they died, they floated above their own body and into a tunnel of light. Their loved ones who had died were waiting for them at the end of that tunnel.

If that's true, then I can be with her again. But that means I'd have to commit suicide.

I read the article again that evening in bed. There's also something about spirits. There are people who claim that all dead people live on as a spirit and that spirit stays around those they loved. That seems a spooky idea to me; I get frightened by it.

If that's so, then my mother has to be around here somewhere. I look around the room but can't see anything. The wardrobe door is open a crack. Could she be in the wardrobe? I lie as stiff as a board in bed. The gap is staring at me. I get even more frightened. I don't dare go and shut the wardrobe door. I pull the covers over my head and creep as far down in the bed as possible with my hands tight over my ears, scared that I'll hear something.

Then suddenly there seems to be a hand on my shoulder. I don't dare move any more; I just shake the hand off. Slightly relieved, I stick my head out of the covers again and then I really do see the shape of a hand lying on my leg. I kick at it; it was a fold in the blanket.

You see, I am going mad. I can't help bursting into tears.

Marian comes into my room. She heard me crying and thinks I've had a nightmare. I just say yes. It makes me feel so stupid.

4 May 1976

Since I've been living with Marian I haven't smoked a single joint but I've been feeling numb recently, as if I'm permanently stoned. Everything flows past me like a silent film. I rode my bike into the back of a car at a red light the other day. Just because I reacted too slowly.

I don't think about anything except my mother. I sleep with the light on now because I'm so afraid of the dark. I have to leave the door to my room open at night, the wardrobe has to be closed and there mustn't be any space between the curtains. I've put all kinds of things under the bed; otherwise I'm scared there's someone lying under it.

During the day, I keep being startled by people I haven't heard coming. Now I'm even getting scared of the moment I'll be taken by surprise. It feels awful, particularly as I'm always jumping at nothing. It makes me so nervous.

If I get home before the others I don't dare go upstairs. I wait until someone comes home and then I listen really carefully to make sure I can't hear anything. It's wearing me out. I feel as if I'm being followed the whole time.

I think I'm starting to irritate Marian. She keeps saying I'm moping around, as if I have to take a rest after each step. According to her, I'm also really out of breath. It's because I'm terribly tired and scared. I'm sure I'm going mad.

The acting guardian has been round. She talked to Marian for quite a long time and now she wants to talk to me.

She asks me how things are going. Okay, I think. I don't dare tell her anything about my nightmares. Then she says that she and the Engel family are not so happy.

That really gives me a shock.

They think I'm too quiet. They want me to talk about the past, they want to help, but they don't know how. They feel I'm isolating myself.

How come? I ask her. As far as I know, I'm always at home.

She says I don't go with them when the family goes for a walk on Sundays.

Relieved, I reply that I do that deliberately, to give them the opportunity to be without me sometimes. I'm so grateful for being allowed to live here. I was under the impression that things were going really well, I say; I look after the children when everybody's working and I really do my best at school.

The guardian still thinks I should talk more about the past. I think it's awful they're not happy with me and I promise her that I'll try. But I really don't know what I should tell them. I'm certainly not going to tell them what I dream about and that I'm scared of going mad. Besides, Marian knows I'm afraid of the dark. I've told her a little bit about San and about Rob Roberti's circus.

I ask the social worker what I should do to make up for it and tell her that I really don't dare talk to the family. That I wouldn't know

what to say. She says I should write it down then. After all, the family
has a right to know what's the matter with me and what's happened
to me in the past.

Now I feel really terrible. I think it's dreadful that I'm disappointing them. I never noticed. They never said anything about it to me.

When the woman leaves, I go upstairs to my room. I don't dare
look Marian in the face. I don't know how to behave towards her
after what the guardian told me. The family, she said, that means all
of them, not just Marian. That means they've all been discussing me
and they aren't happy.

In my room I write a letter to them, explaining that I can't help
the fact that I don't say much. That it might be because I've been
thinking about my mother so much recently and didn't think of talking about it. That I didn't know I had to and that I was really happy
here. That I'm so grateful to them for letting me live here. When I
read the letter through, I know I won't dare give it to them. I put it
in my folder.

8 May 1976

I always ride past a squat on my way to school. For weeks now, I've
seen squatters busy doing up a little shop. On my way home today
they stopped me and gave me a leaflet explaining that the action shop
was open. Anyone can go there for advice on all kinds of things. If
you're having trouble finding a place to live or if you want to squat
in a house or if you just want to demonstrate against something, then
they'll help you.

A young guy offers me a cup of tea. The shop looks really nice.
There's campaign posters and paintings all over the place. The squatters live above the shop; most of them are students at the art college.

When I get home, I tell Marian where I've been and that I'm planning to go there regularly. I know it's something she'll be interested
in. She's active in the women's movement and they help with dupli-
cating newsletters there, too.

June 1976

Now I go to the squat shop every day after school and often in the
evenings and at weekends. Everyone is really nice to me. I help a bit

with everything and join in the meetings. I pose nude for the squatters from the art college, too. They paint me in oils, draw me in charcoal or sculpt me in clay. They have a lot of fun while I'm posing. I can never think of much to say but nobody minds. I just belong.

Everyone has a task. One of the guys has a drop-in session in the shop and advises people with housing problems. Another one is really daring and when a place has to be broken into for squatting, he does the difficult work. Then there's someone who draws for the squatters' paper, someone who does the editing and someone who types out all the articles.

If a place is being broken into, I'm not allowed to be there because I'm a minor and could get into trouble with the Child Welfare Department. But once it's been occupied, I can go in. I'm allowed to help the group prepare for squatting, too. That happens in the action shop. It's really exciting. A scenario of the break-in is written, so everyone knows who will do what and when. I hardly ever say anything but I pay close attention to everything that happens.

Since I've been hanging out with the squatters, I've realised there are all kinds of things we do at school that aren't good for us at all. We're being kept stupid. We learn to iron, cook, sew and polish silver. We're being trained to become housewives and childminders when, actually, we should be learning other things. Marian thinks so, too. Now I've set up a school council. The council's first campaign point is a weekend without homework. Then we're going to campaign for a better environment. The plastic cups have to go. I do drawings and campaign items for the school newspaper.

I've written a letter to Sandra.

I don't feel at ease here since the discussion with the temporary guardian. I can't stand the idea that I'm a disappointment. Everything irritates me, Marian, the children, the women who keeps coming round to talk to me. I no longer feel I fit in at school either. The teachers are nice, and the girls, too, but they talk about things that don't interest me. Now the Child Welfare has decided I need to see a psychologist. I don't know why, exactly. But they say it'll make me feel better. I'm really dreading it. I don't want to talk. I want to be left alone.

3 June 1976

I went to the psychologist today. I have to go all the way to Eindhoven. He's called Jos and he's got a wife and two small children; he showed me their pictures. He asked me all about my foster family and, luckily, nothing about the past.

Next time he said he wants to know more, but I don't know if I'll tell him about my mother. I'll tell him she's dead, of course, but I can't explain what it was like between us. I don't really know if I can tell him about the circus and Rob, either. When I told Marian something about the circus recently it felt as if I was betraying everything. I don't feel right having talked about Marian to Jos, either. After all she has done for me it seems ungrateful if I say that everything irritates me.

Jos has given me an assignment. This week, I have to write down everything I don't like. Now that's quite a lot. I think the only thing I like now is being in the action shop.

14 June 1976

Rob's written me another letter. He's got a new wife and writes:

Remember, I might not be on my own any more, but I don't think that needs to be a problem for you, you'll understand yourself and that was agreed with Mama at the time, too. Mama knew exactly what kind of man I am. It's no good being alone in the circus. You just don't have the time to wash your own socks and cook your own meals, and you don't feel like it after all that work. I do understand this might be a blow for you, which is why I never mentioned it in my earlier letters. But I do hope you can understand. Otherwise you should come over some time and we can talk about it.

Rob put in some photos of him and his new wife. She's blond, the kind of woman I know my mother would think was common. A completely different type of woman from my mother.

I'm glad he wrote, but I'm cross he's married a woman like that. I don't want to meet her. My mother would never have approved of such a woman. That I know.

August 1976

I've had a letter from San, too, asking me over some time. I was so pleased but now it's come down to it, I feel sick with nerves.

I decided to wear the sarong Ans Buis brought back for me from her holiday in Indonesia. It's the first time I've had it on; I get the feeling I'm going back in time. How proud my mother would have been if she could have seen me in a sarong. She often wore one at home.

Marian and Bram take me to Leiden in the car.

Driving through the town, I see all kinds of familiar things. I see the market where we used to buy material. Vroom & Dreesmann is still in the same place. I can't see the *toko* from the road. Then we drive along by the park, down the road where I always walked when I went to visit my mother in hospital. I've agreed they can drop me on the corner my old street, then I can take my time walking up the street to San's. Marian and Bram wish me luck; they'll come and pick me up in the same place.

In front of me is our street, behind me the precinct where we did our shopping. I notice that the street looks much narrower than in my memory. The buildings are much lower, too, and the square with the shops around it looks smaller. As soon as I'm in the street, I can't think why I put my sarong on. The further I go, the more uncomfortable I feel in it.

San's mother is standing outside looking out for me. She waves; she hasn't changed a bit. She thinks I've changed a lot, though, she says I've got bigger and fatter. Then Sandra comes out. She's changed so much that I would never have recognised her if I passed her in the street. She's got really fat. Her nan and grandpa are much the same and their dog, Nitadog's brother, is still there, quite a bit older and calmer. His muzzle has gone grey. That's how Nitadog would have looked now. The mother dog has died.

I can see they think that I'm dressed strangely. I could kick myself for having worn that sarong.

We have a cup of coffee. Sandra tells me she's engaged. Her cousin Rita, who we used to play with, is married and has already got a baby. They've got news of everybody in the street. A lot of people have moved. There's loads of immigrant workers now, Turks and Moroccans.

I try and tell them everything that's happened to me over the past few years. I can see they don't understand what kind of family I'm living with. I try and explain what the house is like but I can tell by their faces that they can't imagine it. If I say it's a big house, they'll think I mean posh and that I'm saying it to show off.

After about an hour we've got nothing left to say. I wouldn't mind going to the playground but that's a bit silly in this sarong. I search for words to keep the conversation going.

I'm relieved when it's time to go. When we say goodbye, I can tell they're relieved, too. Standing outside again I can see my old house in the distance. I'd really like to go inside one more time, but I don't dare.

Marian and Bram are already waiting for me at the street corner. They ask how the visit went.

Great, I lie. I invent a couple of nice things. I just describe it as I'd hoped it would be.

That evening in bed I can't stop crying. Now I've got no one from the past. It feels so lonely.

What I would never dare say out loud is that I feel as if I've betrayed my mother by going to see Sandra. Why was I so keen on going to see her, even if they did take me in? Sandra's parents were never nice to my mother in the past, were they?

I'm angry with myself. How could I have been so stupid as to go in that sarong?

3 September 1976

I've had another letter from Rob. He apologises for not getting round to writing more often because of all those one-night venues. He's probably too busy with his new wife. I haven't been in touch with him since I found out about her. The letter ends:

> I don't know whether we'll be coming anywhere near you, We did drive past your house six or seven weeks ago. It was in the evening and we were passing through, on our way to Heeswijk I think. I couldn't stop, though; you can hardly park a whole string of circus lorries and vans in the road to pop in and say hello!!!

He could have stopped for a while. I would have liked to have seen him, even if I am cross he's got a new wife. He could have stopped if he'd really wanted to. It is possible. We used to stop sometimes with the whole circus caravan if someone paid a visit on the way. I don't like the fact that he drove past me just like that.

He's inviting me to go to the winter quarters some time in the winter to catch up on gossip. He signs the letter 'With lots of love, a paw from Snowydog and Janette says hello.'

What do I care about that woman?

November 1976

The more often I go to see Jos, the worse things get at Marian's. I feel more and more of a stranger there. They want me to belong but I can feel I'll never be one of them. Marian sometimes says she loves me, but I don't believe her. I think she just does it to be nice.

I feel like a stranger at school as well. Because they helped me in difficult times, I feel I mustn't be any trouble to them now, so I do my best. But here, too, it's like I don't belong. The girls are busy with their bottom drawers and they don't understand me at all. Actually, I don't want to go to school any more.

1 December 1976

Marian's had a letter from Auntie Agnes, warning her against me. According to her, my father is a queer. Evidently Auntie Agnes has become his umpteenth victim. Now she's cross with me, but it's her own fault. I did warn her about him. Marian let me read the letter.

Karin is sneaky and nasty, and she tries to play games with respectable people with higher moral standards. She's just like her father. Upon my soul she is her father's daughter, her behaviour bears witness to it. Her father is a dyed-in-the-wool homosexual who attempts to hide it in the nastiest, most hypocritical manner. He is therefore neurotic in his behaviour, a big sadist and absolutely without conscience. He is unable to speak the truth; his life consists of lies and deceit.

Karin told me he had already wrecked so many families and that he can be so changeable, scitsofrenic. Everything Karin warned me about has come true, but Karin is going the same way. On Saturday I had yet another conversation with authoritative persons. One of them knows Karin, too. He saw her recently in town, as I have myself. In our opinion she looks like she isn't worth five cents. Has very low morals. As far as I'm concerned, every tie with the family is broken. All social (mental) assistance is wasted on them.

Marian says I should take no notice.

I hope she doesn't believe Auntie Agnes. I'm not like my father.

Spring 1977

Sister Van den Berg, my form teacher, has invited me to go round to tea. She lives in a convent; she's a nun. She's really nice to me. She's got something for me, an old-fashioned prayer stool I can have. I'm really pleased, it'll look great in my room. I can go and fetch it at four o'clock today. Until then I'm looking after the kids.

At quarter past four Marian's still not home. If she doesn't come back soon, I'll be late. The children are playing nicely so I decide to go anyway. Marian should be home any minute now.

I ring the bell at the convent. A nun lets me in and takes me to a common room. There are some other nuns there; they look like nice old grannies.

Sister Van den Berg pours out the tea. She takes us for biology at school and she starts talking about nature now, too. She never runs out of things to say about it. We talk for about an hour and then I go home with the lovely prayer stool under my arm.

When I go into the kitchen everyone is sitting around the table As soon as she sees me, Marian stands up. Angrily, she starts to let fly at me. She thinks it was dreadful of me to leave the children on their own; she doesn't know what to say.

I clam up. I can feel she's right, but she was late home and I didn't dare be late for Sister Van den Berg. Annoyed, Marian sits back down. I don't dare look at her. The others say nothing.

I go up to my room.

How embarrassing. I feel awful. I'll never dare look Marian and the others in the eye again. What should I do now? I've ruined everything. I wish I wasn't here. I can't take this any more. I want to die. What does it matter, any of it?

There are some pills in the medicine cabinet. I take all the boxes I find in there and fill a glass with water in the bathroom.

Then I go and sit on my bed and start popping the pills out of the strips. It calms me down. Pill after pill, sip after sip. I just hope I fall asleep, that I don't notice I'm dying. I'm getting dopey already.

Everything is getting hazy. Now it's quite an effort to swallow the pills. I just chew and chew, the dry powder crunching between my teeth. I can vaguely see one of the children standing in front of me with a bowl of blancmange. I think he's shocked. I can't talk any more, I feel like I'm really drunk, I can't see him properly.

Marian is dragging me across the floor to the bathroom. She's swearing at me. She's calling me stupid. So I'm still alive and she's cross. I get woozy again.

Now I can tell I'm lying in bed. Marian is sitting next to me. So I'm still alive, but maybe I'll die in a minute. Marian's shaking me. I can feel myself drifting off again. I can feel tears. I'm sorry; I don't want to die any more. Marian hears me say it and assures me I'm not going to die. She says I have to drink a lot. She pours some water in my mouth. I drift off again.

It's really light in the bedroom; it must be quite late in the day when I wake up. I'm still alive. There's a bunch of flowers next to my bed with a note. Marian's handwriting. *Being angry doesn't mean I don't love you*, is what it says.

I'm even more ashamed of myself now. O God, how stupid that I'm still alive. I want to die but I don't, but how can I explain that to them? Walter pops his head round the door and asks if I've had a good sleep. I nod. I'm so embarrassed. He says I have to drink a lot. He brings me some juice and helps me sit up to drink it. I feel really heavy. He says I should go back to sleep. He's called the school to say I'm ill.

I wish I never had to come out from under the covers again. I'm glad when Walter goes away. I keep remembering flashes. Marian was cross with me when she was dragging me across the landing. If she really loved me, she should have been sad, shouldn't she?

I wish I hadn't taken those pills. Now I'll have to go and see Jos more often. The doctor has given me some tranquillisers and the atmosphere in the house isn't improving.

Jos gives me all kinds of assignments I can't carry out. They're talking assignments. I have to talk to Marian, Bram, Walter and Els. And even worse, he wants me to hold group discussions with them, too.

I can't even talk to one of them, let alone all of them. I just can't do it. I know I can't.

Jos has said I'm not allowed see him again until I've followed his instructions.

June 1977

Jos won't let me go and see him because I haven't carried out his talking assignment.

Now I've shaved my head, as bald as a billiard ball.

Marian thinks it's a shame about my hair. She thinks it looked nice long.

What do I care?

She says she understands it's a phase.

She always pretends to understand everything, but she doesn't understand me. No one understands how I feel. I can't be bothered to explain what I mean any more. Actually, I don't want to go on living here. But if I leave, I'll have to go to a home and I don't fancy that at all.

Every day after school I go to De Blauwe Druif – De Druif, as everyone calls the café. On Friday evenings and at the weekends, too.

It's always packed and there's a good atmosphere. The people who go there are quite a bit older than me. At the front of the café you get the students from the art college. In the middle, men and women in their thirties, rather arty types. At the back is where the gays sit and the owner's family. It's a family business.

I usually sit somewhere in the middle. I know everyone by now. At first, they thought I was at the art college, too. I didn't dare say I was at the domestic science school. Now I just say I'm at secondary school if anyone asks. I lie about my age, too; I'm sure I'm too young to be here.

The bar staff in De Druif are different from the customers. Actually, they remind me of the people who used to live in my street in Leiden. I'm always a bit scared of them. Sometimes they're nice and other times they swear at you. But they never stay cross for long.

They keep playing the same tape all day long. Elvis Presley, Fats Domino and Buddy Holly. The customers who go there like other kinds of music but nobody lets it bother them. Now I know all the numbers off by heart. On Fridays and Saturdays, early in the evening, they push the chairs to one side and turn the music up. The café is crowded then and everyone dances or rocks along. Sometimes one of the barmen climbs on the bar and does an impression of Elvis.

I like to sit and watch everybody. Luckily no one asks me where I live. I wouldn't like to have to say I live with a foster family because they'd be bound to want to know why. Marian doesn't like me spending so much time in the café. She wants me to go to an international work camp in Germany in the summer holidays. She thinks it'd be good for me.

I'm fed up with being moaned at all the time. Why don't I keep my room tidy? Have I done my homework? Marian gets on my nerves and that stupid woman from the Child Welfare, too. All that whining. I don't want to keep feeling that I'm disappointing everybody. They should take me as they find me. I'd be happier living on my own in a bedsit, then at least I could do as I please without bothering anybody. But Marian definitely won't agree to that.

August 1977

Luckily Jos understands why I want to leave Marian's. He warns me that it won't be easy to convince the Child Welfare but he's promised to help me by giving a positive recommendation. He doesn't think the foster family has any right to keep me but I could well end up in a home if things don't go well for me. The Child Welfare will probably try to get me into a supervised accommodation project. Jos says that's a kind of home. He's advised me to have a talk with my guardian and tell her I want to leave, otherwise I'll run away. Maybe then she will come up with a solution.

I've let Marian and the guardian know that I want to move to a bedsit. Since then, Marian's been acting nervous with me; she thinks she's not doing her job properly. I've tried to explain that it hasn't got anything to do with her. I just don't feel I belong here. I'm terribly grateful for all she's done for me but I really want to leave. I want to live by myself now. And I'm sure I can manage it.

The guardian has made an appointment for me at a supervised accommodation project. There, she says, you live in a house with a couple of other girls. Everyone has her own room and there are two leaders to teach you how to live independently.

The project isn't in Den Bosch, but just outside. At the entrance to the driveway is a board with the name of a home. You see? Jos was right; it *is* a home. I pretend to the guardian that I haven't seen it but I know already they're never going to get me in here.

We're seen by a man. He starts explaining the intention of this meeting but he can see from my sullen expression that I'm not keen on the idea. Reproachfully, he snaps at me that I have to want to come here, otherwise there's no point in the meeting.

I get up, saying it's not what I want. The guardian sighs and the man says something else to her, but I can't hear it, because I've already walked out, without saying goodbye.

Inwardly I'm rejoicing. It makes me feel so good. Who do they think they are? I'm my own boss, that's for sure.

I walk down the path. A real children's home path; it takes ages to get to the exit. Behind me, the social worker starts her car. She draws up next to me and asks if I will please get in. Well, okay then, seeing as she said please.

In the car she tries to persuade me to stay on with Marian. She says the Engel family is really doing its best for me.

I agree that the Engels are good to me, but I don't belong there any more, I belong by myself, and I'll prove I can manage. They can give me a chance, can't they?

When we get home, the social worker comes in and talks to Marian. For the first time, I couldn't give a damn what they say about me. I'm leaving. That's settled.

Marian stays in her room all evening. Either she doesn't understand how I feel or she's cross with me. Tough.

Jos had already warned me that this would probably be a stressful time. He's helping me. He thinks it will work out. Otherwise, he says, I'll just have to threaten to run away. The Child Welfare doesn't like that happening; it causes them too much bother. He's noticed before that they're wary of it. He does ask me to be understanding with Marian, though. She will think she has failed. I've assured him that of course I sympathise with her, but she shouldn't act like they've lost, either.

When I get to the café Druif that evening, I announce to anyone who wants to listen that I'm looking for a room. Everyone promises to help me find one.

The very next day, I hear from the barman that someone's found a room for me. Jan, a guy I hardly know, has got an empty side room. It's small and dark, though. There aren't any windows because it's in the basement. He doesn't want any money for it but he thinks I ought to go and have a look at it first, as it's not really much of a room.

I couldn't care less what it's like, as long as I can live there by myself. That's all I want. Now I've got somewhere to go, I want to leave Marian's as soon as possible. I'll ask Jos how to approach it from here. Won't he be surprised that I've found a room so quickly?

4

Herman Brood

September 1977
Today I move to my first bedsit. Everyone has supposedly come to terms with the idea, but I can see they don't approve. Marian arranges a nice farewell coffee morning, all the same.

The children are really sorry I'm leaving. I've promised them I'll come round often.

When we say our goodbyes, I thank them for everything they've done for me. I can see that Marian's really disappointed. I've promised her I'll keep going to school.

There's a lot of nagging from the Child Welfare. I'll get some money every week, which I'll have to go and fetch from an agency where they help families in need. I have to go and meet them this week. And every time I collect the money I have to have a chat. They will want to know how things are going and the guardian will come round now and again, they said.

Bram drives me over to Jan's place. I haven't got that much stuff. Just my folder, some clothes, my school things, a sleeping bag and the prayer stool Sister Van den Berg gave me.

He drops me outside my new place. It's dark and it smells damp. There are three cushions in my room which I can use as a mattress. Jan gave them to me.

Jan doesn't want me having visitors. He doesn't like the idea of strangers walking through his place all the time. He's got a little kitchen in the corner of his room. I can use his loo and, if I want something hot to eat, I can use his gas ring. But I don't use it. I can't be bothered to cook. Now I'm on my own, I only want to do things I enjoy. I just want to go to De Druif.

The first week ends in disaster. I've got a tickly cough. It gives me a headache, day and night. And I have to vacate my room. The land-lord doesn't believe I'm just staying with Jan and not paying anything. He thinks Jan is sub-letting and wants me to leave.

If the Child Welfare hears that, then I've got a problem. Before I know it, I'll end up in a home after all. For Marian, that would only go to prove I can't manage on my own.

October 1977
Jan's agreed that I can continue to use his address for a while for the Child Welfare. He realises I'm having a difficult time and thinks it's really mean of his landlord. He's promised to give me any letters that come for me.

When I tell them what's happened in De Druif, a couple who are going to the Canary Islands for a week offer to let me house-sit for them. Then at least I can look after their cat. In the meantime, I have to find a room but I keep going to school so that no one finds out I'm already out on the street.

When the couple come back from the Canary Islands, I still haven't found anywhere to live. I'm really supposed to leave but I've got nowhere to go to. I haven't got a cent so I can't rent a room. Luckily, they say I can stay with them for a bit. They're hardly ever at home and when they are they argue. Still, it's a nuisance I can't find my own room.

I hope the Child Welfare doesn't find out. Up till now I've been able to meet the guardian in the station restaurant, but she's starting to insist on coming to visit me in my room.

The Child Welfare rules are stupid. I can get extra money for fur-nishing my room but only if I give them the receipts for the things I've bought. And I haven't got enough money for a cup of coffee in De Druif.

I always hang around with the same crowd at the café. I have a lot of fun with two guys, Wim and Joop. Wim's unemployed and Joop's at the art college.

108

They never go around together but the funny thing is, if Joop isn't there, Wim is, and the other way around. Actually I'd love to be Wim or Joop's girlfriend. More Wim's than Joop's, I think.

Joop and I often go out together at night. Sometimes he nicks a car, always a Citroën 2CV, while I keep a look-out. As soon as he's started the car, I get in and we go for a drive. If there's enough money for petrol, then we go a long way. Joop loves joyriding. When we've had enough of racing around, he parks the car somewhere in town and we go to his house. Then we sleep together.

During the day, we go shoplifting together. Food, clean clothes and sometimes LPs. He knows all the tricks and he's teaching me. What a shame I didn't know all this in Leiden, it would have been so easy. When I'm hungry, I often think back to those days. If I'd nicked stuff then, I could have given my mother something nice now and again. She'd have been bound to ask where I got it. Then I would have said that San's mother had given it to me for her.

Wim's far more serious. He likes having friends round, then they all watch football together. He often has English people staying with him; they're brickies and nearly always drunk.

Wim is more trustworthy than Joop. He always keeps his word. Joop's a hothead. Someone's only got to say one wrong word to him when he's had too much to drink and he picks a fight. Wim never has a girlfriend but Joop goes to bed with different girls all the time. Still, I like both of them.

When De Druif shuts at night, I go with Wim or Joop to De Papillon. That's a disco where only gays go, but we're allowed in, too.

I can't be bothered with school any more. Seeing as I go out at night, I can't wake up in the morning. I wish I could go and live with Wim.

November 1977
John's about forty. A short man with a bald head. He's always rushing around. He goes to De Druif, too. John's been in prison loads of times already. Now he's selling waterbeds. He works in a strip club as well. No one knows exactly what he does there, but he earns his real money through dealing. Mostly he deals in dope, and coke or speed,

too, if he can get hold of it. When John has a party people talk about it for months afterwards.

I've been hanging around with John quite a bit recently. Wim and I have been invited to his next party.

The party's at his house. A bar's been set up at the end of the garden and the big room's been turned into a dance floor. He's got a girl walking around in a waitress uniform, with a big tray of ready-rolled joints. You can take them for nothing.

There's a separate room where you can get something harder if you pay for it.

Wim says you can get yourself injected with speed there; apparently it gives you an immediate kick. Not many people at the party go into that room. A young guy brave enough to do so comes out with a piece of cotton wool pressed against his neck where he had the injection. I can hardly bear to look at it. What an awful place to be injected.

In the garden, a couple of people are smoking a hookah together, but that always makes me want to throw up.

Wim's obviously made up his mind to get totally legless on the free booze. He's well on the way already.

John introduces me to a friend of his who works as a barman in the strip club. He knows I'm broke and says he knows a way I can make some quick money. He explains how I can easily pick up a couple of clients after closing time. You don't have to go to bed with them. There's always clients who want to get themselves wanked off for a tenner or more. It hardly takes any time. He knows exactly which nights I'd have the most luck. If I want to do it, I only have to tell John. Then he'll tell him and he'll let the punters know. John knows how it works, says the barman. He's got several girls working for him.

The party's really rocking, now. Everyone seems to be high or drunk. I can't see Wim anywhere. Finally, I find him pissed out of his head in John's bed. I crawl in next to him and listen to the sounds of the party, which seems to be going on for ever.

27 November 1977

Tomorrow, a couple of guys who sometimes come into De Druif are going to break into a place to squat. If they manage it, I'll get a room there, too. It's a big shop that's been empty for ages. It looks really good, but I'll have to watch out that I don't get any problems with the Child Welfare. We've agreed that I won't turn up until there's a new lock on the door, there's some furniture in the place and the police have been round.

I can hardly sleep, I'm so excited. Just imagine. If it works out, then I'll finally have a room. It's a real shame the place is so far from De Druif. It's at least half an hour's walk away.

I watched them breaking in from a distance. After waiting all morning until the police have been, I knock on the door. One of the guys, Jeroen, sticks his head out of the window and a couple of seconds later I'm inside. Everything went off without a hitch. Jeroen says we can stay here for the time being.

We go upstairs. Jeroen shows me the rooms I can choose from. I don't care which one I have, as long as I can sleep. He's chosen the attic for himself. He asks me to come up and have a house-warming beer. A couple of his friends are in the attic. I've seen them now and again in De Druif. They'll be living here for the moment, too.

When I'm finally back in my own room, I can't believe how easily it all went. We've been really lucky. My room's not big, but it's very light. It's got a thick carpet on the floor, which makes it nice and warm. There's a loo in the corridor. The kitchen's downstairs but I won't be using it, because there's a basin in my room I can drink water from and I never cook at home in any case.

Jeroen goes to his old house on a delivery bicycle to fetch some mattresses. He's got one for me, too. He's a really clever bloke. He's managed to get the heating and the electricity going; he's good at negotiating with the owner and he's even got us permission to live here for a bit.

I go and collect my folder, my clothes and my school stuff, even though I'm not going to school any longer.

8 December 1977

Well, I've got a room at last, but the annoying thing is that I've never got any money. I've borrowed off everyone and I can't pay them back. The barman in De Druif won't serve me any more.

I usually get up at about two o'clock. At around five I go to De Druif. If I haven't got any clean clothes left, then I nick something in town.

Yesterday John took me to the club where he works. He showed me a little square where I can easily earn some money. At the side of the square, right by the church, is a quiet, dark spot where you can wank men off without being seen. There's quite a few girls who do that. It takes no time at all, John says. He'll find the punters. I only have to take some loo paper with me. A hand-job costs a tenner but sometimes you can charge more.

I've agreed to be there at about twelve tonight. I only have to let the doorman of the club know I've come for John and I have to tell him when I leave, too.

I turn up at midnight, as arranged, and go and stand in the place we've agreed. It's not long before an old man comes up to me. He obviously knows why I'm here. Without me asking for it, he gives me ten guilders and undoes his trousers. I'm not sure what to do or say. I stick my hand inside his underpants and kind of move it around a bit. I can't get at it properly.

The man's panting heavily and grabs hold of my jacket. He wants me to do it faster. After a couple of quick movements, my hand's dripping wet. I'm shocked at how quickly he comes. I wipe my hand with loo paper; he takes a bit, too. Then he goes off without saying another word.

John, who's obviously been watching from a distance, comes over and asks if it went all right. He's got another punter, if I want. I tell him I've got enough money now, but I don't mind doing it again tomorrow. This is easy money.

On the way to De Papillon I feel something wet on my jacket. When I get there, I go and wash my hands first. In the light of the loos I can see a damp patch on my jacket. It feels nasty. I rub it out with soap and water. When I go again tomorrow, I'll take a soapy cloth with me.

The owner of De Papillon is noticeably surprised at me turning up so early and even having enough money for a rum and coke. I usually only have a drink when someone buys it for me.

9 *December 1977*

I've said I'll meet John again as I do want more clients. Apart from the loo paper, I've got some soap with me as well, and a wet towel in a plastic bag. I go and stand in the same place as yesterday. It's ages before anyone comes. There's a woman walking her dog; I hope she doesn't realise what I'm up to.

Just as I've had enough of waiting, a man comes up to me. He's not that old and he's wearing a smart suit. He asks if I'm new. I say yes and he gives me a tenner. He promises to give me more if I do it well. He undoes his belt and trousers himself, too. Through the split in his underpants I can feel a really tiny willy. I start squeezing and rubbing and feel it getting stiffer and bigger. The man asks me to stroke him under his balls. I rub up and down with both hands. It takes a while, but then he comes, luckily not as much as the man yesterday. He wipes my hands clean with his own handkerchief and does up his trousers again, then gives me an extra two-guilders fifty. He thanks me in a friendly way and kisses me on my hair.

Twelve-fifty I got for it this time. Just one more man now and I can buy a round for the whole of De Papillon.

I wait around a bit for someone else to come along, walking up and down and keeping an eye on the door of the club. From time to time someone goes in and from time to time someone leaves. Then a man comes out and I see him heading in my direction. This man wants to stand with his back to me while I wank him off.

I wonder what John's told them in there. I just hope he picks nice blokes for me. These men have obviously done it before. They don't need many words to make it clear what they want.

The man drops his trousers right to the ground. I'm dead scared someone will come along and see us. It might be dark here but the way this man is standing, with his trousers round his ankles, is really noticeable. He asks me to wrap one hand around his balls and wank him with the other. I grab his balls firmly. I've hardly moved before he comes. Luckily not in my hand or against my jacket. I don't like the feel of sperm.

He thanks me nicely and gives me twenty-five guilders. I go to give him his change but he doesn't want any.

Once he's gone, I knock on the door of the club and tell the doorman I'm going. I've got enough money for tonight. I go off to De Papillon again.

I'm really pleased with this little job. This way I can afford to go out every day. I can even pay off my debts.

Christmas 1977
It's Boxing Day. Everyone in the house is away. Luckily De Druif's open today. Yesterday it was closed.

The barman's in a generous mood. I've been his only customer all afternoon. Together we wait for some company. I hope Wim comes in. In the meantime I drink a couple of free jenevers on an empty stomach. I can feel I'm getting pissed fast. The barman's hands start wandering. Well, I can't be doing with that, so I get up and go. I'm going to find Wim.

It's only when I stand up that I realise just how pissed I am. The whole world is spinning around me. Outside, in the cold air, I feel a bit better. I notice I keep falling over, though. I smash my head against a shop window.

A car stops. Two policemen are standing in front of me. They grab hold of me. I try to get away; I want to go to Wim's.

They shove me into the car, folding me up on the back seat. An officer sits down next to me. Bastards.

A few minutes later I'm at the police station and being taken to the cells. They make me take everything off except my trousers and shirt. Even my shoes.

They push me into a cell. I fall on the floor.

The door closes with a clang. I hear the bolt grinding. It's cold here and there isn't even a bed to lie on. Everything's made out of concrete.

I don't know how long I've been asleep. I awake to the sound of a door opening. A cop comes over to me and asks me how I'm feeling.

I've got a splitting headache. I feel sick as a dog.

What a rotten bloody trick to throw me in here, I yell at him. Let me out. I shove, scream and swear. He's about to leave again without letting me out so I grab hold of his leg and bite it as hard as I can.

He kicks me away. The door slams shut.

I feel so sick, I can't hold it in any longer. The puke splatters on the floor around me. The smell makes me feel even worse. My head's bursting. I have to lie up against the wall; otherwise I'll be lying in the sick.

Some time later, a hatch next to the door slides open. A cop asks me how I'm getting on.

Let me out, please.

I hear him drawing back the bolt and the door opens. A policeman is standing there, a different one from before. If I behave myself, I can go, he says. I promise.

In the corridor, I get my clothes back. It's much warmer there than in the cell.

The policeman tells me to go with him to the first floor, where they're making out a report.

Shit.

Five or six policemen are sitting in a big room filled with desks. They say hello.

I sit down opposite an older officer. He asks if I'd like a cup of coffee.

Thanks. Then I can finally rinse the sour taste out of my mouth.

The officer puts a sheet of paper into his typewriter and starts asking all kinds of questions. What my name is and where I live. As a precaution, I give my mother's surname. I'm scared the Child Welfare will find out. I live in a squat and I haven't got any parents. I don't feel like telling them anything else.

The officer pulls the paper out of the typewriter and tells me that, just this once, he's destroying the report, seeing as it's Christmas.

He invites me to come and sit with the other officers.

They're sitting round the Christmas tree. An officer offers me a piece of cake. I eat it up but then I want to go, go home. I've still got a terrible headache.

Spring 1978

I've got a place in a squat on Stationsplein through a guy I know from the action shop. I hope I can stay here for a while. It's a nice place, right near the centre, I've got a big room and it's only ten minutes' walk from De Druif.

There are four guys already living there; all of them are at the art college and go to De Druif now and again. We've got a communal room with a telly, which means I'm at home more often now. At the weekends it's quiet in the house because the guys always go home to their parents with a bag full of washing.

I get on well with them. Particularly Tom. He's quite small and always thinking up really huge works of art. I often help him making the kinetic installations he invents. He's really serious about art. A lot of people don't understand what he's on about, but I do.

The guys are sometimes a bit childish. They laugh a lot. They always cook and eat together and share a household kitty. I can't be bothered with all that. I'd rather be in De Druif around dinnertime. I wouldn't want to miss a single evening there.

I'm starting to get worried because I'm broke again. I've already borrowed money off everyone. John's nowhere to be found and, without him, I can't earn anything through the club. The doorman doesn't dare send the men to me; he's scared of his boss. I'm still receiving benefit from the social services via the Child Welfare, but that money's usually gone the day I get it. It's making me depressed. I just can't handle money. And I'm always hungry, too.

Joop comes round sometimes. These days we spend a lot of time wandering around demolition sites in town and then we fantasise about the treasure we hope to find there. Joop's my mate. Recently he's been really angry about the children's home he used to live in. He's grumpy with everyone except me.

Part of the ground floor of our house is being used by the feminist movement. They've made it into a women's meeting place. Men and boys over twelve aren't allowed in. Marian goes there, too.

We wanted to rent out the empty hall we've got for parties or pop concerts, hoping to make some money. But after only two parties we had problems with the hotel next door. The guests have been complaining. We've agreed with the hotel owner that we won't hold any more parties there. Then a girl who sometimes goes to De Druif wanted to move in there. She's the daughter of a children's book author.

I pop in and see her now and again. She collects dolls, in all shapes and sizes. Actually I don't know what her name is. If I ask her, she doesn't answer. She's got a really dreamy look. She's got long, thick blond hair down to her waist and a very pretty face, but there's something about her that's not right. She keeps asking if I'm going to give her a doll. Very occasionally I nick one for her, then she plays with it.

The past few days I've seen her walking a round with a pram. She tucks her dolls in really carefully.

I've asked Tom about the girl, but he doesn't really know much about her, either, except that her mother is a famous children's writer. She never comes upstairs to us, but I think she likes it when I go down for a cup of tea. She hasn't got any friends.

I came home to find a whole load of strangers in front of the house today. The children's book author's daughter has committed suicide. Just like that.

I daren't ask how she did it.

2 May 1978

Wim's been round. He's planning to go to Spain. I feel sad about it; the idea that he's going away makes me miss him already. He tries to make me feel better by promising I can go over when he's found a job and somewhere to live. Maybe I can find a job there as well. He's leaving in a couple of weeks.

I go down to De Druif with him. There's a lively atmosphere in there. A photographer who goes there a lot has just come back from a trip to England where he was doing a report for a magazine. He puts some photos on the table and explains that there's a new craze in London. The pictures are all of blokes and girls looking really rough. They've got tattoos and torn clothes. Their hair's all in bright colours and standing straight up. They're wearing worn-out motorbike jackets and tights with holes and ladders in. They've put safety pins through their cheeks and ears with chains hanging from them.

An electric shock goes through me. Now that's just the style that would suit me.

The photographer says the new craze is called punk. And there's music to go with it. He's brought a cassette of punk music with him. The barman lets him put it on for a few minutes. The music is really chaotic, like there's all kinds of electric sounds jumbled up together. There's no tune. Now and again, the singer makes some gagging sounds into the mike.

Suddenly I get all excited. This is what I want. I want to be a punk. I'm really struck by the music and with what I've just seen in the pictures. It's the perfect style for me. That's what I want to look like. Why didn't I think of it myself? I take another good look at the photos and decide to go home.

This is the first time I've gone home at this time of day. When I get there, everyone's busy cooking and they all look surprised at me rolling in when I'd normally be in the café. I explain to Tom what I've seen and that that's what I want to do, too. He knows what I mean without having seen the pictures.

He goes and gets a pair of tights off a girl who's staying in the house. I've still got a black leather skirt I pinched once and never wore. I cut the sleeves out of an old T-shirt and tear holes in it.

When I go back down, I tell the others about it and ask if anyone's got a safety pin. I could also use a chain. No one understands me, except Tom.

I get the scissors and cut off some of my hair. Tom gives me some paint to make some blue streaks in it. I've made my eyes up really black and torn enormous ladders in the tights. For the first time, I'm enjoying doing myself up in front of the mirror. I stick a safety pin through the hole in my ear, which has grown over.

Done. From now on I'm a punk. I hurry back over to De Druif. Won't they be surprised?

Everybody I meet on the way turns to stare at me. I feel really tough and walk in a rough but casual way. As soon as I go into the café everyone starts cheering and clapping. Punk, punk, they shout. The barman gives me a free drink. Of course they think I've just dressed up for the fun of it, but I'm never taking these clothes off again, that's for sure.

Wim thinks it's a bit over the top, but starts getting everybody excited, all the same. We want punk, he keeps shouting, and the barman puts the punk band on full blast.

The photographer shows us how the punks in London dance. You jump up and down to the music and now and again someone shoves someone else really hard. A few minutes later, everyone's pogo-ing up and down, shoving each other and shouting, 'Punk!'

17 May 1978

I've discovered two other punks in Den Bosch. Patty and Frits. The first time we saw each other, we were too shy to speak, but now they come into De Druif, too. They've got loads of cassettes of punk bands. Johnny Rotten's going to be on here, soon, and the three of us are going to the gig. None of the others at De Druif are joining in the craze, but they like the way we dress. The problem is, the way I'm dressed makes me stand out so much that it's getting difficult to nick things.

28 May 1978

Tom's dead. Joop came to tell me. He ate something that was bad and died of food poisoning.

I can't believe it. He's already been buried. His parents didn't want anybody to go to the funeral. Now we keep playing his favourite music. Elvis Costello. As loud as possible.

6 June 1978

It's my birthday and no one knows. I'm eighteen today. I ask the guys in the house if we should celebrate this evening with chocolate and dope. Since Tom died, the atmosphere in the squat is so gloomy. The guys promise to get the wine and chocolate and I'll go and ask John for some dope.

He gives me a good big chunk. In the evening, we sit around in the living room playing music and smoking one joint after another. The guys are reading comics and keep having laughing fits. Normally, it's me who's rolling up but I'm feeling a bit down tonight. I can't stand them having so much fun so I go and sit out in the corridor.

In the background I can hear Lou Reed singing *The Kids*. The words drone through my head. The lyrics repeat incessantly, as if the LP has got stuck.

My mother. I haven't thought about her for ages. How did she feel, dying all alone? Was she scared? Did she want to say anything to me? Maybe she wanted to give me one last kiss.

Jesus Christ, Mama, I just hope you didn't die crying. I hope you didn't cry until death took over from you.

Suddenly, I feel myself getting really angry. Everyone always left you alone and then you left me alone. I left you alone when you died. But you're still the loveliest mother I know.

The Lou Reed's nearly finished. Dear Mama, you haven't lost me, never. I hope you can see me. I just hope you know how much I love you.

The guys in the living room are about to put on another record. I go back into the room, my head feeling like it's filled with cotton wool. I want Lou Reed again.

I put the record on really loud and go out and sit in the corridor. Next to me is one of Tom's drawings in a frame. The music resounds through the building. I sing along with the record. In the background I can hear children's voices calling for their mother.

Tom's drawing is staring at me. I shatter the glass with my elbow. Great big shards fall to the ground next to me. One of the pieces stays hanging in the frame. The sound of children's voices crying is slicing through me.

Slowly, I slide my arm over the shard that's stuck in the frame, again and again. My legs are getting warm and wet. The floor is turning red. Someone asks cheerfully if we can have another record on now. And then I hear a lot of shouting. One of the guys is holding my arm in the air. Another one wraps his T-shirt round it and pulls it tight.

They say I have to go with them to the hospital. Someone tells me to get on the back of the bike. Another one walks beside me, holding my arm up.

In the hospital, they put me on a stretcher. They ask me what happened. I tell them I accidentally put my arm through some plate glass. They give me a local anaesthetic in a couple of places and then some stitches and a tetanus injection.

A friendly nurse brings me a sandwich and a cup of tea. I've lost a lot of blood, he says. I'll have to stay lying down for a bit; I'll feel better in a while. I'm lucky I didn't cut my tendons.

July 1978

Wim's gone to Spain and Joop's got a girlfriend. In a few weeks, he's going to America with her for a couple of months. He's got a grant to go and paint in New York. Frits and Patty are planning to go to Amsterdam.

There's nothing left for me here. Everyone I like is going away. John's been in the nick for two weeks again. Now he's out and wants to throw a party to celebrate. I told him he can have it at our place; after all, the room where the children's author's daughter was living is empty now. The guys in the house are against it but I've already promised. We have a row. It's obvious they'd rather I moved out.

John invites everyone and provides the beer. A friend of his organises the music. Halfway through the evening, when John goes out to score some dope, the party gets out of hand. Someone starts throwing empty beer bottles out of the window and a fight starts. In no time at all there are two Black Marias on the doorstep. Then I see John's motorbike approaching in the distance. I'm scared he'll get caught with the dope he's just fetched. I try to warn him but it's too late. I can see two policemen running over and I run after them. Now there's a policeman running after me, too.

John falls. I see him throw something under a parked car as he falls. Then I get a whack on my neck from a truncheon. A policeman pushes me to the ground. They take John and me down to the police station.

I have to wait for hours before they finally get round to questioning me. One of the policemen asks me my name. He asks why I was running away from them so fast. I give them a false name. I say I can't understand why I'm here. I was at a party and when I went outside everyone started running, so I did, too. I put together a pack of lies. The policeman types out my statement and, once I've signed it, says I can go.

The party's over, the house is in a mess. The guys want me to leave right away, as soon as I've packed my things.

I get my folder and some clothes together. Then I go to De Druif, hoping to bump into John there.

In De Druif they think it's really bad luck for John. He was just celebrating his freedom and now he's back inside. A friend of his offers me his attic room. I can stay there for a bit. Actually, I'm not too keen on the idea. He deals and everyone's scared of him. But I don't know where else I can sleep tonight so I accept his offer.

I'll go along with anything. Just as long as I can get some sleep.

18 August 1978

Joop's back from New York. When I see him in De Druif, we fling our arms around each other just like the old days. He treats me to a hamburger and tells me about New York. He's found a studio where he can live, too, and in a couple of weeks' time he's going back for good, with his girlfriend. I'm terribly jealous of her.

We talk nineteen to the dozen. I tell him about John's party that got out of hand and about the attic where I'm living now. Joop asks if I want to go with him to a Herman Brood concert. I'd like to, but I haven't got any money. He hasn't got enough to buy me a ticket. Better luck next time.

Around five, De Druif starts to fill up. It seems like everyone's going to see Herman Brood tonight. He's really great, apparently. I only vaguely know the number 'Saturday Night', which I've heard on the radio.

A bunch of guys comes into De Druif. You can hear they're not from Den Bosch. They're quite rough looking. From the general reaction, I assume this must be Herman Brood's band.

Two of the guys come and sit next to me. They offer me a drink. They order something to eat and ask if I want something, too. I wouldn't mind another hamburger.

The older of the two has ordered soup. He asks what my name is.

Karina, I say, to which he replies that his co-star is also called Karina. When his soup comes, he pours a glass of calvados into it. In the meantime, the other guy is chopping up coke on a pocket mirror and dividing it into lines. They're doing it as if it's the most normal thing in the world. They're really rough types.

They offer me a line, too, but I don't dare say yes. I'm not actually sure it's coke and I don't like to ask.

Then the oldest one asks if I want to go rock'n'rolling with them tonight. The thought suddenly strikes me that this could be Herman Brood himself. I ask him what his name is. He takes my head in his hands and kisses me.

Herman, he says. He asks again if I'm going with them. Okay, I say. I've got nothing to do, anyway. When I say I haven't got any bread, it makes him laugh. You won't need any, he assures me.

The other guys in the group come and join us at the table. A short, balding man with a leather jacket much too big for him is pacing nervously up and down. He's got a funny accent, a bit common, and ends every sentence with an English swearword. He's waiting for the man who's supposed to come and pick us up in the car.

Herman takes my hand and whispers that he thinks I'm sweet.

Finally, the man everyone's been waiting for comes in. He's tall, with a leather jacket, tight black trousers and a bald head. He's called Philip. The little balding bloke tears him off a strip.

I go outside with Herman and a guy with curly hair who tells me he's the bass player. There's an American limo in front of the door. Philip gets behind the wheel. The balding bloke gets in the front next to him. I get in the back with the curly-haired guy and Herman.

The other members of the band are following us in another car. As we drive off, I see that everyone's come out of De Druif to wave us off.

The balding guy is called Koos, but Herman calls him Coach. As we drive, he keeps pressing the button that makes the window go up and down. Wow, man, he keeps saying.

Herman puts his arm round me. Here I am, in the arms of Herman Brood. Won't they be surprised in De Druif, and what will Joop say when he sees me at the concert tonight?

We stop in front of a hall where they often have concerts. There are lots of people waiting outside already.

We go in through a side entrance. Herman's holding my hand. He's head and shoulders shorter than me, which makes me feel a bit stupid. There are loads of people in the dressing room too. The other members of the band are already there with their girlfriends. I get introduced to everybody. I'm probably one in a long line of Herman's girls. They take hardly any notice of me, apart from the guy who was in the car with us. He's called Freddie and he tries to put me at my ease.

Herman downs a fair amount of calvados and gets changed. Then he goes and sits on the loo for ages. Koos bangs nervously on the door and shouts at Herman to come out of there. He gets everything organised and goes on stage with Herman and the rest of the band.

Herman has given himself a shot in the leg. It obviously didn't go very well because his leg is bleeding. He goes off stage again. I go to the dressing room with him. He rinses the blood off at the handbasin. Then Koos comes to fetch him. The band's waiting for Herman. I can hear a buzz from the audience.

Herman asks me to go on to the stage with him. There's a place where I can stand. He gives me sweet little kisses on my mouth and hands and puts me next to a speaker.

It looks like the place is packed. When the audience sees Herman they start cheering. He goes over to the keyboard and the music breaks loose. I get almost shaken to pieces between the speakers, it's so loud. The people in the hall are screaming and dancing.

The other band members' girlfriends come and join me. I hardly dare look at them. They don't speak to me.

Herman gives a good show. He alternates between singing into the mike and playing the keyboard. He's all bent over at the keyboard. He's sweating and there's spit flying out of his mouth. I wonder if he's pissed as a fart or super-stoned. He runs to and fro across the stage, squeezing the breasts of the girls at the front. Then it's the intermission.

Herman leaves the stage, drags me into the dressing room, and starts kissing me wildly. Everybody drinks and snorts a lot in the interval. This time I do dare snort a line, too. After I've snorted it, I can't feel my nostrils. I press them and it's like they're not there any more. This is strong stuff. When Herman has to go back on stage, I take up my place between the speakers. Now I'm really kicking.

At the end of the gig I'm not sure what's going to happen. Herman asks someone where they they're playing the next day. Breda. He asks if I'm going with him. Fine by me. He's pleased. But first he wants to go for a drink somewhere in Den Bosch before driving on to Breda. Philip drives us to De Druif. It's not so crowded now. The others will be back from the concert soon.

Herman takes me out to sit on the terrace; it's still nice and warm out. Opposite us, in the market square, is the fair. The rides have just been closed and they're covering the seats with tarpaulins.

Herman asks me where I live.

Here, there and everywhere, I say. I kind of move around from one squat to another.

He does the same, he says, but recently he's been sleeping in hotels a lot, too.

He asks if I'm happy.

I look at him and shrug. I've never thought about it.

Herman's legs are itchy all the time. He scratches them till they bleed. Philip asks Herman if he's planning to sit there much longer. Herman tells him to relax.

Then the regulars come out of De Druif and sit with us. They obviously want to talk to Herman. He drags me away from the café to the other side of the street. We get into a two-seater car on the Octopus, one of the deserted fairground rides in the market square. Herman doesn't feel like having other people around at the moment.

Sitting here at the fair makes me think about the circus. I tell Herman I used to travel with a circus. He wants to know all about it. I tell him about Rob and the animals and about the tightrope walking.

Herman calls me his circus girl.

I ask him what he meant when he said his co-star was called Karina, too. He says he's been asked to act in a Pim de la Parra film, but he's not sure he ought to do it. The band's been so successful recently. They play a different town every night. He really would like to be in a film, though. He wants to be famous. Actually, he wants to write and paint, too, but he's so busy he never gets round to it.

One way or another, we can't stop talking. I wonder if it's down to the coke.

Finally, Philip comes and gets us. He doesn't want to wait any longer. The rest of the band is already in a motel somewhere, apparently.

Philip drives us over there. Herman's sitting in the front now. They've put some music on. I stretch out on the back seat and watch the lampposts on the motorway whizzing past.

It's the first time I've told anyone about the circus.

I can see everything clearly before me, the bright blue circus trucks with the bright yellow stripes, the thick, red velvet curtains, the props, the painted figures. I can see the posters I endlessly pasted on to cardboard. I can smell the wallpaper paste and the sawdust in the ring. I can remember everything, right down to the smallest detail.

We stop at a motel, somewhere along the motorway to Breda. Herman takes my hand.

My circus girl, he says again. It's obviously made an impression on him.

Philip goes into a little office, comes back with the keys and says goodnight.

In our room, Herman's looking for the mini bar. There's nothing to be found. We lie down on the bed. He's tired. I'm not at all. He gets undressed and I do the same. I hear him peeing in the basin. His back and his legs are a bit bowed. His legs are covered in scabs from the needles and his skin is red from scratching. His arms are muscly and I can't see any needle marks on them.

He pulls me towards him and kisses me tenderly. Then he turns over. He wants to sleep.

I'm relieved. I like him. I'd have done it for him if he'd wanted, but I don't really want to screw.

The sheets are nice and cool. They've been ironed stiff. I take in the smallest details of everything around me and my mind is really sharp. I'm sure I can see and feel everything so clearly because of the coke. I can't sleep because of it.

19 August 1978

In the morning I hear Herman peeing in the basin again. He wants to go out and asks if I want to go for a walk.

There's black hair lying on his pillow. He sees me looking at it and tells me his hair is falling out because of the drugs.

We walk along the edge of the motorway for a while and come to the outskirts of Breda. It must be very early still because there's hardly any traffic. We go into a roadside restaurant. Herman orders breakfast: coffee and rolls and a glass of tequila. The waiter shows his disapproval.

We go and sit out on the terrace where we talk nineteen to the dozen again. Herman wants to know all about the circus and he tells me he's got a little boy he never sees. There's a girl in The Hague he's in love with, too, but they keep arguing. He wrote a song for her.

He asks me if I'm daring. I don't really know what he means.

Would you dare sit here on the terrace with bare tits, he asks.

I pull my top up. He likes that. I pull my top back down again and tell him it's his turn to do something daring.

He stands up, pays the bill and takes me by the arm. He wants to climb walls. He wants to climb on every wall we come across. Like two high-spirited kids, we go down all kinds of little streets and climb dozens of walls. We lose our way and have a great time.

When we finally arrive back at the motel Koos is there and he's completely pissed off. He couldn't find us and thought Herman had done a runner. Apparently he does that quite often.

Herman asks Koos for some speed and booze.

Koos gives him the gear.

Herman goes and sits on the loo and gives himself another shot in the leg. When Freddie comes to ask if I slept well, Herman calls from the loo that I'm a circus girl.

20 August 1978

The gig in Breda is a big success. Now Herman's asked if I want to go with him to Brussels where they're playing at an outdoor festival tonight. Yeah, why not?

Koos organises the trip to Brussels. He wants everyone to get rid of their gear because he doesn't want to get caught with drugs at the border. He frisks everyone. I haven't got a passport but Freddie says they never check anyway. Philip and a couple of guys load all the equipment into a big truck.

Before we set off, everyone's given a line to snort. I get one again, too.

The car ride is fast, but smooth. Herman's leaning against me, stoned. He's out of it. But I'm clear as a bell again.

A big truck like that, packed with equipment, and the way we're driving now, one after another, to the next town, the next gig, it's just like in the circus. I let the memories roll over me as the motorway shoots past.

In Brussels, they drop me off at the venue. Then Koos, Herman and Philip go into Brussels to score. I help the roadies get the equipment on the stage. It feels just like the old days.

Herman's headlining tonight and there are a couple of support bands. It's warm out and there's a good atmosphere. A lot of the musicians know each other and there's much laughter.

Slowly, the field in front of the stage fill up. I get talking to Dany, one of the guitarists in Herman's band. He's from Belgium and likes playing here. Then Herman comes back. He's wearing new pointed snakeskin boots with high heels. Now he's almost as tall as me. He's pretty pissed again as well as stoned. Koos takes the bottle off him; Herman can't get too drunk before the gig. He doesn't protest. Now and again he comes and gives me a kiss. While we're listening to the support acts, he tells me how pleased he is to have Dany in his band. He's the best guitarist there is, says Herman.

When he finally has to go on stage, the audience goes crazy. After the show he's completely out of breath. He's sweating terribly and it's obvious he doesn't feel well. He's dead pale and there's white slime in the corners of his mouth. He's completely knackered.

He goes and lies down in the car. Koos tries to perk him up. Freddie takes me for something to eat.

It's late in the evening when we drive back to Holland. Herman's got over his dip and is sitting snogging with me in the back. He pushes my head down towards his crotch and I suck him off. In the front, I can hear Freddie talking to Koos and Philip. It suddenly occurs to me that this is a really special moment. A sex-and-drugs-and-rock-'n'-roll moment.

We drive all the way from Brussels to Groningen. On the way we eat in a restaurant, where Herman puts calvados in his soup again and takes off to the loo. I feel really at ease with him.

It's night by the time we get to Groningen, where Herman takes me to his local bar. Everyone wants to talk to him. We hang out there until the early hours of the morning. Then Philip comes to collect us. He lives in a village somewhere outside Groningen, where we stay the night.

21 August 1978

I haven't washed for days but I can take a shower at Philip's. He lends me some clean pants, too. Men's underpants with a split in the front, but it doesn't matter. They make Herman randy. It's easier to get at me that way, he jokes.

He's got to play again tonight, but he doesn't feel like it. He wants to write some new songs but all the travelling is stopping him. He's sulky, but he's sweet towards me.

At the end of the day, we drive back to Groningen. Koos gives Herman some speed and he drinks before, during and after the meal. I'm scared it'll be too much for him. He was out cold for hours yesterday, too.

At the venue, he has to go up a spiral staircase to reach the stage. Before the gig, he goes to check that everything's in the right place. I'm standing at the bottom of the stairs when I see Herman fall.

He crashes his way to the bottom, where I'm just able to half break his fall.

For a moment, he doesn't move. There's blood running all over his forehead. Koos is there already. He wipes the blood away and keeps saying, 'All right, man, all right, it's all right.' He's shocked, too.

Herman stands up. He's so stoned he's squinting. This is no fun any more.

He puts on a glittery jacket and goes back up the stairs to the stage. I don't want to look at him any more. I can't understand how Koos can let him play like that, after so much drink and drugs. He's still bleeding a bit. He wipes the blood off on the girls standing near the front of the stage.

After the gig, Herman books into a small hotel with me. He's got the day off tomorrow. The day after that, he's got to play in Groningen again and then we're going on to Dordrecht and Rotterdam.

There's a telly in the hotel room. We get into bed and watch, snogging a bit but not screwing. Herman apologises. He says the gear stops him from getting a hard-on. I don't mind; I don't need to screw.

Herman starts talking about the past, how he hated school and how he wanted to be world famous. I want to be famous, too, but I wouldn't know what for. I can't do anything. He says I should go Amsterdam, to the café De Palm. He goes there a lot, too. He'll introduce me to some people in the film business. He bets Pim de la Parra would have a role for me.

If I go to Amsterdam, he says, he'll help me get famous.

23 August 1978
Herman's awake early again. He's restless. He wants to get out of bed and find a bar. With some difficulty I get up, too. I haven't had anything like enough sleep. I'm starting to feel sorry for him. I wonder how healthy he really is; he seems pretty hooked on drink and drugs.

28 August 1978
There's more touring in the days that follow. After Dordrecht, Herman wants to go back to Groningen. The success is driving him nuts. He's convinced that the audience just stands there cheering when he comes on and no one listens to his music. He's feeling edgy. He wants to write new songs.

Philip drives us to Groningen. In his local, Herman starts writing lyrics on little bits of paper and beer mats. He's restless and ready to move on. He wants to go to Amsterdam, right now. He asks if I'm going with him.

I think he's joking.

He goes off. I wait ages for him. At first I think he must be in the loo but he never comes back. Towards the end of the evening I ask the barman if he's got Philip's phone number. I haven't got any money and I don't know where Herman is.

Philip comes and picks me up. Typical of Herman, he says. He pays the bill for me and suggests I spend the night at his place.

I don't know where else to go anyway. We drive to Philip's house. When we get there he tries it on with me.

I don't care. I'm tired and I'm quite prepared to do something for a bed.

He screws me furtively, as if he can tell I'm only doing it to get shot of him as quickly as possible. When I start moving my hips up and down a bit, he comes suddenly. He's annoyed at having come so fast and accuses me of moving too quickly. But I'm relieved. At least I can get some sleep now.

End of August 1978
Next morning, Philip drives me to Groningen station. We hardly say a word to each other. I wonder if he's Herman's dustbin.

I make up some excuse for the ticket collector. I tell him my bag got stolen. He writes out a slip so I can pay the fare later.

I feel miserable. It was really rotten of Herman to go off without me. He just left me sitting there. I couldn't help thinking about the circus the past few days but now I don't feel anything any more. It's like I'm completely empty.

I find a beer can in the litter bin. I pull the ring-pull off and stick the sharp edge into the inside of my arm. I make little dents and cuts. It doesn't bleed much but my skin gapes open.

I make patterns on my arm. I want to feel something again.

Back in Den Bosch I hurry over to De Druif. It feels like ages since I left. The terrace is full. I go inside, saying hello to a few people on the way, but the barman hardly looks up.

I'm back, I want to scream, but no one seems surprised to see me. The photographer comes over; he's the only one who says, 'Long time no see.' When I tell him I've been with Herman Brood he laughs and asks if it was fun.

Yeah, it was fun, I say. He looks at my arm and sees all the wounds. Then he slaps me hard in the face. He doesn't say anything but somehow I know what the slap meant.

For the first time in my life I appreciate being slapped.

When I order a coffee, the barman asks if I've got any money. I still owe him twenty-five guilders. I haven't got any so I don't get served.

As I walk out, I realise no one else could have cared less that I was away even though I'm sure they must have seen me leaving with Herman. Disappointed, I walk back to my attic room. On the way, I nick *Shpritz*, Herman's latest album.

My room stinks of rotten Chinese takeaway. There's dirty clothes everywhere. I read the sleeve notes; I know the tunes off by heart now. For the first time, I think it's a shame I haven't got a record player, otherwise I would have put the LP on full blast now.

I wake with a start in the early evening. I've been asleep all afternoon. Outside I can hear a car engine running, then the doorbell goes. It's Wim, back from Spain. He's just passing through. He's got new plans; now he's going to live with an old girlfriend in Belgium. When we say goodbye, we promise to keep in touch, but somehow I know we probably won't.

After he leaves I feel down. I make the decision to go to Amsterdam. I can't be bothered with De Druif any more.

Later in the evening, hunger drives me into town. I've got to try and borrow some money from someone. In a side street, I discover an opening party going on inside a shop. There are some people there from De Druif. I make my way unnoticed through the crowd, saying hello to one or two people I know. There's a cold buffet so I eat something. Then a ladies' handbag on a couch catches my eye. Without another thought, I pick up the bag and sling it over my shoulder. Once I'm outside, I go home as quickly as possible.

When I open the bag, I realise I know the owner. I feel a bit bad for her, but there's a hundred and fifty guilders in it. Well, that's it then; tomorrow I'm off to Amsterdam.

Next morning I make sure I get rid of the handbag and the papers in it. I put them in a plastic bag and throw it in a bin on the way to the station. In the bag I've brought are my folder, a few clothes and some makeup.

Then I buy a single ticket to Amsterdam. I hope I'll find Herman in the De Palm café. After that, well, we'll see.

5

Church of Satan

1 September 1978

Amsterdam. The city I've heard so much about yet never visited. In the square in front of the station I stop and stare at the enormous mass of people.

I move through the crowd in the hope of going in the right direction, walking with the flow. Trams pass and the first time I cross a big road I realise you have to watch out. Mopeds, bicycles and cars tear past and, just as I'm about to cross, a tram squeals round the corner.

Like most cities, I guess the widest road leads to the centre. I try and remember the directions Herman gave me to De Palm. Left at the Dam, then straight on and second right. Okay, first let's find the Dam.

I quickly spot the war memorial in the Dam Square; I remember it from television. There are tourists sitting on the steps around it. I wonder if I'll come and sit here a lot. Then I can't get my bearings any longer. Which side do I go straight on from, now? There are so many streets here. Some bloke notices I'm looking for something and comes over. I ask him if he knows De Palm and he points in the direction of a narrow side street. As I start walking off, he asks if I want to buy some dope.

The side street's quiet and dark. I wonder if it's actually sensible to go into it. All around me there are black guys hissing, 'Hashish, hashish.' I decide to risk it anyway.

I go right down the street and back again but can't see a café called De Palm. There are two other cafés, though, De Brakke Grond and Frascati. I go into Frascati to ask the way to De Palm. It can't be far.

Inside it's packed, unlike the alley which seemed deserted. I order a coffee. I ask the barman if he knows where De Palm is. He tells me it's right behind Frascati, by the canal. I pay and walk off in that direction. Then, sure, enough, I see the café by the canal.

It's busy inside. I look round to see if Herman's there, but he's not. I ask the barman if Herman still goes there. The man laughs. You never know with Herman, he says. He hasn't seen him for ages. But I might be able to find him at Chez Nelly this evening.

I thank him. I don't dare ask where Chez Nelly is.

I stroll along the canals for a bit, impressed by all the things I see. The old houses, the little boats, but especially the people walking around, loads and loads of different kinds of people.

In the meantime I try to remember the way. I want to go back to De Palm in a little while. Maybe Herman will be there.

All evening I wait for Herman in De Palm. I get talking to a sculptor, an older guy. One of his arms is paralysed. When I tell him I haven't got anywhere to sleep, he asks if I want to go back to his studio with him.

We take the tram across Amsterdam. His studio is on the east side, in an old school building, where it looks as if there are other artists, too. He lives on the first floor in an old classroom. All his sculptures are of bulls, big and small, in wood, bronze, stone and clay.

There's a raised area in the studio where his bed is. He pours out some wine and makes things cosy. He asks if I mind sharing the bed with him. He's only got one bed, he says, but it's big.

We lie down rather self-consciously. He tells me about his work and his exhibitions and, after a while, starts making a move on me. I let him; he's nice and I'm glad I can sleep here. I feel sorry for him with that paralysed arm.

He climbs awkwardly on top and starts to screw me. Only being able to lean on one arm, he's heavy. He goes in and out endlessly. I catch myself looking around while he's doing it; I don't feel like paying him any attention. He notices and gets annoyed.

He wants to come, but then I'll have to work with him, he says.

I wiggle around a bit, to help him along.

He rolls off. He doesn't want to screw like that.

I turn over, glad it's finished and I can go to sleep.

Next morning I get dressed quickly and sneak out. He's still asleep.

★

I've got no idea how to get back to the city centre. I ask a woman on the street which tram goes to the Dam Square. She shows me which way to go.

The tram takes me back to the station. From there I walk to the Dam and on to De Palm, but the café is still closed. I wander around the area a bit. It's a red-light district. There are rooms all over the place with red curtains and little red lamps. Prostitutes are standing in the windows of some of them, trying to lure men in.

In the afternoon, I take a rest on Leidseplein. I get talking to a girl who works in a café on Thorbeckeplein. She's a topless waitress. I ask her if she knows where I can get a job. I tell her I've only just arrived in town and don't know anybody yet.

She asks which languages I speak. English, German, French?

Only Dutch, I say.

Well it won't be easy, then, she assures me. In the bar where she works, you have to deal with tourists a lot. There's plenty of work in restaurants and bars, she adds, but I'll have to alter my appearance. The way I look now, she doesn't think I've got any chance of being taken on.

They'll think you're a junkie, says the girl.

After talking to her I walk into the shopping area. I've got to change the way I dress if want to find a job, but I've hardly got any money left.

I try to see if I can nick something, but the security seems to be tight in Amsterdam. There are security gates everywhere, or the clothes are chained to the racks. Finally, I manage to get something in Vroom & Dreesman. I put on a smart pair of trousers under my old ones and walk out. I change in the loo in a café. Now I just need a top and I'm all set.

Later on I go back to De Palm in my new outfit. Herman still hasn't been seen there. I go back to the café where I went first, Frascati.

When I go in, it's so packed that most people are having to stand. They've got a really big menu. In De Druif you could only get a hamburger, egg and bacon or a bowl of soup.

Everyone seems to know each other, there's a lot of kissing. I spot a couple of famous faces from a TV series.

I find myself a place to sit. An older man comes and sits next to me and asks if he can buy me a drink. I order yet another coffee. The man introduces himself. He's called Hugo. He asks where I come from.

Den Bosch, I say.

He can tell by my accent, he says. He lives nearby and comes here every day. Now and again he introduces me to people who come over to talk to him. He offers to buy me a meal.

Most of the menu is in French. I've got no idea what it all means so I ask him to choose something nice for me. A few minutes later, two steaming plates are put in front of us. I've got spare ribs, delicious. Hugo's having something fancy. I don't like to ask what it is.

We keep being interrupted while we're eating by people coming to say hello to Hugo. I get the idea that he's very important. Towards the end of the evening, I'm feeling really at home in the café, even though the people who come here are quite a bit older. Around closing time, Hugo leaves. I'm starting to get a bit worried about where to spend the night when some guy asks me if I want to go for a nightcap in De Pieter. Fine. De Pieter is in a narrow, dark alleyway. There's a Hell's Angel at the bar. It's written in big letters on his leather jacket. When he turns towards me, I see his face is disfigured with burns. He's wearing shades. The guy I came in with introduces me to him and buys me a drink.

I tell them I'm looking for Herman Brood and ask if they know where Chez Nelly is. The Hell's Angel knows it and says he'll take me there. He knows Herman, too.

In the middle of the night we walk to Chez Nelly. According to the Hell's Angel it's not far from De Pieter. It's right in the middle of the red-light district.

The streets are crowded. Droves of tourists, mostly men, strolling past the prostitutes. I ask the Hell's Angel how much a room costs here. There are loads of them advertised for rent. He explains that you can rent the rooms for a day or half a day. They're meant for prostitutes. I tell him I'm looking for a room and a job. Then he tells me I can make easy money behind Rembrandtplein. At the end of Utrechtsestraat there's a little park where you can take punters. He knows some girls who do that. He doesn't know how to get a room, though. There are squats in Amsterdam but you've got to be lucky to find something.

Chez Nelly is a tiny old bar which is only open at night. That's brilliant. It means I've got a roof over my head tonight. The barmaid hasn't seen Herman for ages, either. She promises to say hello to him for me if he comes in. She asks me my name three times, and forgets it every time.

'Karina, wasn't it, love?' she says in a thick Amsterdam accent.

I play dice with the Hell's Angel until the early hours. He looks scary and dangerous but he's actually a really shy bloke. He lives in Angel Place, where only Hell's Angels are allowed to live. De Pieter is his local; he goes there every night.

We leave just before dawn. I can hardly keep my eyes open. The Hell's Angel shows me the way to Rembrandtplein. I have to stand at the end of Utrechtsestraat, he says, right by the park. The other end of the street it's mostly Moroccan boys picking up tricks. Then he goes off.

I walk across the square and into Utrechtsestraat. It's a shopping street and I can't see any guys there, or any girls either. At the end is a little park with a fountain. I lie down on a bench for a bit, using my folder as a pillow. I drop off in the warm sun.

In the afternoon, I explore the area. The park's got plenty of places where you can stand without being seen and the fountain is handy for washing your hands. Rembrandtplein's really nice. There are lots of terraces and cafés. A bit further on, I can see Thorbeckeplein with the topless bars the girl I met earlier was telling me about.

Towards evening, I spot a couple of Moroccan guys walking up and down by the tram stop on Rembrandtplein. They're obviously not waiting for the tram. Now and again one of the guys goes off with somebody or gets into a car. Further up Utrechtsestraat I can see some girls hanging around. I walk over towards the park and stand on the corner to see how they handle it.

When a car stops, a girl gets in or exchanges a few words with the driver and then she walks off to the park. I follow one of the girls to see where she's going to stand. There seem to be an unusual number of men around in the park. On the right-hand side I see one coming out of the bushes; he's obviously just been wanked off in there by one of the girls.

I wander about a bit and it's not long before someone approaches me. Suck, fuck or hand-job, he hisses.

I look at the man. Hand-job's a tenner, I say. I act like it's the most natural thing in the world. He walks with me into the bushes and gives me a ten-guilder note. I undo his flies and wank him off in a routine way. He groans a bit too loudly for my liking when he comes. I tell him to keep the noise down. He apologises and walks off. I rinse my hands in the fountain.

This is a pretty handy spot, better than in Den Bosch. A girl who's also trying to pull is sitting on a bench, smoking. I go and sit next to her. I tell her I'm new at this. I want to know what the prices are and what she does. She tells me she never gets into cars. You can earn more than enough in the park. Mostly it's blow-jobs. Hand-jobs are fastest, and screwing also pays well, but it's difficult. There's nowhere to lie down. She always does it standing up against the little wall by the fountain. There's a couple of blokes who try to get it for nothing, they're always hanging around here, she says. But after a couple of days you know most of the punters, it's always the same ones. She buys her Durex at the chemist's up the road. They have a nasty rubbery aftertaste so she always chews gum.

I thank her for the tips.

She tells me it gets busy after eleven in the evening. Everybody's got their regular spot. You can get into quite a row with the girls if you go and stand in someone else's place. She shows me all the regular spots and her own patch.

12 September 1978

I've been working in the park for a week, now, and I've done everything a few times. I know most of the other girls and the punters and I earn enough to live on, but I can't find a room. And it's getting colder out. Sometimes I go home with someone from De Pieter or Frascati to get a good night's rest. The barman in Frascati knows I'm looking for somewhere to sleep and as soon as I get talking to anyone he warns him I'm a whore, the bastard.

One night I ask Hugo if he can help me find a place to stay. I want to get off the streets. He offers me his spare room; his house is big enough. I should have asked him earlier.

It's after twelve when we walk back to his house. We go through the narrow streets to the Herengracht. As we cross the bridge, he points to a corner house in the distance, with red-and-white wooden shutters. That's easy to remember. It's got several floors, with little staircases all over the place, and it's decorated in a really interesting way. The spare rooms are right at the bottom, in the basement. The biggest one is for me. Hugo says I can stay with him for a while; it'll be company for him. He makes it clear that I can't bring people back to the house, though. Then he shows me where the towels are and the light switches and says goodnight.

20 September 1978

Hugo shows me around in Amsterdam. He thinks I should go to the Social Security office to apply for benefit. I don't dare; I made such a hash of it in Den Bosch. But I don't tell him that.

I'm usually in Frascati now from about five until late in the evening. A lot of actors go there, and film and TV producers and journalists. Hugo knows what everybody does. I get a lot of drinks bought for me now. Sometimes I pop over to De Palm, in the hope of catching Herman there.

One evening, I'm sitting at the bar in Frascati, surrounded by the hum of voices. Everyone's busy talking. Diagonally opposite me are a couple of men, deep in conversation. I've never seen them here before. One of them's blond with a beard of about two days' growth. I'd put him at about thirty, but there's something very boyish about him. As if he can feel me looking at him, he turns his face towards me. Our eyes meet for a moment. I jump from the shock that goes through me. My heart is racing.

I can't keep my eyes off him and it's making me terribly edgy. A little while later he looks at me again. He's probably realised I'm looking at him. I give him a big smile, out of nerves. Not long after, he gets up, holding a leather saddlebag with two metal clips to attach it to the luggage rack of his bike. He says goodbye to the others. I catch something about a train. He leaves the café.

I feel really confused. What a gorgeous bloke. He must live in another town. But two days later, just as I'm leaving Frascati to go to Hugo's, I spot the guy who made my pulse race. He sees me, too.

Our eyes meet for a moment. Shyly, he says hi and then goes into Frascati.

My heart's thumping like mad. So he comes in here regularly. I'd love to get to know him.

26 September 1978

There's a little café on the Spui called De Zwart. A couple of people I know from Frascati go there. Apart from that, it's all old men. You can sit on the terrace and watch the people going by. Round about five in the afternoon, the café fills up. Everyone's packed shoulder to shoulder, talking and drinking lager.

Unlike in Frascati, I have hardly anything to do with anyone here. I sit in the corner at the bar. Just as I've decided to leave and go back to Frascati, I see the face of the man I'm now madly in love with.

He sees me and I smile at him.

Taken aback by my smile, he looks the other way, but I can see out of the corner of my eye that he keeps looking over in my direction. I wonder whether I should go over and speak to him. What should I say?

The mass of bodies stops me. I'm smiling openly at him now, and I can see that he keeps looking back, smiling. Just briefly, but it's definitely a smile. He goes outside to sit on the terrace. If I want to get to know him, I've got to do something now, before he's gone.

I go out on to the terrace. There's a seat free next to him. Sitting down, I say, Well, we've smiled at each other so often now, it's about time we talked.

He introduces himself as Peter.

I ask if this is his local.

He comes here every day except Sundays, when the café's closed. He asks if he can buy me a drink and tells me he's just going on holiday to France. Cycling with some friends. He's got to buy some wellingtons and asks if I feel like going with him.

Now I'm actually talking to him, I fancy him even more than I dared imagine. I'm completely head-over-heels in love. I don't think I've ever been so much in love with anyone.

As soon as we've finished our drinks, we get up to go shopping. We're going to buy wellies. He takes his bike with him.

On the way, he asks me where I live and I explain that I'm staying at Hugo's. I tell him about Leiden, my mother, the foster family and my life in Amsterdam the past few weeks. No details, just an outline. I don't dare tell him about my work in the park. I daren't tell him my real age, either, and add a few years on. He's already thirty-one.

He might know of somewhere for me to live, he says. He lives in a commune with a number of people. One of them is staying somewhere else for a while. He'll ask if I can use her room while she's away. He'll let me know more in a couple of days.

I have to get a grip on myself not to show how much in love I am with him. I'm worried it'll scare him off. I've really got to go about this with a bit of discretion.

We buy some wellies in a sports shop. Peter invites me to go for a Chinese. I'd like to but I haven't got any money. Doesn't matter, he says, it's on him.

At the restaurant, we talk about his past. He comes from Enschede. His father was a bricklayer. He built those old, high, round chimneys that factories used to have. His mother worked in a textile factory from the age of fourteen. Peter was an afterthought. His mother was already in her forties when she had him. He gets on well with his parents and goes to visit them a couple of times a year.

He came to Amsterdam to study educational theory when he was twenty-one. He played the star role in a film and with the money that earned him he travelled around Africa for a year. Now he lectures in video studies at the university.

He asks about me. I find it difficult to give up my secrets just like that, but he asks the questions in a way no one has ever asked them before. The way he acts makes me feel comfortable. To come across as normal as possible, though, I invent all sorts of things.

After dinner Peter has to go to work. He writes his address on a piece of paper and tells me to call him about the room the day after tomorrow. Then he gets up and kisses me quickly on the cheek.

27 September 1978
Early next morning I'm already in De Zwart in the hope of meeting Peter again. I've just laid out my last one-and-a-half guilders for a coffee when he comes in. He was on his way to work and saw me

sitting there. He presses a twenty-five-guilder note into my hand, says I don't have to pay him back, and he's off again.

I sit there, amazed. It's the first time a man's ever given me money without wanting anything for it. I'm so in love with him. I've got to get a normal job. Peter definitely wouldn't approve of me working in the park. I don't want him to find out.

That evening, I go back to Hugo's early. I can't get Peter out of my mind.

28 September 1978
I might have a job as a barmaid. I've spoken to the boss of De Brakke Grond and he has agreed to try me out this evening. I had to lie and tell him I'd had experience. He asked me to pour a beer, which worked by pure luck. Exactly two fingers of head, stopped the pump just in time, really pure luck. I hope I can manage this evening. Tomorrow I'm going to speak to Peter again. I really hope I can move into the house with him.

My trial shift was a success. It's terribly difficult to remember what people order and it's even more difficult to work out how much to charge them. But I managed it and have been asked to come back tomorrow evening. I don't earn much, five guilders an hour.

Just one more day and then I can speak to Peter again.

29 September 1978
Today, finally, I can call Peter. The last two days have seemed like weeks. I call him from De Brakke Grond.

I hear his voice at the other end. I listen for any hint of him being pleased to hear from me, but his voice sounds neutral. Quite calmly, he tells me I can move in tomorrow and the rent is a hundred and fifty guilders a month.

I arrange to go over tomorrow at four. He'll make sure he's home. Hugo doesn't mind me leaving. He's enjoyed having me, but I can tell he's relieved, too.

30 September 1978
Peter lives in the Jordaan. I only know about the Jordaan from songs. I hadn't any idea how to get there so I went to the Tourist

Information office to ask the way and buy a map. My stuff is all packed in a bin bag. I bought a bike off a junkie with the first money I earned. For Peter I buy a rose. A subtle hint.

I think roses are so romantic.

On the way, I get one of the bicycle wheels stuck in the tram rails and crash into someone opening a car door. The rose stem's broken. I hope it doesn't bring bad luck. After searching around the winding streets, I finally find the address I'm looking for. It looks like an old factory. Peter's name is on the door.

I press the bell. A few seconds later, I see Peter's head poke out of a window.

Come on up, he calls.

Again, my heart skips a beat. Jesus, I'm really in love.

Peter opens the door and I step into a big room. He says this is the communal sitting room. It's got an open kitchen where he introduces me to two guys and a girl. They live here, too. The other two are expected back around dinnertime. Behind the sitting room is a corridor with seven rooms off it. Everyone's got their own room. Peter takes me to mine. It's big and everything looks nice and tidy. Plants, books, a made-up bed. The girl who lives here has gone off for some time.

Then he takes me two doors further up and shows me his room. It's small, but really tidy, too. There's a cloth on the table. His bed, a mattress on the floor, is nicely made up. He's got loads of books. There's a teapot on the table, over a pot-warmer, and the radio's on. There's all kinds of photographs on the wall, large, small, black-and-white, colour – loads of them with girls on.

When he sees me looking at the pictures, Peter says they're all his ex-girlfriends.

I wonder if he's trying to make it clear that he hasn't got a girl-friend now.

He can't be long, he says. If I want to stay in his room, then by all means do so.

October 1978

Most evenings now I work in De Brakke Grond. I really like it. The beer pouring is going fine and I get better at the mental arithmetic every day. I've got to know a lot of new people in the past week. I buy new clothes with my tips and in De Bijenkorf I bought some makeup for the first time, instead of nicking it.

Peter comes home around eleven every evening. In the mornings, he has breakfast at his table at half past seven. Radio on and the newspaper. I'm amazed to see he sets the table properly for himself.

I'm even more in love with him than I was before and I wonder desperately why we're still not going out together. I can tell he fancies me, but that's as far as it goes.

Recently I've started getting him to wake me in the morning by knocking on the door. Then I wait for him, after I've made myself up, lying with my top half bare and the sheet draped over my tummy, pretending to be asleep, in the hope that he'll want to make love. But he doesn't do anything. He just calls me. Then I get dressed and go and have breakfast with him.

We listen to the news on the radio together in his room. Then he goes to work and I clear away the breakfast things. He gives me a kiss when he leaves, but it's more like a peck. I don't know if it means anything or it's just a habit.

Actually, I'm getting more insecure by the day. I can't work Peter out. He's nice and friendly but a bit strict, and so different from any other man I've ever come across. He's really calm and serious.

On the evenings when I'm not working, I sit and wait for him to come home. He gets in on the stroke of eleven. We're all generally sitting in the communal room watching telly. Peter just says goodnight to us and goes off to his room.

About a quarter of an hour later, I pop in to see him. By then he's already in bed, with the bedside lamp on and a book in his hands, the sheets right up to his chin. Now, I dare to go and lie down beside him and chat for a bit. Then I go to my own room. I can never get over the disappointment of not getting him to make love to me.

22 October 1978
Today Peter's going to France for a week. Just another half-hour and then his friend's coming to pick him up. I help him pack his saddlebags. I put a new zip in his tracksuit by hand. It was a hell of a job but I'd do anything for him.

We have a last cup of tea together and then, out of the blue, unexpectedly, he puts his arms round me and kisses me tenderly. My heart starts racing. I nestle into his arms. And then, just as suddenly as he took me in his arms, he stops kissing me. He walks out of the room, saying goodbye.

'Just a minute, I'll come and wave you off,' I say, running after him. I'm so happy, I could dance.

His friend's downstairs by the car. Peter gives me a kiss, an ordinary kiss, brief, gentle, but with nothing of the tenderness of just now. All the same I'm so happy, so happy that I wish his friend a good journey and kiss him, too. Elated, I wave Peter off.

You see? He does feel something for me.

The week Peter's not there, I can't stop thinking about him. I count the hours until his return. On the day he's coming back, there's a postcard. It's addressed to everybody, but my name's first. That must mean something.

That afternoon, he comes home. He's brought presents for everybody and for me a bottle of almond liqueur. I decide to keep it for the rest of my life, my first present from Peter.

Once everything's been unpacked, an insecure feeling creeps over me. Are we going out or aren't we? Peter behaves as usual. He's really nice and tells me about France, but he doesn't take me in his arms. When he goes to bed, it's just like before. I make jokes and tease him a bit but nothing happens. He kisses me goodnight and I go back to my room.

29 October 1978

We finally made love. It was different from any other time I've done it, but still, we did it. I was sitting on the couch with him watching *Toppop*. My favourite record was on, Meat Loaf's *Paradise By The Dashboard Light*. Peter thinks it's a good record, too. I turned the sound right up, went and stood in front of him and sang loudly, 'Do you love me, will you love me for ever, do you need me, will you never leave me?' When it got to the chorus I sang it again, as loud as I could. Then he started kissing me and asked me to go to his room with him. He locked the door and we tussled around until we were lying naked in each other's arms. That was it.

I didn't dare make the first move; I was too scared of putting him off. I just moved the way I thought he wanted me to. It didn't get any further than lying naked next to each other.

Then I had to go back to my own room. I would have so loved to fall asleep in his arms, but he told me can't sleep with someone next to him. I just hope he gets used to me so that he can.

Back in my room, I can't get to sleep. I'm so happy. I'd love to tell my mother about Peter. For the first time in ages I miss my mother again. I write her a letter, which is a bit like telling her. I put the letter in my folder.

8 November 1978
There's going to be a video presentation at the university and Peter's asked me to do the commentary between the films. I've got no idea how something like that works, but I'll do anything for him.

I have to read out the commentary in a studio, in front of the camera. The films are going to be presented in a big hall, with my bits, live, in between. We've rehearsed it a couple of times. I have to look straight at the camera and recite a script off by heart. I can't remember the script. Every time the man behind the window in the studio says 'Action!' and I look into the lens of the camera, I forget where I am and what I'm supposed to be saying. I get the giggles, but five minutes before the presentation, I manage it after all.

Ten seconds to go, I hear the man in the studio say. He counts down and then I say exactly what I'm supposed to, straight into the camera.

The films aren't very long. Some are five minutes, the longest fifteen. One time I forget the script and have to make it up as I go along. Afterwards, Peter tells me the audience was cracking up when I did that.

It went really well, considering it was the first time.

End of November 1978
Peter and me are girlfriend and boyfriend. Now we really make love and I'm allowed to sleep with him. He's introduced me to his friends and his parents as his girlfriend.

I don't go out any more. I do the shopping, I cook and I've stopped working in De Brakke Grond. Now we're really living together I watch telly every evening.

I'll have to tell Peter my real age soon. I'm scared he'll find out my date of birth. He wants to go abroad with me next summer and then I'll need a passport. It was stupid of me to ever lie about my age. The longer I'm with him, the more difficult it gets to come out with it. His friends already think I'm much too young for him. They're all about fifteen years older than me.

I don't like his friends much. They always make such a big thing out of everything. They always have to have an opinion about things. They never just enjoy them for what they are, except *Monty Python*. They come round to dinner every Sunday night and then they watch highbrow documentaries. Whenever they talk about anybody, it seems like they're only one of them if they've been to university or if they've got an important job. Nobody lives together; if they do have a relationship, it's a complicated living-apart-together one.

All their girlfriends keep telling me I'm getting too dependent on Peter. They think I should get myself an education. But I couldn't be without him for a day. None of his friends want children but I'd love to have lots of children with him.

I've had Peter's name tattooed on my arm. I want him to know I mean it. That I want to be with him for ever.

January 1979
They always need people to help out on Peter's video course at the university. That's how I fill my days. I like the work. One time I'll be acting, another time I'll be helping with the production or I'll do the catering.

April 1979
I bumped into Herman on Rembrandtplein the other day. We went for a drink and we just picked up where we'd left off, as if we'd known each other for years. He looks better than he did in Groningen. I told him about what I'd been doing and about Peter and that I'm acting in videos now.

I notice he's had a tattoo done on his arm, too.

DOREEN, it says. That's his big love. We're amazed we've both had a kind of banner tattooed on our arms. Him on his right arm, me on my left.

He says he's doing well. Someone's writing a book about him, there's plans for a film, his music's taken off and he might be going on tour in America. Then he'll be world famous.

We drink the whole evening. He's still drinking heavily. As for me, it's the first time since I moved in with Peter that I've spent so long in a bar.

Before we say goodbye, Herman stresses that I should go and see Pim de la Parra. He's still making the film Herman was going to be in. He gives me the address.

Next day, I just turn up at the address. It's a big building on Geldersekade. There's a brass sign by the door: SCORPIO PRO-DUCTIONS. *Pim de la Parra & Wim Verstappen*. I ring the bell.

When a woman opens the door I ask if Pim de la Parra's there. She shows me in; his office is upstairs.

As I go into the room, a short, skinny guy comes over. He introduces himself as Pim. He asks if I'd like something to drink and what I've come about. He's got a foreign accent. It sounds a bit Indonesian. I ask him where he comes from.

From Suriname, he says, delighted that I didn't know. Apparently everybody knows that.

I tell him Herman gave me his address, that I'm acting in videos at the moment but would really like to act in a real film.

Pim says he's doing a film he thinks I'd be good in.

I can hardly believe what he's saying. Just like that? He doesn't even know if I can act.

The film is about a tourist who meets various women in Amsterdam, who he then has all kinds of adventures with. It's going to be called *Dirty Picture*. It's something Pim's been planning for years. He had had Herman in mind for the main role but now Herman can't do it he's going to play it himself. Pim says his girlfriend, who's called Karina, too, is going to play the female role. I knew that already from Herman.

Inspired by my visit, he wants to have a think about what kind of role he can give me and says he'll be in touch.

Jumping on my bike, I feel like I'm floating. I really have to concentrate on the traffic. It's incredible. Now I'm getting a film role. It seems as if everything is working out the way I want.

Peter's pleased for me but he bombards me with questions. Just exactly what kind of role is it? Will I have to appear naked? Pim's known as a director who works with a lot of nudity, he says.

I can't answer him. We didn't talk about that. And I don't care, even if I have to take off every stitch of clothing. There isn't anything I don't dare do, even stunts if I have to.

Peter warns me to be careful.

May 1979
I've been feeling sick in the morning recently. When I get out of bed I almost have to throw up. Maybe I'm pregnant. I sneakily bought a test and, yes, it's positive. I know for a fact that Peter won't want to know about it. He's working and studying and when he talks to his friends about children it's clear he's not ready for that by any means.

I wouldn't mind having a baby. Maybe if I handle him carefully he might like the idea once he's got used to it.

As soon as he comes in, I ask him to sit down.

I'm pregnant, I blurt out.

Nervously, Peter gets up. 'You can't be,' is the only thing he says and walks out of the room. Shocked, I stay behind.

A little while later he comes in with some tea. Tensely, he starts asking how it could have happened. I'm on the pill, aren't I?

I don't dare to say I fibbed about it. I tell him I forgot it one time.

He gets cross. He thinks I'm careless. He says I've got to arrange to get rid of it.

The words hit me like a slap in the face. Get rid of it?

I ask him if he wants a couple of days to think about it. I tell him I quite understand he's shocked.

We drink our tea in silence. I can see that Peter feels awful about it. I promise to get rid of it if he really doesn't want it.

After two days, I can see he won't change his mind. I tell him I'll keep my promise, but under one condition. I want to know if he ever does want children.

Peter swears that he'll definitely want a baby in a few year's time, but now's really not the right moment. We've got hardly any money, nowhere proper to live and he wants to finish his studies.

Now I know I've got to get rid of it I can't wait a minute longer. It's such a horrible idea that there's a baby growing in my belly by the minute.

I make an appointment at the Rutgershuis Clinic.

6 June 1979
It's going to be done next week. According to the procedure I have to take two weeks to think it over, but that time's passing so slowly. Peter feels awful about the abortion, too.

We go out to dinner for my birthday at De Reiger. They're looking for staff and the owner asks if I'm interested. He says I can start in mid-June. I decide to do it.

Over dinner I tell Peter my real age. I'm nineteen today, I tell him.

He looks at me in surprise. Then he laughs. He thought I was going to tell him I was older than I'd said. He doesn't mind me being four years younger. Now there's thirteen years between us.

12 June 1979
Today is the abortion. Peter's going to work. I don't want him going to the clinic with me.

There are eight other women in the waiting room. They divide us into two groups, those who are going to have a general anaesthetic and those who are going to have a local. I've opted for the general. I can't stand the idea of being aware of what's happening. The thought of being hoovered out is too much for me.

A nurse explains to us exactly what happens, how long it takes and how we can expect to feel over the next few days.

I keep trying to tell myself the baby is still just a blob, that it hasn't got any arms or legs yet, but I'm not sure about that bit, especially as I don't really know how far gone I am. The doctor who gave me an internal examination says it's nine or ten weeks. I hope it's only a blob.

Seeing as I'm having a general anaesthetic, the nurse wants to take a blood sample. Bloody hell, why can't they just get on and give me an injection and then I'll wake up in a bit and find it's all over? The nurse comes and sits next to me and asks if I'm sure I still want to go through with it.

Yes, I hear myself saying, but suddenly I can't help bursting into tears. I can't do anything about it, it just happens.

Concerned, the nurse asks if anyone's coming to fetch me afterwards.

Sobbing, I nod.

After she's taken the blood, I have to go to a ward with beds in it. Then I'm given a pre-med, to calm me down. Bed and all, they wheel me into the room where it's going to happen. There, I have to change over to a table with stirrups. A friendly doctor helps me but as soon as I lie down and have to spread my legs, I'm in floods of tears again. Jesus Christ, why haven't they put me out yet? I feel a needle going into my arm and see the doctor touch my face. He strokes my forehead and I'm just about to say something, but I already can't feel anything any more.

From far, far away, I hear the nurse. She's nodding at me in a friendly way.

Wake up, she says, it's over.

I'm relieved. I'm back in the ward. I can feel a big sanitary towel between my legs. They bring me a cup of tea and some sandwiches and I apologise a hundred times for having cried like that.

I don't dare move, any moment I'm expecting some terrible pain, but luckily I don't feel anything. I'm just bleeding as if I've come on.

Once I've eaten the sandwiches and been for a wee I'm allowed to get dressed and go to the waiting room. Peter's not there. Outside, when I feel the cool breeze on my body, I'm glad it's all over. In the distance a car stops. It's Peter, with a friend. For a moment I'm disappointed he didn't come alone.

14 June 1979

Two days after the abortion I start my new job as a barmaid in De
Reiger. Luckily I haven't had any pain. I'll be working three shifts a
week.

At De Reiger I meet Yvette. While we're working, she always plays
Dusty Springfield or Millie Jackson and then we sing along at the top
of our voices. We get on really well together and often get the giggles.

Pim de la Parra called. He's thought of a couple of roles for me and
wants to do some film tests.

7 July 1979

Today Pim's going to see how his ideas for some possible roles for me
work out on film. He hasn't got any cut-and-dried roles in mind yet.
His fantasy goes in all directions with me, he says.

He wants to do something with my height. Him as a short, naked
man and me as a tall, naked woman. But that quickly turns out to be
too comic. We improvise a number of scenes. Then he wants to do
something with the wild, exotic look he thinks I've got.

We go to the Herengracht canal. He's seen a big tree there with a
branch hanging out over the water. The round-trip boats sail up and
down the canal. He thinks it would be great to see me lying naked,
or dressed only in a tigerskin, on that overhanging branch.

We decide to do it. Someone organises a tigerskin.

When the camera has been installed on a bridge some way from
the tree, as the idea is to slowly zoom in on me, a couple of men hoist
me on to the branch. High above the water, I pull myself forward
until I'm almost at the end. For a moment, it reminds me of the circus
where I often climbed high in the ropes.

My tigerskin has come loose from shuffling along the branch. The
round-trip boats stop underneath me, the tourists gaping up at the
almost naked woman in the tree. They take photographs and film me
with their camcorders. They probably think I'm a tourist attraction.
Pim is so far away with his camera that they can't see this is for a film.
All they can see is a naked woman on an overhanging tree branch.

I smile at them and wriggle around on the branch a bit more to
amuse them.

When Pim's got enough material, the men call to say I can come back, which isn't easy from my position. I can't turn round, so I shuffle backwards. As soon as they can get near me, two men help me out of the tree.

Pim thinks it's terrific material. I'm just glad I didn't end up in the water. My thighs, tummy, breasts and arms are all scratched from the rough bark of the tree.

We try out a few other possibilities in a building in Singel, until late in the evening. Pim wants to see what a blond wig does for me. That's a real laugh. Then he wants me as a high-class whore, then again as a cheap whore. By the end of the evening, he's finished. I'm going to be a kind of young version of Anna Magnani, who he bumps into at various locations in Amsterdam. What exactly he means by that, I'm not sure.

I've really enjoyed working with Pim, especially trying out all the roles. I decide to try and get some more film work and register with a casting agency.

A couple of days later I get invited for screen tests by various production companies. I get a couple of parts in TV mini-series and act in some short films the film academy students are making. In the meantime, I'm still working on Peter's videos.

It's quite hard on top of working at De Reiger and I decide to hand in my notice there, even though we really need the money. I hardly get paid anything for most of the film work.

August 1979
Pim's finished recording. We've had a great time. We get on really well and sit deep into the night talking about films we're going to make in the future. He wants to explore the boundaries between pornography and eroticism on the silver screen. I don't mind experimenting with him at all.

Beginning of October 1979
I was invited to the film festival in Arnhem. Pim introduced me to loads of people there, mostly directors and producers. The fact that I have no objection to appearing naked gets producers

interested. It seems as if everyone can see a prospective role for me as a prostitute.

End of October 1979

I got a call from the casting agency. Don Siegel, an American director, is in Amsterdam. He's filming scenes here for the film *Rough Cut*, with Burt Reynolds and David Niven. He's looking for someone to play a hooker and they thought of me. Could I come to the Hilton for a screen test?

I'm not letting this chance slip away. I don't speak any English but I don't mention that.

In the Hilton someone takes me to the room where Don Siegel is. Apparently Belinda Meuldijk is also up for the role. We both wait nervously for our turn.

Don Siegel's sitting in a chair in an enormous hotel suite. He's a little, grey-haired man with a friendly face. We shake hands. He gets me to step back a few paces, walk backwards and forwards, turn around and then I can go. I don't have to do or say anything else.

See you later. Goodbye, he smiles. Before I know it, I'm outside again. Next week I'll know if I've got the part.

5 November 1979

I've got the role. I've just signed the contract. I've never been paid so well before.

Part: *Hooker*, it says. Film: *Rough Cut*. Fee: *650 guilders*, and that's for one evening's work. They've booked a room with room service at the Sonesta for me, even though I live just round the corner from the hotel. But that seems to be the American way.

I don't have to do much. I have to lure Burt Reynolds into my room in an alley in the red-light district near the Sonesta. I only have to go up to him and take him in inside. That's all.

The afternoon of the shoot a wardrobe lady measures me up. I'm going to be dressed in black. Short skirt, tight top, stilettos and stockings.

I spend the evening in the hotel room. In costume and made up, I lie on the bed watching television. I talk for ages on the phone to Peter, who's lying in bed at home with backache. I can order what

I want from room service and I call the waiter a couple of times, just for the fun of it. Pity I'm on my own in this room.

Around midnight, I'm on. They take me to a street where there are normally prostitutes but all the rooms have been rented for the event. I have to go and stand in the doorway of a window brothel. The American crew works quickly and efficiently. We rehearse a couple of times with a stand-in for Burt Reynolds and everything goes fine.

Then it's action. Burt Reynolds walks up. He's quite a bit shorter than me. I flirt as if I'm completely used to it and usher him into my room. We get it in one take.

They take me back to my hotel room. I can spend the night there if I want, but I'd rather go home and tell Peter all about it.

Spring 1980

From now on I'm going to take my film career seriously. I'm registered at the job centre in the artists and musicians section as an upcoming film actress. I've had some pictures taken, too, and sent a portfolio with a letter to a few directors and producers.

No big parts have come along yet, but there's plenty of work in smaller productions. The disadvantage is that I hardly get paid anything. On the other hand, I am meeting a lot of people in the film business and the experience I'm getting is worth something, too.

20 June 1980

I've had an invitation to the showing of Pim's *Dirty Picture*. It's premièring in ten towns on the third of July. My name, with my mother's surname, is featured prominently on the poster and there's a lot of media interest.

The media are talking about a Pim de la Parra comeback. At the same time as *Dirty Picture* is showing in the cinema, they'll be showing some of his old films on TV. He's pleased as Punch.

Whenever we see each other, we still experiment. Pim's obsessed with the pimp-and-prostitute theme and is looking for backers. He's got a couple of scripts ready, with a main part for me.

The showing of *Dirty Picture* is really disappointing. The film's in black-and-white, without sound. It's meant as a silent film.

Pim, who plays the role of the tourist, watches one woman after another pass him by, I see myself go past on the screen, as various characters. He's used the material from the test filming in the tree, too.

I'm afraid the film's going to be a big flop. But maybe I'm wrong. Maybe it's meant as a cult or art film and, who knows? Maybe he's done it right, in that case. I think it's a shame Herman didn't play the main role. He would have been good in it.

3 July 1980
Pim's film is being badly received by both the press and audiences. I really feel sorry for him after trying so desperately to make a success of it. He'd really hoped for a comeback. He's terribly disappointed. But he's not giving up. He's still looking for a backer for his next film, which I can star in. Well, we'll wait and see.

Luckily I've got plenty of work over the next few months. I've been asked to play the main part in Marian Bloem's short film *Breasts*. Pieter Verhoef wants to make a short TV film in September, under the title *Sex and Violence*. He's asked me to play one of the leading roles. I've agreed to both of them.

December 1980
I've had a pretty busy year. The past few weeks I've been working intensively with Pieter Verhoef on *Sex and Violence* in an old convent in Driebergen. Now he's editing it. The Marian Bloem film has also been shot and is in the process of being edited. Even though I played main roles this time and put in long, heavy days during the shooting, I only got my travelling costs and expenses paid.

Peter's complaining that we can't manage financially any longer. He's still studying and only working three days a week.

Now I've been asked to do another role, nude again, for expenses only, but I would have to be mad to take it on. I've had enough of the film business. I know I can earn far more money some other way.

I'm fed up with never having any money. I'm fed up with Peter always worrying about it and the moaning it causes. It reminds me of the past and that's something I don't want to think about.

17 January 1981
Wanted: Girls for topless work in nightclub. Info. after 13.00 hrs.

Shall I go for it? Peter'll have a fit, that's for sure. That afternoon I call the number. A woman answers. I ask about the job.

If I want to come along this afternoon, she can explain everything to me, she says. She gives me the address, Oudezijds Achterburgwal 37, first floor. Ask for Michelle.

I don't dare to ask any more questions and arrange to go round at the end of the afternoon.

When I tell Peter, it starts a row. He doesn't want me to do it. The address is in the red-light district; it can't be a good sign.

I try and convince him. What difference does it make if I'm serving beer with my tits bare or walking round with a bare bum in a film? Everyone can see me like that on the beach at Zandvoort, can't they? At least I'll get paid for it.

Peter thinks it sounds dodgy.

Well, I'm going anyway, I say. I want to earn some good money for a change.

Peter realises he's not going to stop me and gives up objecting. He kisses me before I leave and asks me to please be careful.

Of course I promise I will.

I padlock my bike to a tree opposite the address the woman gave me. It's an old canal-side building with shutters painted with bare ladies. In the basement is a sex cinema. There are punters everywhere.

I go up the steps and ring the bell and a little hatch slides opens. Someone asks me who I want to see. When I say Michelle, the door opens. As soon as I step over the threshold I can smell stale beer and cigarettes but it smells of perfume, too. It's dark inside. A man takes me into a room with a huge bar, where a number of men are sitting. He introduces me to Michelle.

We go and sit in a corner and she offers me a drink.

It's no ordinary bar. There are red leather cushions on the counter, with girls lying and sitting on them. I see they're all wearing black stockings. Some girls are wearing see-through black body stockings; others are topless.

Michelle asks how often I can work.

Every day I say.

She tells me the shifts here are long, from four in the afternoon until four in the morning, but you do get a break. You also get a meal and a retainer of a hundred guilders for every day you work, which is paid out on Fridays. When it's busy you get a bonus.

I ask her what the work involves. She explains that you serve the customers with drinks, talk to them and try and make sure they have a good time, to keep them here as long as possible. Then all the girls are allowed to offer the customers something extra of their choice, or the customer's choice. You can dance with a customer, for example, let them give you a massage or give them a little show, anything you like. You decide your own price. For everything you do that the customer pays you for, you can keep the money yourself.

She asks if I'll do it.

Yes, I say.

Then Michelle wants me to go upstairs with her for a moment. There's another bar there, with a dance floor, which is only open at night when there's a DJ playing records. There's a floor above that but I won't be going up there until I've been working here for a while. She leaves me on the dance floor with a girl called Nancy, who'll fill me in on the rest and arrange when I can start.

Nancy's an American; you can hear it straight away. She asks me if I've done this kind of work before. Then she quickly runs through what I have to bring and therefore have to buy.

There's a strict dress code. Black stockings with or without suspenders and a black body stocking. Towels are provided. If I want to give shows, then I have to bring my own massage oil, vibrators, bananas and lubricant. She shows me a little room with a basin and shower where I can freshen up between shows.

Nancy explains that, like downstairs, here too you always sit on the bar with the cushions. You make sure the customers get their drinks and chat with them; you can offer them a little show or dance with them. Dancing can be with or without a body stocking. With a body stocking it's a tenner and fifteen guilders without. The DJ makes sure the dance doesn't last more than three minutes. I'm overwhelmed with information.

It makes Nancy laugh. She puts my mind at rest. The first time it takes some getting used to, but after a couple of days it's as if you've never done anything else, she assures me. She'll show me the ropes tomorrow. The first night I can just serve drinks if I want and watch what the other girls do. I'll earn money anyway, with my retainer. She asks if I'm still interested.

Sure. It's not badly paid, especially if you can do other things to make a bit more money.

Then Nancy tells me there are a couple of other rules as well as the dress code. She explains that the club is called Saint Walburga Abbey. A lot of businessmen who come here call it Le Boudoir. All the girls are sisters of Saint Walburga Abbey. You call each other sister. You never call each other by first name alone. First you say sister, and then the first name. Most girls don't use their real names, but that's up to you.

When a customer comes up to the bar, you welcome him to Walburga Abbey. Then you introduce yourself as Sister Karina and ask what he would like to drink. When you're talking about it with the other girls, you can call it a show, but if you're talking to a customer it's called a ritual. So you never ask if they want to see a show, but always if they want to see a ritual or take part in one. And they have to pay extra for a ritual.

You always have to wear a medallion round your neck when you're working.

Nancy shows it to me. It's a black disc hanging from a black ribbon, engraved with a pentacle and a devil's head.

When you work here, you belong to the Church of Satan; the Abbey's part of it. I will have to learn the welcome phrase off by heart, she stresses.

Those are the most important things, she says. She takes me back downstairs and shows me the dressing rooms where we can wash in between clients and where we can take a rest, get a cup of coffee and have something to eat. The doormen bring you whatever you want to order, chips, kebab or Chinese. Everyone's got their own locker and a dressing table.

She'll expect me an hour earlier tomorrow, as she's got to explain a lot more.

★

On the way home I think about what I should tell Peter. Maybe just that I serve beer topless and there are striptease shows. If he gets to hear what it looks like and what goes on in the club he'll never agree to me working there. But the retainer alone is more than I've ever earned anywhere.

I make up my mind to work as many days as I can. I've got nothing else to do anyway. Just imagine, seven days, that's seven hundred guilders a week. And even more if I do anything extra. Won't Peter be surprised at me earning so much money?

Peter doesn't like the sound of it. And I haven't told him about everything I saw by any means. I do understand it's not exactly the most normal job, but what does it matter? I'm not being forced to do anything and I'm old enough and wise enough to decide for myself how I earn my money.

Peter thinks it's dangerous working at night. I try to reassure him by saying I'll take a taxi home every night. I earn enough.

I'm sure he'll worry less when he sees how much I'm going to earn tonight. Then I'll be able to take him out to dinner tomorrow.

18 January 1981
Before starting my new job, I go into a sex shop in the red-light district and buy stockings and suspenders and a body stocking.

On the way to the Abbey I continually get approached by punters. With a friendly wave of the hand, I let them know I'm not interested. That's enough. They don't push it any further. Outside the Abbey, there's a crowd of people milling around and two guys are drumming up clients. I go up the steps and, again, the little hatch slides open. The same doorman lets me in as yesterday.

Tonight Michelle is dressed in a long, black nun's habit with a wimple. She's wearing a medallion, too. She takes me to the dressing room where she shows me my dressing table and locker. There are two other girls who she introduces me to. They speak English and give me a friendly nod. They're putting on their makeup.

Michelle gives me a medallion. She says there are often men who want to know more about the Church. I just have to refer them to the Mother Superior, which is her. That's how I have to address her.

When she's not there, Saskia's the Mother Superior. If the Mother Superior is occupied and someone insists on having information about the Church of Satan, then there's a pile of leaflets and brochures above the bar. They're printed in seven languages.

She gives me a towel for when I want to freshen up in between clients and says I should tell them that all the money collected from the rituals goes to the Church. Then I can put it in my own locker over the bar. That's where I have to put all the other things I need while I'm working.

While I'm getting changed the other girls ask if this is the first time I've done this kind of work. They can see I'm nervous and try to put me at my ease. After the first night it's not scary any more, they say. They ask me if I'm working upstairs or downstairs.

Upstairs, I think.

They tell me I shouldn't worry. In the beginning you get back-ache and knee-ache from all that bending over and crawling on the bar, but upstairs you can get off the bar now and again.

Nancy comes to fetch me and take me upstairs. She gets me to climb up on the bar and shows me the compartment above where I can put my wallet and other stuff. I notice there's a bell every few feet along the bar. Those are for our safety, she explains. If there's a client who wants to hurt you or a fight breaks out, you have to press the bell. Then the bouncers will be straight upstairs.

She shows me how the beer pump works. It's a kind of hose you pull out of the bar, with a button on the top. When you push it, beer comes out. In the middle of the bar are the glasses and a glass washer. The spirits are kept on a shelf above the bar. There are soft drinks there, too. The customers can drink whatever they want. It doesn't cost them any more.

Nancy tells me that each girl has developed her own ritual. She, for example, can smoke cigars with her pussy. I stare at her in amaze-ment. She explains that she learned it in Bangkok through yoga. I'll see in a minute, she says. Almost all the girls do banana and vibrator shows. I could perhaps do a lesbian show with another girl, or rub myself with massage oil or let someone do it for me. She advises me to watch the others closely and to stick to dancing for this evening.

Finally, she warns me to always agree the prices with the girls I work with, otherwise it can lead to a row. There are different girls working here all the time and they all charge different rates. If you do a show with another girl, you share the money. There always has to be a girl on the bar. So you can't both go to the loo or take a shower at the same time.

Nancy swamps me with instructions. I'll never be able to remember them all, and she still hasn't finished. See that pole in the middle of the dance floor? If there are enough customers, you can pole dance and go round afterwards collecting money. They usually slip you something.

Tonight I'm working with Elvira and Nancy. Elvira comes from Suriname. She looks a bit like Grace Jones, as dark as her and really muscular. She can't be bothered tonight, she sighs. Nancy organises her locker above the bar. She's got several different vibrators, a bunch of bananas and a box of cigars. Carla is the DJ tonight. She promises to play some good music and sets herself up at the turntable. She only plays records and doesn't do anything with the customers.

The customers will be up here any minute. The bar downstairs is already full, apparently. I quickly pop to the loo. I wonder what on earth I should do if a client wants to see me do a ritual tonight. It'll look so stupid if I can't do anything.

A group of men comes in. I take a deep breath. I hope it'll go all right. Carla gives me a wink. I hear Elvira saying the welcome phrase. Then she asks what they want to drink. I help her serve them.

The gentlemen want to dance.

A tenner dressed, fifteen naked, Elvira whispers to me.

As if it's the hundredth time I've done it, I get down off the bar and make a deal with my first client. He wants me dressed. Carla puts on a slow number and we shuffle awkwardly across the dance floor. Just as the man starts pressing himself up harder against me, the record finishes and I climb back on the bar. I know for sure I left him with a hard-on.

One of his friends wants to dance with me, too, but naked. I ask him for fifteen guilders and I'm amazed at how quickly the notes are in my hand.

I attempt to remove my body stocking as gracefully as possible. I keep my stockings on. We shuffle across the dance floor, egged on by my client's friends. They call out to him to put his hands on my bottom. He doesn't dare.

Back on the bar I get dressed again as elegantly as possible. Well, I earned my first twenty-five guilders quickly and easily enough.

The men go back downstairs and Elvira and I go and put on some makeup. She thinks it's going to be busy tonight.

Half an hour later, a middle-aged man comes upstairs. Elvira slides off the bar. I can have him, she whispers; she doesn't feel like it tonight. Nancy's nowhere to be seen. I don't know where to begin. The man looks smart; he must be a businessman.

As soon as he's sitting down, I pluck up the courage to crawl over the bar to him. He doesn't even give me time to say my bit, but says I must be the new sister. The sisters downstairs have already told him about me. I nod and introduce myself as Sister Karina. I ask him what he would like to drink.

He doesn't want a drink, but asks me to do something for him. He pulls me over towards him and asks if he can see my bum. How much should I charge for that, for God's sake? I decide to ask him for twenty-five guilders, which he hands over straight away. I put the money away safely in my compartment.

I turn my back to him. Wiggling my hips, I roll my body stocking down past my buttocks. I hope it looks convincing.

As soon as my bottom is bare, I hear him whispering to me, asking me to bend over and spread my buttocks. He wants to look at my arsehole.

I'm embarrassed as hell; I really hope no other customers come up right now. I bend over low, wiggling from side to side, and spread my buttocks for him. Then I turn round slowly and look at the man. I can see he's trying as hard as he can to keep the image of my arsehole imprinted on his retina. As soon as I've got my body stocking on again, his eyes go back to normal.

I feel rather shy; after all it's a bit strange, showing someone your bum like that. And he was willing to pay twenty-five guilders for the privilege. Is he a bit warped or something? Luckily, Elvira comes back just then and gives me an enquiring look. I think she's used to this customer. As soon as he's gone, I tell her what I did. She says the price I charged was normal and that this man comes in every week.

Now the place is filling up fast. Elvira gets a few customers together and says everyone has to pay a tenner if they want to see a banana ritual. She asks me to take care of the drinks.

Elvira keeps her bananas above the bar. I see her take one and quickly rub lubricant on to it. The customers don't notice. Carla puts a swing number on. Elvira starts dancing and removes her body stocking quite skillfully, with the clients standing round encouraging her. She rubs oil on to her skin and asks a customer to help. The man who's pushed forward by the others hardly dares touch her. Then she gets the banana and slides it all over her body. She lies down on the counter and opens her legs wide. Then she bites off the hard end of the banana and slips it into her fanny. When the banana is halfway in, with legs wide apart she slides towards the men. When she's lying right in front of them, she deftly peels the banana and asks, with it still inside her, if any of the men would like a bite. Everyone cheers and laughs. Then the bravest one, accompanied by loud cheering, takes a bite. Elvira slides back on to the bar, stows the banana away and gracefully gets dressed again.

We offer the men more drinks and ask them if they'd like to dance. We make sure they stay as long as possible. When they leave, Elvira gives me a tenner because I helped her with the drinks while she was doing her show. She's earned herself seventy guilders from this group of customers in a matter of minutes. You often get coach-loads of tourists, she says. With those kind of big groups you can make a hundred guilders a ritual.

Nancy works the whole night by herself on her own side of the bar. She makes a lot of money with her cigar ritual. She can really inhale smoke through her fanny and blow it out again. She's good with vibrators, too, but she's sitting just too far away for me to see how she does her shows.

The rest of the night I spend alternating between the bar and the dance floor. I put away one tenner after another. Most of the customers don't really dare get up close. Three minutes is just long enough. Just as they're beginning to relax and want to do more, it's over and I detach myself with a friendly remark. I keep wondering if they feel they're being taken for a ride.

The last client leaves the building at four in the morning. Elvira's hardly done anything the past few hours; she's knackered. She's got a two-year-old daughter who's up and about at seven every morning.

I can hardly walk. My back and knees hurt from all that pouring drinks. But I'm delighted with my fat wallet. I've lost track of my takings during the evening. I'll count the loot when I get home.

The girls who work downstairs ask if I want to go for a kebab on Zeedijk.

Another time, I promise. I want to go home to Peter. Won't he be surprised at how much I've earned?

As soon as I'm dressed, I call a taxi. But at this time of night they're hard to get, apparently. Elvira suggests I should walk over to the Nieuwmarkt; you get cruising minicabs there. Luckily the doorman doesn't mind dropping me off. He lives in the Jordaan, too.

When I get home, I see the light is still on. Peter sighs with relief when I stick my head round the door. He's been awake all this time.

I pretend I've just been serving drinks topless and done a bit of pole dancing. I throw him his dressing gown and ask him to come into the sitting room for a minute, then we can count the money. I put my wallet down on the table. Peter can't believe his eyes. He smoothes out the notes and lays them in a pile.

It's roughly three hundred guilders, and that's not even including my retainer.

23 January 1981

I've been working at the Abbey for a week now and today I get my first retainer. To get paid, I have to go to another address, diagonally opposite. There'll be someone at Oudezijds Achterburgwal 46b the whole afternoon organising the payments.

An hour before I have to start work, I go and collect my wages. I ring the bell at the address they've given me. A guy opens the door and asks me to follow him to a room at the back of the building. He's got an iron strongbox on the table with envelopes in it. On them are written the names of the girls and the number of days worked. Mother Superior keeps a register.

He asks my name and finds the envelope. There's a form attached to my envelope with a paper clip. He tells me I have to fill it in.

I ask him what it's for.

He says it's so that I don't have any problems with the tax office. All the girls have to fill in and sign one of these forms. Otherwise Maarten gets into trouble.

I ask him who Maarten is.

The boss, is all he says.

Cost of entry in the Church register, NLG 9, please enclose, is written in the top left-hand corner of the form.

The guy says I don't have to pay the nine guilders. That's for if you don't work here.

Then there are two questions to answer.

YES/NO *Enter in the Church register as a member of the order of principle O°*

YES/NO *Please send me further information on membership, meetings, teachings, contacts. Only applies in the event of entry in the Church register.*

I asks the guy what on earth 'the order of principle O°' means.

He doesn't know either. He only knows that I have to answer YES to the first question, and NO to the second. Then I have to fill in my name, address, telephone number, year of birth, sex, marital status, height and weight and the colour of my eyes and hair.

Then comes *Name and date of birth of your spouse, Number of children, Previous religions and societies, Nationality, Special Interests, Talents and Gifts.*

I fill in what I'm asked to, even though I don't understand some of it, and wonder if it's really wise.

In the bottom left-hand corner of the form a space has been left. *Please do not write in this space, intended for Church use.* Just above the place where I have to sign it says, *Endorses the principles and philosophy of the Church of Satan as described above and acknowledges it's hierarchy, power and influence.*

I sign the form and hand it back to the bloke. He says I should always check in his presence that the content of the envelope corresponds with the number of days worked. Then he can still do something about it if there's been a mistake. This time there's no extra bonus. It wasn't so busy this week.

There are 500 guilders in the envelope. That's correct. There's a timetable in it, too. If there's anything wrong, I have to sort it out with Mother Superior, it's nothing to do with him, says the man.

This coming week I see I'm scheduled to alternate between upstairs and downstairs. I haven't worked downstairs yet. They do more kinds of shows there than upstairs.

Fine by me.

I'm over the moon. This week I've earned more money than ever before, even without the retainer. And now I can add this on, too.

It's true what the girls told me at the beginning. After the first evening it stops being scary. Now I've already done a banana show and some vibrator shows and danced with loads of customers. When I start downstairs, I'll do more shows. I'll get rich.

In the sex shop I buy some new stockings and another body stocking. I get some different vibrators and a big tube of lubricant. There's a snack bar on the corner where they sell bananas, too. I carefully pick out a bunch according to size. They mustn't be too curved or too big, I've noticed. That hurts. The owner of the snack bar charges two guilders a banana. What a rip-off. Tomorrow I'm going to get them from the greengrocer's.

Peter doesn't know anything about this. I don't dare tell him, either.

April 1981
Now I'm working five nights a week. Peter thought seven was too much.

I earn so much money I can afford to take it a bit easier, he says. He still doesn't like me doing this kind of work. I cautiously started telling him what some of the girls do on top of serving beer, but he doesn't want to hear about it.

Well, I don't care. Peter's always moaning about something. When I finally find a job that pays well he's still not satisfied. He doesn't have to spread his legs, does he? I don't mind doing it, I just flick a switch. It's not real. It's just a show. It would only matter if I enjoyed what I do with the customers. But it's just an easy way of earning money, nothing more. Well, I won't tell him anything else, then. I'd never be able to explain the difference between real and show anyway.

He does like the things I buy for him, though, and we can buy anything we want now. I bought a Bang & Olufsen television for Peter in an expensive shop in the Spui and a video recorder with remote control. I've ordered a really big Auping bed, with adjustable head and foot. You pull a string and you automatically sit up or the foot comes up. And soon I'm going to have the whole house done up.

I know all the girls now. Downstairs, five of you work on the bar, upstairs three. I like it better downstairs than upstairs. You earn slightly less because the shows are shorter but somehow it's more of a laugh. We pick banknotes out of glasses with our pussies. You get a customer to fold up a five-guilder note and skilfully take it out of the glass, without using your hands. Tenners we take off their noses. We ask them to turn round and lean against the bar with their head back. You fold the note over the customer's nose and descend elegantly until you've got it.

We've also thought of something for customers who haven't got so much to spend. We lie down with our legs open and they can throw guilders at us. If a guilder lands on your pussy and stays there, then they get two back.

Upstairs you get more men with special requirements. Sometimes I get really sick of them. There are some real maniacs amongst them. We always warn each other about nutters. The other day one of the girls was bitten until she bled.

The regular customers with special privileges are a particular drag. That's because of the predictability of their bizarre requests.

Every Friday night, a man comes and stands in the shower room. The only thing he does there is make coffee for us, in the nude. Or clean the shower if we've used it in between. He doesn't say anything.

Sometimes, just before opening time, there's this man who wants one of us to pee in the glass washer. He pays a hundred guilders for it, but it's quite a job to pee to order. You have to pretend to be serious but you can hear smothered laughter from the girls in the background.

There are also clients who are out to give us an orgasm. They're a real pain. We usually leave them to Vivian. She takes care of the minge munchers, as we call them. As far as Vivian's concerned, it's the ideal way to make money. You lie down and the customer exhausts himself licking your pussy. She can relax completely, come sneakily several times and get paid a bomb for it into the bargain.

If you get customers who want SM then you refer them to Oudezijds Voorburgwal 59. There's a special department there. Actually, that's where the real Church of Satan is, where all kinds of heavy rituals take place. It's pretty creepy looking.

Some customers want to watch fucking. We send them to Oudezijds Achterburgwal 88 where they give live sex shows. A couple of the girls who work here do live sex on stage there as well.

For the odd stray gay we've got a special place, too. Oudezijds Voorburgwal 136.

Down in our own basement customers can pay to watch hard porn films.

We've got something for everybody, really.

The taxi drivers get a percentage if they bring clients to us. A couple of travel agencies have got a deal with us. That's where we really cash in. We have fixed arrangements with some tour guides for which shows we give and how much they cost. They think they're getting a special deal with us, and we like them to remain under that impression.

The customers pay twenty-two guilders fifty for half an hour and the rent of a glass. For that they get free drinks and can look around. For an hour they pay forty-five guilders. They get a ticket when they come in with the time of entry on it. If they stay longer than arranged, which we do our utmost to make them, they have to pay a surcharge per minute.

Most customers stay much longer than they'd planned and hardly drink anything. We're usually too busy with our rituals to pour drinks or they're so busy watching that they forget to order. Most of the men drink beer because they're not aware that anything stronger is available. I'm starting to get to know the clients quite well, and to distinguish between them.

Sometimes there's loads of tourists. We can tell immediately when there's a trade fair going on at the RAI exhibition centre.

You have to watch out with the Japanese. They're hard-handed and like to give us an unexpected pinch.

The most generous are the businessmen. In general, they're experienced night-clubbers and bid against each other in their generosity. Sometimes you get businessmen who want to make a private appointment with one of us in a hotel. They're generally staying at the Hilton, Caransa or Americain.

There's not much to be earned from the unsuspecting tourists who are talked inside by the doormen. They can't get over their amazement and just want to look over the shoulders of other clients.

I sometimes worry about the spotty teenagers. Usually they come in in twos or threes and they want you to use the biggest banana or the biggest vibrator. They really have a ridiculous idea of what women enjoy. They seem to think this is the height of ecstasy for us. I can imagine they'll have a lasting inferiority complex about the size of their own little willies after visiting us.

The most irritating kind you get in are the snooty fraternity students. They're really insecure and, one way or another, they always manage to humiliate us. Not only do they ask a lot but they don't want to pay much for it. At the end of it they're never satisfied either. I can't stand that. It always makes me so aggressive. Sometimes I feel like knocking their spoiled, baby-faced heads together. With those students we drag out the shows deliberately so that they have to pay extra when they leave.

My favourite customers are the little old men who've decided they'd like to see a naked woman from close up one last time. All they want is to look between your legs for a while; they pay up without any fuss and are truly grateful to you. I never keep them talking, because every minute costs them money.

After work, we always go for a kebab on Zeedijk. It's difficult to get a taxi in the middle of the night but now I know which minicab drivers I can trust. They always park in the same place in the Nieuwmarkt.

28 April 1981

Today's the première of Marian Bloem's *Breasts* at the Kriterion. Even though I'm playing the main role, I don't feel like going. Film doesn't interest me at all any more. It'll be on the telly in the autumn, so I'll video it then.

Sometimes I feel a bit guilty that Peter doesn't know about everything I get up to. I feel overburdened by too many secrets recently.

I've hardly told him anything about the past. He knows in general terms about my mother, the circus and the foster family. But he doesn't know anything about Zaltbommel.

Somehow I'm scared of telling him I've actually got a father, brother and sister. I'm still embarrassed about the way I had to pretend to be a cousin in Zaltbommel. If I tell Peter that, maybe he'll start having doubts about me. If even your own father, brother and sister don't want anything to do with you, then there must be something wrong with you, mustn't there?

He'll think they must have had a good reason.

He'll think he's got a right one here. First I lie about my age, and now I come up with a father, brother and sister.

And if he finds out what I really do for a living, then he'll never want to stay with me.

May 1981

I work regularly with a girl called Ann. She fled the Israeli army and has been working at the Abbey longer than any of us. She's thin as a rake, with hardly any breasts or bottom. She reminds me of my mother when she was ill. What would she have thought about me working here?

Ann's really popular with the customers. She speaks a charming kind of broken English and has dark, curly hair and blue eyes with thick, dark lashes. She's got a dreamy, sensual look she uses to seduce men. I've taught her a couple of Dutch expressions which she says to customers in such a way you immediately want to cuddle her.

Ann's always feeling cold and picking up infections. At first I thought she used heroin, as I know she takes private clients upstairs to the third floor with a girl who's on drugs. I hardly ever go up there.

It seems the idea was that there would be a Church of Satan restaurant there, where clients could dine served by the sisters. But nothing came of it. Now the floor's empty and some of the girls go up there with their clients.

As Ann's here illegally, she's scared she'll be sent back to Israel if she goes to the doctor. She asked me if I'd get a prescription for her from my GP, too, if I ever get an infection in my pussy. A lot of the girls suffer from infections. Luckily I haven't had one yet. It comes from the bananas. If you give a lot of shows, the inside of your pussy gets grazed by the hard end of the banana. As a precaution, we bite it off before giving a show and use lubricant, but Ann thinks it's also got to do with the pesticide they spray the bananas with.

I do sometimes notice that it feels fiery and itchy if I've done a lot of banana shows, but if I stop doing them for a while the infection gets better by itself. That isn't the case with Ann. With her it's sometimes so bad she can't work. I don't think she's got much resistance because she's so thin.

I don't dare go to my own doctor so I go with Ann to the drop-in surgery of a general practitioner we found in the phone book. She's explained exactly how it feels and I pretend I've got what she's got. I did a lot of banana shows last night so the irritation is pretty visible.

The doctor is a friendly man. A little embarrassed, I explain that I've got something of a strange problem, that I give banana shows for my work and that's what's caused the trouble.

The doctor asks me what I do with the bananas.

I tell him how the show works.

He wants to examine me. I lie on the couch and put my legs in the supports. He swivels a lamp round. I can see him carefully examining me and repeat what Ann told me.

The doctor says it's a bit red but it looks all right apart from that, nothing unusual, no wounds inside. I tell him it hurts to pee, that it's sometimes terribly itchy and now and again I get a smelly discharge.

He explains about the acidity level in the vagina and tells me not to work with bananas any more, not to wash myself with soap and not to use any lubricant, then it'll get better by itself. Putting some yoghurt in the vagina sometimes has a relieving effect.

Now I say the smell is unbearable and I have to keep working. Surely there must be something to cure it? Colleagues of mine get medicine from their doctors when they have what I've got, I say.

Finally, he writes me out a prescription. From now on I can ask the assistant for repeat prescriptions if I need them. I've done it.

Ann is pleased and relieved. She treats me to lunch.

While we're eating, she asks why I never go private with any of the customers. It pays well, she says.

I say I've never told Peter what I actually do as it is, and he would never accept anything like that.

Ann shrugs. It's just work, she says. You can earn more in fifteen minutes than you do in half the night at the Abbey. She tells me about her clients. She's got a couple of regulars in the Church and a couple in hotels. I can take over one of them if I want. He's a nice-looking guy who comes to Amsterdam every couple of weeks and stays in the Americain.

I ask her if she's ever scared. In the Church we've got an alarm bell and the bouncers. But in a hotel room they can do what they like to you without anybody noticing.

Most clients she knows from the Americain and the Hilton are okay, Ann says, and she tells me what she does with them and what I have to watch out for. You have to take your own Durex because they always want to do it without. Then you agree a price. She charges a hundred and fifty guilders for screwing with a Durex, two hundred with a blow-job as well and for special things you name your own price, like they do at the Abbey. They have to pay up front. First you have to wash their prick and take a good look to make sure there's no discharge and they haven't got a rash. You make sure they get a hard-on, put the Durex on immediately and then it's usually over before you know it. You have to be nice, but strict and businesslike at the same time. You never let them kiss you. If they have any special requests, you tell them exactly what they can and can't do. They usually do as they're told, but if they don't you just stop and leave immediately.

Ann says I can fill in for her for a while but she wants it understood that it's only temporary. They're still her clients.

19 May 1981
Ann's got a private client for me. He's expecting me at the Americain. She's taking over my shift in the Abbey.

I'm a bundle of nerves.

It'll be fine, she reassures me. I have to ask for Henri in the Nachtwacht Bar at the hotel.

The waiter shows me where he's sitting. Henri is a guy of around forty. He's wearing a dark-blue suit, white shirt and tie. His hair's blond and he's beginning to grey at the temples. He gives me a friendly smile and asks if he can get me a drink and if I mind his friend coming, too.

I act like it's the most natural thing in the world and tell him it doesn't bother me as long as his friend pays as well. I don't want a drink. I want to get down to business.

The friend is wearing a suit, too. Like Henri, he looks very respectable.

The three of us go upstairs to a room with a view of the terrace. Henri draws the curtains. I can hear the buzz of voices and the street musicians through the closed curtains. I'm trusting that Ann hasn't set me up.

There's a big double bed in the room. I ask them exactly what it is they want.

Henri wants to screw and his friend wants a blow-job, preferably at the same time.

Well, I'll give you a special price this time, I say, a hundred and twenty-five each. They think it's a good deal. I remember Ann's words. *Be nice but businesslike.*

They hand over the money. I ask if I can use the bathroom and tell them to lie down on the bed. They do as I say. In the bathroom, I take a flannel and cover it with soap. I can hear muffled laughter. At first I'm not sure how to go about it. Two at a time is a bit much.

Henri undresses himself; I give his friend a bit of help. As if I've done it a million times before, I give their willies a good soap and try to get a good look to see if there's anything unusual. Henri is circumcised, but not his friend. Neither of them is that big, luckily.

Then I get some Durex out of my bag and I ask, very professionally, if they would like to choose one from the packet themselves. In the meantime, I get undressed.

Henri asks me to lie across the bed. He doesn't want to touch his friend while he's screwing me, but he does want to be able to watch me sucking him. I lie down so he can take me and I can get to his friend, who's kneeling by the bed. Henri is in a hurry. I feel him entering me. I hold his friend under the balls and suck him, holding the Durex on with my hand. God forbid that it should come off and I get his sperm in my mouth.

Henri thrusts hard. I'm stuck in an impossible position and can't do more than move with him. Like that, the blow-job takes care of itself.

Just for a moment, I feel myself getting turned on. Images from porn films flit through my head. The feeling of excitement and lust confuses me. I think of Ann. *Be strict and businesslike and never let them kiss you.* I recover and let Henri's movements do their work.

He comes, groaning. His friend needs a bit longer, but now Henri's got off me, I can deal with him alone. For a change, I grab hold of his buttocks with one hand, holding the Durex on with the other. Then I feel it swell up in my mouth, as he comes. Luckily all I can taste is rubber.

In the bathroom I wash myself and rinse my mouth out.

When I leave the hotel it's still busy on the terrace. I get the feeling that everyone can see what I've been doing. I don't take a taxi, but walk home through the dark, all the way down Marnixstraat. I need time to wind down.

Right now, I'd really like to be sitting on my breakwater in the Waal River. That used to calm me down. I feel so confused. Normally I flick a switch when I'm working. Then it's as if it's not me when I'm doing a show, but this time I got turned on. That didn't feel right. I can't do this to Peter and, actually, I didn't even really enjoy it. It just happened and I couldn't do anything about it.

Halfway down Marnixstraat I have to turn off into the street where I live. But I still don't feel ready to go home. I'm afraid Peter will notice I've had it off with someone else. I feel guilty. I just hope he never finds out.

I try to think of what Ann said. It's just work and it pays well.

6 June 1981

I'm twenty-one today. To celebrate, we go out to lunch at the Chinese restaurant in the Damstraat. The big, round tables are surrounded by Chinese families. Grandads, grandmas, fathers, mothers, nephews, nieces and little kids. They're eating unidentifiable steamed dishes. There are big pots of tea on the table. It looks really cosy.

The families remind me of the paper dollies I used to play with. The families I made from paper were always large, too.

As always on my birthday, I miss my mother. And suddenly I find the courage to talk to Peter about Zaltbommel. I want to tell him I've actually got a father and a brother and sister.

He's surprised. To my relief, he doesn't mind the fact that I didn't mention it before. But he does ask whether he can expect any more secrets in the future.

I nod. I say there are some things I can't tell him just like that. Too much has happened.

Peter says he loves me. No matter what.

9 June 1981

The boss of the Church of Satan, Maarten, wants to meet me. He receives me at the Oudezijds Achterburgwal 46b, the same building where I collect my wages every week. I'd put his age at about thirty-five; he's much younger than I'd imagined. He's dressed in a tight black suit. Around his neck hangs a silver chain with a silver pentacle.

He asks me to follow him. A narrow staircase takes us to the first floor, where we walk along a corridor to the back of the building. The door's fitted with electronic security. He punches a code in. Then we enter a room that reminds me of a castle, decorated in a highly baroque style, with lavish furnishings. Heavy curtains, big bookshelves and lots of paintings. The chairs are upholstered in black-and-green velvet.

We sit down at a heavy wooden table with silver candelabra. Maarten asks me how I like the work.

It's fine, I say. Sometimes I find it difficult, but the pay makes up for a lot.

He asks what I've done before and I tell him about my film work. He says he was directing theatre productions before this. Then he says he's noticed that my shows in the Church go down well and asks whether he can film me. He wants to make a video of the rituals that take place in the Abbey and show it in the window of the building where we are now, to attract more customers. He's got a professional cameraman lined up. It won't be any kind of vulgar exhibition. What he wants to capture is the magical, satanic atmosphere of the rituals. He'll pay me well for it.

I hesitate for a moment. What would Peter think? Actually I don't care. It's only tourists and punters who come to the red-light district. I've appeared naked in other films and I didn't get paid for those.

I agree.

The video will be shot in one morning sometime when the Abbey is still closed. Maarten sees me out. I'd been expecting rather a nasty piece of work, but he's quite nice, actually, a bit of a softie even.

29 June 1981

Maarten's really satisfied with the results of the filming. Scenes from the video are now being shown on a monitor in the display window under his apartment. He feels it's good advertising for the Church of Satan. Now he wants to see me about something else.

This time we arrange to meet at the Abbey. As soon as he comes in, all the girls get nervous. The boss is here, they whisper, and they seem to try just that little bit harder to do their best. He takes me up to the third floor, where we can talk in peace.

He's planning to make a television show which will be broadcast on cable. It's going to be a kind of erotic magazine programme in which people can ask questions about their sex problems and an expert gives them advice. They already have programmes like that in America and they're a big success but it will be breaking new ground in Dutch television. He thinks I'm perfect for it. He's already thought of a title, *Patricia Privé*. And I'm Patricia. He promises it'll be a properly thought-through programme and he'll be directing it himself. He's got a sponsor already, too, the boss of the porno magazine *Chick*, who's willing to make a substantial investment. The broadcasts will be once a week, only at night.

I say I'll do it. It sounds like fun and it'll make a change. Of course if Peter knew he wouldn't approve. But he did say he loves me no matter what and that he'll stay with me. Anyway, he's asleep at night.

July 1981

I'm rich. What I always wanted is coming true. I've got money; I earn a terrific amount. I find it really difficult to sleep during the day. I live in a haze of excitement about all the money I earn every night and I want to spend it as fast as possible.

I've earned enough to have our house completely done up. A couple of people in the commune have moved out and now we rent their rooms, too. I want to knock all the walls through so we can have a great big sitting room. I want a new kitchen as well, and new carpets. I've ordered some furniture from a shop on Rozengracht, two sofas, a couple of cupboards and some other nice stuff. I'm having some curtains made at Metz & Co. I want to make things nice for Peter. He likes to stay at home and read. On the other hand, he can't stand mess, or change, so it hasn't been easy to get him to agree to having the work done. But I've found a good solution: I'm sending him on holiday to the south of France with a friend. I've booked the flight and the hotel and I'll make sure the workmen are finished on time so that when he comes back everything will be shipshape.

Peter hesitantly agreed. Typical of him. He always needs time to get used to anything new. He always raises an objection or sees a disadvantage, or else he feels guilty. It's amazing we still get on so well. We're exact opposites in every respect.

12 July 1981

Me, Maarten and a cameraman and sound technician are busy with the recordings for *Patricia Privé*. We're filming at different locations, but today we're starting in a brothel on Overtoom; Maarten's arranged it with the owner. There's a great big Jacuzzi and he feels the rooms make the perfect backdrop. We arrange to meet there early in the morning.

A woman lets us in. We enter a kind of lounge where, to my amazement, I see Herman sleeping off a hangover on the sofa. The woman is about to throw him out, but I stop her.

Herman's a friend of mine, I say, and I don't mind him being there during filming.

He looks terrible. His clothes are grubby. Things are obviously not going well with him.

Maarten has already gone upstairs, where he's going to set things up in one of the rooms. I wait until they've finished and then change into my Patricia costume. In the meantime, I talk to Herman, who can hardly stand up and grunts more than talks.

I ask him how it's going with the band. I've haven't been following Herman since I've been working at the Abbey. I don't even know what kind of music is in now. I lead such an eventful nightlife that I no longer know what's going on in the outside world during the day any more.

He can't be bothered with music any more, he groans. He wants to paint and people are always moaning at him. Everybody's cross with him and Koos doesn't want anything to do with him. He's looking for a girl to give him some comfort, he pouts.

I try and cheer him up. I don't mind comforting you, but first I've got to comfort other people, I joke. I tell him we're just about to record the *Patricia Privé* programme and how I have to comfort all kinds of men over their sex problems.

Herman leans against me. I need comforting, he groans.

I put my arms around him. Then Maarten calls to say we can start recording and Herman leaves, walking with a stoop. He whines for a kiss like a small child.

The recording goes without a hitch. I answer so-called letters from readers, making sure the magazine *Chick* is visible in my hand during the presentation.

The boss of *Chick* comes to see how things are going during the recording. He makes embarrassing remarks and keeps touching me in a dirty way. He stinks; he's got long, greasy hair and his fat belly hangs over his trousers. His arms are covered in scratched-open spots. He asks Maarten if he likes looking at young, peachy little cunts, too.

When we take a break he leaves and I'm relieved. I've rarely met such a slimy man. I ask Maarten how well he knows him but he just shrugs and says that he's paying well so I shouldn't complain. He wants to get on. Now I have to play with myself with a dildo in the Jacuzzi.

Today we're going to film outside at the Oudezijds Achterburgwal, too. I have to cross the street in a mini top, miniskirt, stockings and high heels. I'm not wearing any pants. They film me walking along and when I open the street door to Maarten's house, I have to bend down to pick up the post. Then they film my bare bum.

25 July 1981
The first broadcast has been transmitted. I haven't seen it but Maarten is satisfied with the programme.

Peter stayed up to see the broadcast. He doesn't like me doing this at all. The reception was really bad and Peter reckons there's so much interference because the broadcasting is illegal. He's glad about the crackling. He hates the fact that everyone can see me.

I've tried to tell him he shouldn't make such a fuss about it. It's all show. None of it's real.

Maarten called to say that journalists keep ringing since the broad-cast, wanting information about the Church of Satan. There's a good chance I'll come across them in the Abbey. He stresses that I should say nothing about the Church or the programme. If they want to know anything about either, I should refer them to him.

That evening two men come and sit at the bar. They don't act like the other customers. They look around in an investigatory kind of way and want to talk to me. They want to ask me a few questions about the Church, they say.

I tell them that, as a sister of the Church, I only perform rituals and they'll have to see Maarten if they want to talk about the Church.

They're persistant and keep trying to draw answers out of me.

In the end I crawl over the bar to another customer.

They look round for a bit, then slope off.

End of July 1981
Maarten has invited me to meet a friend of his who's over from America with his wife. He's the big boss of the Satanists there.

Maarten was taught by him and it was through him that he had the idea of setting up a Church of Satan in the Netherlands. I have to report to the church, or temple as Maarten prefers to call it, on the Oudezijds Voorburgwal.

He notices I'm hesitant and talks me into it. I always find it a bit spooky in that church. Everything's black and there's a coffin with a mummy in it and loads of skulls. There are heavy chains hanging from the wall, all kinds of machinery and an altar with loads of stuff for doing special rituals. It reminds me of my mother's stories about the dark arts and spirits.

Maarten's really splashed out in honour of his guest. Huge candelabra full of candles are burning in the middle of an enormous table, with a skull in the centre. The table is set for a feast. A waiter pours the wine for us.

Maarten's girlfriend is in a black velvet dress. She fits in well with the decor. I recognise the face of the American friend from a big oil painting Maarten's got at his place. He's bald, with a goatee and a piercing look in his eyes, as if he's looking right through you. He's wearing a long, black leather coat over a suit and tie. He doesn't take his coat off. His wife is blond and looks friendly.

He shakes hands with me, introducing himself as Anton. His wife is called Diane.

I can't really talk to them, as my English is limited to a few words. Now and again Maarten's girlfriend translates what they're talking about for me. In the meantime, the waiter lavishes all kinds of dishes on us, which he has laid out beautifully on silver platters. Maarten's girlfriend tells me that Anton used to be a lion tamer in a circus and now he advises Hollywood directors who want to make films with a satanic theme.

They talk and talk. I can't follow the conversation but the food is delicious and it makes me feel really spoiled to be served by a waiter.

After dinner, Maarten invites us to have coffee in the library. He points out a trapdoor in the floor, just before you go into the room. He had it installed for unwanted guests, he tells me. He's holding something that looks rather like a torch. That's the remote control, he explains. It's for drawing the curtains and opening the doors and shutters.

He presses on the remote and the door opens automatically. We enter the library, where classical music is playing. Everything is very rich, in the same style as his flat on the Oudezijds Achterburgwal. From the street you'd never guess that it was fitted out like a fairy-tale castle inside. One wall is lined with high bookshelves and a fire is blazing in a huge hearth. I see an altar covered in dishes and skulls.

We sit in the dark green velvet chairs by the open hearth. The waiter serves the coffee. Listening to the buzz of voices, I watch the flames and think about the circus.

I think about the French trapeze artiste with her net stockings. I've recently swapped my stockings for nets, too. It slims your legs down. The colour of the flames reminds me of the Frenchwoman's gold leotard. If I could speak English, I'd have liked to tell Anton and the others that I come from the circus, too.

August 1981
The builders have finished and Peter's back from holiday. When I come home in the afternoon with bags full of shopping he puts a cup of tea in front of me and asks me to marry him.

I'm startled. Get married? That'll get a lot of comments from his friends. I don't believe him, but he says he means it.

When I realise he's serious I say yes. I'd love to, but I can't imagine he really wants to marry me. Would he still want to if he knew exactly what I do? I wonder if I ought to tell him first. Marriage is something sacred. I don't dare. Maybe I'll do it one day.

I really want to marry Peter. Then I'll take his name and be rid of my father's. I'll be Mrs Schaapman from then on. I'll solemnly swear always to be true to him. Even if I have sex with strangers. But that's not real. Not like when I do it with Peter. Maybe I should stop having sex with my private clients. Yes, I'll have to, and just get married without telling him.

Peter doesn't want to make a big thing of it. He wants the simplest possible wedding, down to the town hall, signatures, and out again.

I suggest we ought to make something of it for his parents' sake. They've been on at us for ages, asking when we're finally going to get married. Then it'll be nice for them, too.

10 August 1981

Maarten now goes around with two bodyguards. I think it's because he's set up a foundation for broadcasting as a TV pirate station. SBC TV, it's called. The Satanic Broadcasting Corporation. There are several TV pirates and now a row has broken out between then. They interfere with each other's broadcasts. Videotapes are being stolen on both sides, including tapes with me on. Now they're even broadcasting each other's tapes, apparently.

The TV pirates want to meet up in the Caransa hotel to sort out the row about broadcasting. They want to negotiate mutual agreements on who broadcasts when. And they want to unite as a group. They've suggested that Maarten should be the chairman. He was wondering whether he ought to go to the meeting because he doesn't trust the situation. In the end he went and the meeting turned into a fight at the hotel. Maarten got out just in time.

All this fuss with the TV pirates is making me nervous. It can't be allowed to get out of control. I don't tell Peter anything; he'd immediately get stressed. I just hope he doesn't find out. I hide the paper with the report of the fight in the Caransa from him.

In a couple of days' time, Maarten's holding a satanic disco party with some other TV pirates. I'm not going. They'll only start fighting again.

2 October 1981

I'm getting married today. In West India House on Herenmarkt. We're keeping it simple. Peter's parents are my witnesses and his sister is his. His brother-in-law is taking the photographs and his two little nieces are coming, too.

I think of my mother as Peter slips the wedding ring on my finger. From now on I'm a married lady. Mrs Schaapman.

Half an hour later we're standing outside again.

October 1981

More and more articles on the Church of Satan have been appearing in the paper. A whole debate has broken loose over whether it's actually a real church. I'm amazed everybody's making such a fuss about it.

It's making Peter nervous. He's scared I'm committing illegal acts but I don't think things have gone that far. There's loads of things that aren't allowed in the red-light district.

I often do lesbian shows, now, with Afa. She's my best friend at work. She's a Moroccan who was pushed into an arranged marriage and ran away. She doesn't want to do any banana or vibrator shows, because she's scared of losing her virginity that way. When we do lesbian shows she always penetrates me with a strap-on dildo.

She lives in an attic room in Govert Flinckstraat. I've been round there a couple of times. Actually, where she sleeps is a storage area. It's in a communal attic which is divided into different compartments with wooden fences. Everyone who lives there has one of those storage spaces.

Afa's scared to go out on the street. She's frightened of bumping into her father, her brothers, her cousins, her uncles. Outside she always wears a headscarf because she's not allowed to leave her hair uncovered. She's been working here longer than me but she's an illegal immigrant. As she lives a nightlife, she doesn't know how to organise some things so I often give her a hand.

In the beginning I helped some of the other girls, too, but I'm getting a bit tired of it. It seems like there's no end to their problems.

Vivian only does live shows now. Her boyfriend's on drugs and needs a lot of looking after. She can't manage to work all night any more. Elvira's got a new boyfriend who waits outside for her every night. She has to give him all her money and even so he beats her up regularly. Nancy's actually the only one who's got her act together. She performs her rituals very efficiently, doesn't get involved with anybody and never moans. She saves and invests all the money she earns. She drives a white Porsche.

16 October 1981

Now a real pirate war has broken out. We've stopped filming *Patricia Privé*. I still work five nights a week at the Abbey. Now and again I stand in for Ann and see a client privately in the Hilton or the Americain. Since the fight with the pirates in the Caransa hotel I don't dare work there any more. A lot of guys from the red-light district go there and I'm scared they'll associate me with Maarten.

November 1981
I feel like an old hand in this business. I used to really do my best, but now I try and make as much money as possible with as little effort as possible.

When I'm showing new girls the ropes I find myself being less and less concerned as to how they feel. At the beginning I really tried to put them at their ease. Now I just explain some of the basic rules. After a week you've picked it all up anyway and after a month nothing's strange about it any more and almost every night's the same.

The thrill of all that money is beginning to wearing off. It's amazing how quickly you can get used to money.

The work's starting to become a drag. I get more and more irritated by the customers and with the girls' fussing.

Now and again, Michelle gives me a client for the third floor. She thinks I ought to get into specialities.

There are customers who'll pay a packet for something extra. They're mostly experienced businessmen who've already seen or tried everything at one time or another. They visit brothels and nightclubs all over the world on their travels. You're only allowed to go upstairs with them if you've been working here for a long time.

I don't mind it. It makes a change from the grind of the evening and it pays well.

23 December 1981
I'm feeling lonely and depressed, like I always do around Christmas. We've got to go out for a meal with Peter's parents and that always rubs in the fact that I haven't got any parents to go and see.

There's a letter from Rob amongst the Christmas cards.

Dear Karina!
Just found an address book of mine with your old address at that lady in Den Bosch's. I called her immediately and she gave me your address. Even though we haven't been in contact for 'donkey's years' I'm writing straight away, because I've been planning to look you up

for yonks (no really!!!). I gather everything's going all right. Well, for me too, partly.

I'm not travelling with a circus any more. I only do two subsidised winter circuses in a big theatre in Groningen and in the new Vredenburg Music Centre in Utrecht and, for the past six months, I've also been working as tour manager for a troop of German motorbike acrobats (the Hell Drivers). Not to be confused with the Hell's Angels, because those are child rapists! And I'm in a big caravan here, with a little printing machine and we muddle along like that.

I heard from the lady in Den Bosch that you've got a nice job. And you've ended up more or less in show business after all. If you have any problems, my phone number is still the same (should I enclose a quarter? Ha ha ha) Just a little joke, but seriously, give me a call some time.

     Lots of love,

     Rob Roberti

It's a long time since I heard anything from Rob, but it looks as if he hasn't forgotten me. The letterhead is printed with stars and the Circus Roberti logo. I can't help smelling it to see if I recognise the sweet smell of the circus, but I can only smell printing ink. I'd love to see him again but I don't dare. I'm scared I'll start missing my mother again. I don't want to feel like that any more.

I read the letter again. Yes, I suppose it is a kind of show business I've ended up in. But the Hell's Angel I met wasn't a child rapist. Maybe I'll tell Rob about him some time.

I stick the letter in my folder.

Maybe I should go with Peter to visit my mother's grave, but I don't dare do that, either. I don't think I can stand the idea of being so close to her yet.

January 1982

Peter wants me to stop working. He just can't get used to it. In fact, it bothers him more and more. Now he's taking sleeping pills and they give him stomachache.

Well, I couldn't care less what Peter thinks about my job. I seem to be getting harder and more indifferent all the time. And I don't care what I do with the customers any more, either. Nothing surprises me. I don't even really care about the money. The fun of buying things has worn off.

Everything seems such a drag.

February 1982

We've got a new girl starting and Michelle's asked me to show her the ropes. I can't really be bothered because it means I'll have to turn up for work an hour earlier, but it doesn't look as if anyone else can do it. Michelle obviously can't be bothered to do it herself, either.

When the bell goes I hear the doorman talking to the new girl. It takes a while before he shows her in. She's blond, not very old, and fat. We've got girls in all colours, types and sizes, but we've never had one that fat before. She's got an open, friendly face. She's wearing a tracksuit and no makeup. She hardly dares look at me.

I'm afraid it's going to take quite a bit of work to get her spruced up, but there'll be a market for her, too. I take her upstairs and, routinely, explain what's expected of her and what the dress rules are. She's relieved that she doesn't have to take all her clothes off and she can decide for herself how far she goes.

She's starting straight away but she hasn't got any money to buy stockings or a body stocking. Well, okay then, she can borrow some of mine.

We go to the dressing room where I give her some things and tell her she can use the makeup in my beauty case. Then I get changed. I can see that she's shaking with nerves so I make an effort to put her at her ease, after all.

I ask her where she lives.

In Rijnstraat, she says. She's got two small kids and a husband.

While she's changing, I notice the long, red stretch marks on her tummy. I ask how old the children are.

The youngest is three weeks old.

She squeezes herself into my body stocking and, even though it's elastic and stretches for ever, it's tight on her. I spot the blue string of a tampon hanging between her legs and ask if she's having her period.

No, she says, she's still bleeding from the birth; that goes on for about six weeks.

She can't work with a tampon in, I tell her. It looks awful if clients can see the string hanging out.

Well, she hasn't got any intention of taking off her body stocking anyway, she says.

I suggest that, to be on the safe side, she puts a sponge in instead. If she does end up taking her clothes off, then no one will see it.

She's never heard about sponges. I point out a bag of natural sponges next to the shower cubicle. They're about the size of an egg and there's no string on them. You just pop one inside and no one can see you're on your period. They're pretty good and quite handy; it means you can go on working. Some girls use them as a contraceptive if a client wants to have sex without a condom. After you've used the sponge, you rinse it out with Dettol and water. You can always use it again. The only problem is that it can sometimes get deep up inside, after a banana or vibrator show. Sometimes you can't get at it to pull it out for yourself. If that happens, I tell her, she should ask one of the girls to get it out for her, and I see her blush.

I give her a sponge and tell her to put some Dettol on it first and then rinse it out thoroughly with water. If you leave the Dettol on, before you know it you've got a fungal infection.

She takes the sponge with her into the shower. I feel a bit sorry for her, actually. She's already so nervous and now this. Well, I remind myself, the first night is always a bit scary but then you've got it over with.

A few minutes later, when she's standing in front of me in the stockings and body stocking, I give her the medallion to put around her neck and a towel. I tell her to make herself up quite heavily; the makeup gets lost in the dark and under the red light. She rummages around awkwardly in my beauty case. She's got no idea what to put on. I go and sit next to her and get out some lipstick, blusher, eyeshadow and mascara. Actually, it looks quite good on her. She takes a look at herself in the mirror and I can tell she doesn't like the effect.

Keep an eye on what the other girls do tonight, I tell her. You'll be working upstairs with me. I'll give you a hand. Just stay on the bar; all you'll have to do is pour drinks. I really do feel sorry for her.

I ask her what her name is.

Anja, she says.

I tell her she'd better think of another name. She chooses Eve. Sister Eve; one way or another it suits her.

The next day, Eve's near to tears.

She watched carefully yesterday, she says, and she'll never dare to do all the things we do.

Oh, you get used to it, I reassure her. She's really popular with the men. Everybody wants to dance with her or wants her to do a show but Eve doesn't dare.

Halfway through the night, Eve's sitting in a corner of the bar. In a quiet moment, I ask her what she's so scared of. Maybe she ought to look for another job; she'll never last out like this. At some point you have to do something with the customers.

She bursts into tears and tells me she doesn't want to do this at all; it's her husband who's making her. They've got a lot of debts and this is the only way out.

I try to comfort her and then send her off to the changing room; we can't have a snivelling sister. I feel bad about it. What a bastard to force her into it. I tell Michelle to send a girl up from downstairs. I'm not going to sit up here on my own with all these nutters.

When Michelle hears that Eve is sitting in the changing room, she goes and tells her to leave. You can't work here if you're not prepared to do anything. Eve is inconsolable when she hears that she has to go.

I crawl back on to the bar. They send Afa up, but she hasn't got any enthusiasm either. She puts her things into her compartment with a grumpy face.

It's not easy to get me upset but I don't like this business with Eve. Suddenly I'm overcome with a tremendous rage. I've had it up to here with all these nutters. I can tell by their build what their preference will be. The tall, lanky ones with an intellectual look and thin, straight hair hanging in the wrong direction, those are the arsehole observers and muff divers. They've got slightly hunched shoulders and a gawky torso that hangs loosely at the hips. You can tell them a mile off. Oh, don't they just fancy themselves! They make their eyes shine, but it's a fake shine. Their long, gangly arms taper into long, narrow fingers with finely shaped fingertips which grab your hand and kiss it tenderly, like some poncy gentleman. Jesus! They try and humour you with pretty words, but their mouths are always dry and, patting and purring, they dive into your muff with lip-smacking vigour. Puke.

I think I've reached the limit of disgust. Now I'm really feeling aggressive. If I see another sly wanker tonight, I'll yank his hands up above the bar.

Sly wankers are either too skinny or too fat, almost always wear glasses and always with the wrong frames, their hair is wiry and they wear it short and slicked down as if they use wallpaper paste, but of course it could be their own spunk. They disgust me. They wear dreadful jackets and usually have a little leather wrist wallet dangling from their arm. Their shirts smell of sweat. Do they honestly think I can't see them sitting there shiftily wanking off? That I can't see the trembling flesh of their rancid bodies? Do they really think I don't notice when they get that blank look and start going red in the face and beads of sweat appear on their foreheads? Or is that actually the kick? They don't even say goodbye when they leave, the sneaks; they just slide from their stools with their hands in front of their crotch. I'm rigid with tension and aggression now. In the meantime, Afa's got a client for a lesbian ritual. She asks me if I want to do it with her.

Okay, I say. We take his money. I have to stop myself from snatching it. The client wants me to take Afa with a strap-on dildo. That's what he paid for, he says, but Afa doesn't want to do it that way round. Afa should bloody well grow up and stop being so fucking hypocritical. It's always me that has to get fucked, just because she finds it so damn necessary to stay a bloody virgin. Well, she shouldn't have come to work in the fucking Abbey, then; that's asking for trouble, isn't it?

Afa gets the client to choose a dildo. He wants the medium-sized one. She gives me the bottle of oil, we rub it into our hands and then our ritual begins. Routinely, we fondle each other's breasts, belly and thighs. As always when we do our little show, Afa turns round, gets her dildo and straps it on while I stroke her hair. She's got really long, black, curly hair. I wonder if the client who's watching us now realises how lucky he is to be able to see Afa's hair. Actually we ought to charge more for this show. She turns back round. It's time to be taken. I turn my back to Afa and bend over. The client watches breathlessly as two women fuck each other. Doggy fashion. Never from the front, always from the back. Afa slides the dildo in carefully. She doesn't want to hurt me. She pushes it gently in and out and I start getting angry again.

Jesus Christ, this is so hypocritical. She should bloody stop all that stupid culture rubbish, it just doesn't go with working in the Church of Satan. She observes Ramadan and remains a virgin but at the same time she's fucking women with dildos.

We're like animals. That's probably why we do it doggy fashion. I've had enough.

I look up at the client; he's obviously satisfied. I want Afa to stop. I'm sick of this. I go and take a shower. I feel so dirty.

I stay in the shower a long time. I've got to calm down. I still feel so aggressive I'm shaking. The hot water relaxes me a bit.

Good thing it's not Friday night, otherwise that nutter would have been in here in his bare bum. He's incredibly lucky because I would have kicked his bare bloody arse out of the shower. There's nothing to come cleaning in here. No matter how long I let the water run, it just won't wash me clean. It's as if all the filthiness is sticking to me. The oil makes the water glide off my skin.

I feel dirtier than I probably really am. Everything seems magnified.

Something's not right but I can't quite put my finger on it, I only know it's got something to do with Eve. In some way, that's what's put the lid on it for me. Eve could have made a lot of money, that's for sure. Men like a soft, fat woman with big breasts. There would have been a lot of men who'd have liked to eat a banana from between her fat thighs. In the dressing room you could clearly see the traces of her pregnancy on her belly, but in the red light of the bar they weren't noticeable. A three-week-old baby. Eve didn't have the nerve, and a good thing, too. It made her cry, and so it should have done. If you're still bleeding after giving birth then you are as good as immaculate.

As immaculate as Afa, who has never done it with a bloke because in her culture you're not allowed to have sex outside marriage.

Afa and Eve. Two sister who strayed into the wrong church – the Church of Satan's Walburga Abbey.

Good evening, I'm Sister Karina of the Church of Satan. What can I do for you? How often must I have said that?

The worst thing is that it was us who made all those blokes believe it's so great to be a sister in this Church. We were the ones who liked to choose the biggest dildo, even though it hurt us. And we kept smiling as seductively as possible. Jesus fucking Christ.

I asked Eve to do what was expected of us sisters. In doing so, I actually forced her, just like that bastard husband of hers. Why do all those nutters who come here actually want us to do this?

I wouldn't mind taking Afa for once; I want to experience the feeling of power, too. And of course that's why I feel so dirty. It's as if Afa was raping me. Jesus Christ. Oh, it's nice and easy for those nutters. They let us fuck ourselves so that they don't have to. Then they won't have to feel bad about it afterwards. Let's face it; they paid for it, didn't they? They pretend it's a fair deal, but it's not.

I don't want to let myself get fucked any more. Not by Afa and not by nutters. I'm not assisting in my own rape any longer. Maarten can fuck off. Super pimp.

That's it.

I dry myself off and, against all the clothing regulations, go downstairs with nothing on. Afa's already busy with the next client.

In the dressing room I come across Menno, a nutter with self-bestowed privileges. Because he's been coming here for years, he's allowed to take pictures of us if he pays for it, but most of the time he doesn't pay us. And on top this, more and more often he's doing it without asking. He gets a kick out of photographing us at our vulnerable moments, while we're making up or eating. What he'd really like to do is deeply penetrate us with his zoom lens, for ever and ever, I know he would. Our inner depths are still not deep enough. Sometimes we talk him into taking a nice picture of us and then the prick makes a dirty photo out of it anyway. And the cunt wants us to pay for the prints, on top of it. He's fucking us in front of our noses.

I tell him in no uncertain terms exactly where to go. I've got no time for Peeping Toms tonight.

Suddenly my mind is made up. It's so sharp and clear that it feels like I've been using really good coke.

I'm quitting. Right now.
They can keep my retainer and my things, too.
I'm finished with this for good.

6

Mother

March 1982
It's a couple of weeks since I stopped working and I've already run out of money. I haven't yet dared work out how much I've gone through in the past year.

Peter's perfectly all right again now. The stomachache's gone and he's sleeping without pills. He's so pleased I've stopped working. Good thing I never told him exactly what I was getting up to. He would never have got over it. Sometimes I try and tell him something about it, but Peter stops me. He just says he doesn't want to know.

I've had a letter from Pim. He's in the Antilles and wants me to come over. He's got a role for me in his new film.

Well, I don't want to be in any more films. I don't want to appear naked again. Never again.

I want to lead a quiet life. I don't care if we haven't got any money. Actually, now I'd like to become a mother.

April 1982
Peter and I went to have dinner with a colleague of his. His wife, who's Indonesian, had made a full Indonesian meal. The taste took me right back.

I asked her if she'd teach me to cook Indonesian.

The next day, she took me to a *toko* on Ferdinand Bolplein, where she helped me buy the spices. She's written out some recipes for me and now she's teaching me Indonesian cooking.

May 1982
Now I cook Indonesian food every day. I've been trying out the recipes one after another. I want to treat Peter to nice meals as

much as possible. I feel as if I've got so much to make up for.

I've bought the *Keijner Cookery Book* which has Dutch, Chinese and Indonesian recipes in it. *The Keijner was originally written for Dutch housewives in Indonesia*, it says on the back. The ingredients are all written in Malaysian, the method in Dutch. It's the ideal cookery book for me. I know the names of all the spices in Malaysian. I recognise the smells and flavours from long ago. It's how our house used to smell.

The Indonesian food gives me a comforting feeling. It makes it easier to talk to Peter about the time with my mother. I still don't dare tell him everything. I keep telling him little bits; feeding him pieces of the past through the food. Over the *soto ajam* I tell him about the pigeon my mother cooked for me; over the pudding I tell him about the lumpy milk puddings at the domestic science school and about how hungry I was when I was alone at home.

Peter's a good listener. He always asks the right questions and never asks too much, just enough.

For years, all I've been able to think about is the bad things connected with my mother's death. The smell of the Indonesian spices is releasing all the good memories. It makes me feel strong. Maybe I should go and visit my mother's grave some time and show Peter all the places from the past in Leiden.

Actually, I'd really like him to see what our street looks like, and the playground. I want to show him the *toko* and the park, and Vroom & Dreesmann. I don't know if I dare go and see San's mother. I still haven't got over the disappointment of the last visit.

24 July 1982
Today Peter and I are taking the train to Leiden to visit my mother's grave. It amazes me how quickly we get there. In my memory, Leiden's worlds away.

At the cemetery, we ask the caretaker where my mother is buried. He looks it up in a register. He gives me a number and a plan.

The cemetery still looks like the big park I remember from the funeral. It's still a long walk to reach the grave. On the way, here and there we read what's written on other gravestones. They offer comfort. Sometimes there's fresh flowers. I can see a few freshly dug graves and most of those are covered in fresh flowers. I think about the trowel-full of sand I threw into the black hole with the coffin at the bottom and the thump of the sand on the lid. I've got no idea what state the grave's in now. I've never thought about it before.

When we get to my mother's number, we look for her grave-stone. I'm taken aback when I see a pole at the spot where she's lying. One pole in amongst all those gravestones. It's small and grey, with several numbers engraved on it. According to the care-taker's note, the lowest number is my mother's. The numbers on top of it are other people's. None of them's got a name, just a number.

I lay the flowers next to the pole. I'm disappointed my mother hasn't got her own pole. Now she's got to share the flowers I brought for her with other people. All the same, it's not as bad as I'd expected. Nothing like as scary as I'd always dreamed. Now I'm standing here, right on top of her, it just feels desolate.

Peter hugs me. He can't help crying.

I still haven't got any tears.

We decide not to go into Leiden after all. I want to go home. On the way back to Amsterdam I tell Peter about my aunts in America and the dollars they used to send us. He says why don't I get in touch with them. They must still be alive.

August 1982

I've decided to look up my mother's sisters, Auntie Bea and Auntie Lucia. Peter's been helping me. In amongst my mother's papers in the folder, I found Auntie Bea's husband's surname and, through the archives in Rotterdam, I've managed to find her address. They moved from Rotterdam to Los Angeles some years ago.

I've written to Auntie Bea and had a letter back from her.

She was pleased to hear from me. She writes that she and her hus-band tried to find me when they visited the Netherlands in 1975. They even went to the hospital where my mother was and asked about me. But nobody could give them any information.

She says she's passed on my address to Auntie Lucia and there's a letter from her on its way. She asks me to come and visit them in America some time. *Your mama will be so happy we have found each other,*

Karina, don't forget that, and in a way I think she knows it, is how she ends the letter. I read that final comforting sentence again and again.

My mother would certainly have been glad I was in contact with her sisters again. And that I'm leading a quiet life with Peter now. I think that, like Peter, she'd have been horrified to hear about the Church of Satan. With the good things in my life, I hope she's watching me from a cloud, but with the bad stuff, I hope she can't see me, or otherwise forgives me.

Auntie Bea and Auntie Lucia must believe in the dark arts, too, and in life after death, like my mother. I don't understand how people can believe in things they can't see. It does offer comfort but I still don't think it's a nice idea. If my mother is still anywhere, I want to be close to her again.

November 1982
When I was working at the Church of Satan, I hardly ever saw Yvette, but now I see a lot of her again. She's my best friend. She knows hardly anything about my past and I don't dare to tell her the details, either. She was living in Spain when I was at the Abbey.

I go for a cup of tea with her every day in the De Reiger café where we used to work together. She's taught me to knit and now we knit jumper after jumper. I go round to her place first thing in the morning when our husbands have gone to work. Then we chat and make ourselves up. About eleven we go to De Reiger.

I get all broody when I talk to her about children. She doesn't want any yet, but I do. I asked Peter if he wants a baby, too. He wasn't sure, as usual, but I managed to convince him.

I'm going to stop taking the pill. We'll see what happens.

March 1983
Yvette and I never seem to stop talking and laughing. Now and again we tell each other something about the past. She lived by herself from the age of fourteen. Her mother's a Jewish war victim. She's so busy dealing with her own traumas that she's got no time for Yvette. She still has her lucid moments. As a child in the war, she was the only one of her family left. Now she sometimes thinks everybody wants to murder her, or that her parents are still alive and living in America.

Yvette doesn't let it bother her. She's used to having a mother like that.

Like me, Yvette hasn't had any education. She wants to do evening classes and, if that works out, go on to university. I don't want to work or study. All I want is a family with lots of children. And to treat Peter to nice dinners.

June 1983
Still not pregnant. Since I stopped taking the pill, I've been late or even early every month. I want a baby so badly.

Peter wants me to stop buying pregnancy tests. He thinks it's getting too expensive. They cost thirty guilders each and I buy one every time I'm late. If the first test's negative, then a couple of days later I buy another one, just to be sure. It's got to be positive some time.

Now that we have to get by on Peter's salary, things are a bit tight. He's still studying and working part time. I'm starting to regret the fact that we haven't got very much money. I keep having to stop myself pinching stuff. I find myself looking for the security cameras in department stores.

I've got that old feeling from Den Bosch back again. As if the way I survived then is still in my system. Very occasionally, when we're really strapped for cash, I think how easily I could make some quick money, but I've made up my mind never to backslide. I want to be a good wife to Peter. He never lets me down and always looks after me. I can't do it to him. Going back to doing something he can't stand. I'm going to look for an ordinary job so that I can contribute something to the housekeeping.

July 1983
I now write regularly to Auntie Bea and Auntie Lucia. Their letters are so different. Auntie Bea writes about her children and grandchildren. Auntie Lucia talks about the things she does. She's quite old but she still works and she's studying, too. Both of them keep asking when I'm going to go over to America. I don't really know how to answer them. I don't know them well enough. I promise I'll do it one day.

I've applied for a job as a barmaid in a café called De Engelbewaarder, and they've taken me on.

20 August 1983
Today a boy got stabbed to death by a skinhead. Because he didn't like his colour, they said on the radio.

The story's knocked me for six. I keep bursting into tears.

A customer at De Engelbewaarder asks me why I'm so quiet. I tell him I'm upset by the stabbing, that it worries me that there are more and more skinheads in Holland and that the Nationalist Party is gaining popularity.

A heavy debate on the Nationalist Party starts in the bar. I'm shocked to hear someone saying he thinks the leader, Janmaat, is all right. There are far too many foreigners in this country. They should bloody well go home, the man adds.

The remark numbs me. In my head I hear echoes of the insults that were so often thrown at my mother and me. *What are you doing here? Go home, bloody foreigners.*

Look, I haven't got anything against foreigners, I hear someone else say, but there's so many of them.

It hasn't got anything to do with numbers, I'd like to scream at him; there were just the two of us, my mother and me, and they wanted us to go home, too. But I keep my mouth shut. I see the angry looks from the past, on the stairs, in the street. I hear the hissing, *Bugger off home, peanut chinky*; I hear snowballs exploding against our window.

It scares me. The customers in this café are all well educated. I always thought it was only people like those in our street in Leiden who made discriminatory remarks, just out of ignorance. That's what my mother used to say. But the customers here are writers, journalists, students. Surely they ought to know better.

November 1983
I'm a week late and I've sneakily bought another Predictor. I couldn't help it. The result's positive.

I'm pregnant.

To celebrate, we go out to dinner at De Reiger.

7 December 1983

Today we heard the baby's heart for the first time. It was a really fast, strong heartbeat. It's due on the twenty-second of June.

It looks as if I'm continuing a tradition. There's loads of June babies in my family. My brother, sister and I all have our birthdays within ten days of each other, me on the sixth, my brother on the eleventh and my sister on the sixteenth. My mother's birthday was the thirtieth of June and she was born on her mother's birthday.

If the baby arrives a week late, then it'll come on my mother's birthday.

Christmas 1983

We're staying in Enschede, at Peter's sister's. His parents are here, too, and one of Peter's aunts. While the Christmas dinner is being prepared, Peter's aunt takes him aside. When he comes back, I can see he's shaken and angry.

I've never seen him like that before. I ask him what happened and at first all he says is that he wants his aunt out of the house, right now. Then he tells me what his aunt said to him. She couldn't understand how he could have married a half-caste.

I can feel myself going red. My heart starts hammering. I run upstairs to the spare room. Defeated, I sit down on the bed. I can't believe she said that.

Peter comes up to comfort me. We hear a door slam downstairs. He says his aunt's gone and she's never going to set foot in the house again.

So now there'll be a family row because I'm here.

Peter tells me not to think any more about it, that it's just stupidity, we're out in the sticks here.

It brings back my mother's words to me. Whenever I asked her why people looked at us so crossly, she would take my face in her hands and give me a penetrating look. *It's the narrow-mindedness of a chilly, damp country, girlie*, she would say. *The people don't know any better, they can't help it. Don't let it bother you.*

Peter's words comfort me, just as my mother's do, even after all these years. When I'm feeling better, I go back downstairs.

Shoulders back, chin up and chest out, my mother always said. Going down to the sitting room I'm very conscious of my posture.

Bolt upright, with my pregnant belly even further to the fore, I walk into the room where the family's waiting to celebrate Christmas.

Everyone's shocked and apologises. Luckily they don't share the aunt's opinion.

March 1984
My belly's getting too fat and I've got to stop working at De Engelbewaarder. I don't fit behind the beer pump any more. It's a shame because I like the work and I've got nice colleagues who keep sending me sweet little notes about my prospective motherhood. I feel fit and strong and incredibly proud of my growing belly. I would have liked to go on working for a while.

At least Peter's got a full-time job now. Together with a partner he's going to set up a migrant workers' television channel in Amsterdam. That means he's going to be working day and night for the foreseeable future. It's pretty handy financially, because up till now he hasn't been earning quite enough and I don't want to have to work any more when the baby comes.

I want to look after it day and night.

30 June 1984
Today's my mother's birthday. The baby's a week overdue.

My belly's enormous. I really hope the baby is born today and I try everything to get the contractions going. I take a brisk walk through town and masturbate madly, but it doesn't do a thing. I hadn't worried about anything until now, but when I see how huge my belly is, I wonder how on earth the baby can get out. A great big baby will never fit through such a small hole.

I didn't go to any antenatal classes because I didn't feel like huffing and puffing with a whole group of pregnant mums. Now I'm beginning to wonder if it might not have been a good idea after all.

1 July 1984
Today our son was born. He weighs almost ten pounds and is perfectly healthy.

The contractions started at four o'clock in the afternoon and three hours later he was lying in my arms. I gave birth on the floor of our sitting room. Peter and Yvette were there.

It's a miracle.

My child feeds from my breasts and now and again he opens his little eyes.

I'm a mother.

7

Family

Spring 1991

On 13 April my fourth child was born. I now have two sons and two daughters, so my family's complete. I'm a full-time mother and I wouldn't want it any other way. Peter's got a new job where he's really happy.

I enjoy my children. We've moved to a house alongside a canal, with a big communal courtyard garden where the children can play in complete safety in the heart of Amsterdam. My kitchen door's open all day long and the neighbouring children are in and out all the time.

Since I've been a mother myself, I often wonder how my own mother used to do things. I try and imagine what she would have been like as a grandma. Sometimes I feel it might be nice to be in contact with my sister Diana. Maybe she's got kids now, too. Who knows? Maybe she's curious about her mother, too. I often imagine telling Diana about my mother, our mother. But maybe she doesn't want to have anything more to do with me. Or she'll tell my father and brother everything.

I'm still frightened of them. It's that fear that stops me looking for her. Since I've had kids, I feel vulnerable. I don't want my children being bothered by my father, my brother or my past.

Of course it's possible that Diana isn't in contact with them any more. Maybe my father's dead by now. In that case, there's nothing stopping me. Just recently I've been thinking I might risk calling her if I can get hold of her telephone number. If her reaction is off-putting, or I feel uneasy, I can always hang up.

8 May 1991

I go to the main post office with the children. They've got telephone directories for the whole of the Netherlands there. I only hope Diana still lives in Zaltbommel, otherwise I might as well forget it.

I look for her surname in the Zaltbommel section. There is, indeed, a van Dijk listed. I note down the number and stroll home with the kids. As soon as they are playing nicely, I go to the phone. My hands are shaking as I pick up the receiver and dial the number.

Someone picks up the phone at the other end. It's a woman's voice, but it's not Diana.

I ask for her, but the woman says she doesn't know any Diana.

I ask if by any chance she knows if there's another van Dijk living in Zaltbommel but she can't help me.

21 May 1991

I finally managed to find out through the town hall in Zaltbommel that Diana's living in Hedel now. I dial the number they give me.

Diana van Dijk, says a voice. I recognise it immediately.

This is Karina, I hear myself saying. Remember me?

Silence for a moment. I can hear Diana getting over her astonishment at the other end.

Of course I remember you, she says quietly. I can tell by her voice that she's pleased. Where are you living? How are you? She bombards me with one question after another. I do the same to her.

She tells me she's been married but she's divorced now and lives with a disabled man. She hasn't got any children.

I ask if she still sees Johan.

She hardly has any contact with him, she says. He's in and out of prison and only just came out after being inside for a year and a half. He's got a wife and child now. Diana hopes he's going to mend his ways now that he's a father.

I ask her not to tell him about this call. I can feel myself getting scared again. Then I ask her about her father. I can't bring myself to say the word 'my' or 'our'.

She says he hasn't changed a bit. Now he's married to the umpteenth woman. She won't tell him we've spoken, either.

We're over the moon. We think it's so great to talk to each other after so many years that we keep on speaking at the same time. We agree to meet again as soon as possible.

Tomorrow, says Diana, and I agree. She'll come over to my place. Just for a moment, the thought crosses my mind that it might not be sensible to give her my address but the urge to see her is stronger than my fear of her passing it on to Johan or my father. We arrange for her to come over tomorrow evening. Then she can meet Peter, too.

I can't get to sleep the whole night. Finally, I'm going to be able to talk to Diana about my mother. I'm dying to tell her the way she was and the things she did with me. I'm curious to see what Diana will want to know about her. Maybe she hasn't even got any idea what she looked like.

I want to know all about Diana, too; what she was like when she was little, for instance. I think of all kinds of questions I can ask her. I'm so curious to see whether she still looks the same as she did and if, now we're grown up, you can tell we're sisters.

22 May 1991

I wait for Diana, together with Peter and the children. We said seven o'clock and, finally, the time comes. Every car that passes makes my stomach go into a knot from nerves.

Then a car stops outside. Diana gets out and waves to me.

I run outside and give her a hug. She hasn't changed a bit.

Diana thinks I have, though. She asks me to give her a hand getting her boyfriend Dennis out of the car. We walk round to the back. It's a kind of delivery van. I'm taken aback when I look through the window and see Dennis sitting there. I had no idea he was so seriously disabled.

As soon as we've got him out on the street with his wheelchair, I introduce myself.

Diana explains that he's paralysed and can't shake hands, so I lay my hand on his and say welcome. She wheels Dennis on to the pavement and then, together, we carry him up the steps in the chair. He makes all kinds of incomprehensible noises but Diana seems to understand what he means. I gather he's only physically disabled but I find myself saying simple things to him because his head leans to one side, he pulls faces and talks unintelligibly.

My children creep behind me. They have to get used to the strange man in the wheelchair.

Diana tells us how, after her divorce, she went to work in a nursing home. That's where she met Dennis, who had ended up a paraplegic after a motorbike accident. He had been in the military police and suddenly found himself as a young man among all those old people. Diana fell in love with him, took him away from the nursing home and started to care for him at home.

For her that means intensive care day and night. Dennis can't eat or drink by himself. He empties his bowels via a catheter. He is held upright by a harness. That means it's hours before she can get him into his chair in the morning. When Diana washes him, she has to dry every fold of his skin, otherwise it can get chafed. And he can't even feel that. She has to get up twice in the night to turn him in bed. She never goes anywhere any more. They have to stay indoors from October to May, in any case, as Dennis can't regulate his body temperature properly. She can't stop talking about Dennis. Her life follows a strict routine and every hour is spoken for.

I ask her about Johan. She can't actually tell me any more than she did over the phone. The same goes for her father.

Peter takes the kids to bed and I make some more coffee. I don't really dare talk about my mother. Diana doesn't seem to be curious about her at all.

While we're drinking the coffee, Peter gives Dennis some squash with a straw. Peter's always considerate. When Dennis chokes, Diana's there immediately. She thumps him hard in his stomach. It gives me quite a scare. She explains that Dennis can't solve the problem himself if he chokes. Peter lets Diana take over giving him the drink. It gave him a shock, too, when she thumped him.

Then, finally, Diana asks me what happened after I left Zaltbommel.

I tell her how I was forced to stay with Auntie Katrina and about Marian and the foster family. It's soon clear that Diana has heard quite another story. She even casts doubt on my version in order to defend her father.

That makes me angry, but I try not to let it show. I can imagine it's really difficult for her to be confronted with the nasty side of her father. After all, I had no bond with him, but they're still in contact.

Cautiously, I ask her what she knows about my mother. I find I'm talking about 'my' mother and 'her' father, and ask her to excuse me. Our mother, I should say. It takes some getting used to.

Diana says she knows practically nothing about her, only that her father spoke badly of my mother. He told her and Johan that they got divorced because she tried to poison them.

She says it's not important to her to know who her mother was. It's all so long ago. She'd rather look to the future.

I can hardly bear her lack of interest. I feel I have to defend my mother.

I tell Diana what a lovely mother my mother was, that she would never do anything like that to her children. She never hit me, I add, trying to persuade Diana to look at it differently. Your father hit us for the slightest thing.

Well, we weren't such little angels, either, and we deserved to be punished sometimes, replies Diana.

I can hardly believe she's defending his behaviour like that.

Maybe I'll be able to tell her more about my mother when we've talked more often. We barely know each other.

As soon as they leave, I'm overcome with impotent fury. I hate my father even more than I did already. How dare he says such things about my mother?

Peter has sympathy for Diana. He thinks I should give her time.

I could shake her till her teeth rattle. I feel terrible. I'd imagined this evening quite differently.

Peter talks me round, trying to get me to see how complicated this must be for Diana. He manages to wear the sharpest edges off my anger. After all, he says soothingly, the truth will out, as the saying goes.

Before I go to sleep, I promise my mother not to let it go at that. Diana has to know who she was.

28 May 1991
Diana called to say that, without even knowing we'd been in touch, Johan is looking for information about his mother. In doing so, he's found some people who lived next door to her in Indonesia.

Then Diana startles me by saying that she told Johan about our meeting. Luckily she didn't tell him where I live. Johan asked her to give me his number so I can contact him. It's important for him to find out more about his mother now that he's got a child himself. His father refuses to talk about her.

Diana gives me Johan's number. He lives in Belgium. She makes it clear that she's doing this for her brother. She doesn't feel the way he does; she'd rather leave things the way they are.

After she's hung up, I'm overwhelmed by a sense of triumph. Finally recognition for my mother, perhaps. Johan was the last person I'd expected this from. We've still never spoken to each other and now he wants to talk to me about my mother.

I can't wait to call him. I'm frightened as well, but the desire to tell Johan about my mother is stronger than my fear. I wait till Peter comes home and ask him what he thinks.

Go ahead and do it, he says, nothing can happen over the phone.

I dial the number Diana's given me. A man's voice answers with the name of a company. Without giving my name I ask if I can speak to Johan van Dijk.

That's me, says the man.

This is Karina, remember? I hear myself saying.

Johan stammers. I stammer. I'm still scared of him.

Johan tells me about his little boy. It turns out that he and my second son were born within a week of each other. Since he's had a child, he tells me, he's been trying to find out about his mother. He wants to know what his background is. His father won't tell him anything about the past and he hasn't got any pictures of his mother, only a few of himself as a baby. He tried to get his father to talk about her, but the only thing his father would say was that she was a bad mother and neglected her children. And that she tried to poison them.

My brother can't understand it. If that's true, why does he look so healthy in the baby pictures?

I find it difficult to believe that it's Johan who's looking for information about his mother, while Diana doesn't want to know anything about her. I don't doubt him any more. I don't feel any more fear, either. What I'd really like to do is tell him everything, absolutely everything, about her right now. We arrange for him to come round with his wife and their little boy.

As soon as I've hung up I burst into tears. I tell Peter, who's trying to comfort me, that these are tears of joy because Johan wants to know all about my mother. I catch myself saying 'my mother' again. I'll have to be careful to talk about 'our mother' when he comes. After all, she was his mother, too.

It's not easy to have to share my mother.

2 June 1991
Johan's coming today. We're all sitting nervously waiting.

I've spoken to him a couple of times this week and I can't understand why I was so scared of him. Diana knows we're meeting up but she's less enthusiastic about the reunion. She's told me she doesn't really get on with Johan's wife and she's suspicious about his latest business. After all, he's gone straight for a while several times, but things have always gone wrong again in the end. She doesn't share his interest in my mother.

Diana seems to approach everything rationally. Johan is far more emotional.

A dark blue Mercedes sports car stops in front of the house. Johan gets out. He looks different. He's bigger than me and much fatter. He's got short hair and a moustache and he's wearing a gold chain round his neck. Actually, he looks the most Indonesian of the three of us.

We kiss each other.

Hi, I hear him say. Shyly, I turn to his wife, who has now walked over to us. She's got bleached blond, bouffant hair and a lot of make-up on. She introduces herself as Priscilla. She's carrying their son. He's a strapping lad.

Priscilla does most of the talking. She explains how they met. Johan was in the prison where she was working. Her family hasn't accepted their relationship.

Johan tells me she's an ace babe. Always stands up for him. He rolls up his shirtsleeves, exposing a heavy gold watch. His hands and arms are covered in tattoos and all kinds of other symbols and signs including three dots between the thumb and forefinger. He shows me his biggest and best tattoo.

Had it done for Priscilla, he says. He's had their son's name added. Priscilla beams.

I tell him I had Peter's name tattooed on my arm, too. My tattoo is quite modest in comparison with his, but it gives us something in common.

Johan is awkward in his manner and Priscilla keeps on apologising for him. She explains that he has difficulty in adjusting because of his past.

Irritated by her apologising for him, Johan says it's because of his father. Priscilla agrees and, slowly, I feel a wonderful kind of joy rising up from my toes.

I've got allies. I'd always thought Johan was on his father's side because he never hesitated to harass other people on his father's instructions. It seems like he's changed.

I ask him what he's been doing all these years.

He settles himself into a comfortable position, legs apart. He did some odd jobs that got out of hand. Fighting, break-ins, some business with contractors, that kind of thing, and once he did an armed robbery. Now and again it landed him inside. There he got in with the wrong crowd.

He doesn't do things like that any more, he says. Since he's had a child himself, he's changed. Now he's in vitamin pills. He lives in Belgium because he'd never get a job in Holland with his history.

Johan tries to convince me that he's a good guy now.

Hey, I've done things that don't bear thinking about, either, I say, to reassure him.

He's visibly relieved, and Priscilla even more. She explains that Diana doesn't trust Johan and she really hates that.

Now Johan would like to know more about our mother.

I tell him about how my mother and I lived in Leiden. I tell him how sweet she was and how poor we were. I don't say anything about Rob and the circus, but I tell him about how she got ill and how she died. Somehow, I want to spare Johan's feelings so I just sketch the outlines.

When I tell him how she died, he wants to know where she's buried. He wants to visit her grave.

In Leiden, I say, but she hasn't got a real grave, just a little pole to mark it.

I can see he's getting emotional.

We've got to do something about that, he says to Priscilla. My mother's going to get a beautiful grave.

It moves me to see how much Johan feels for my mother, without having known her.

I tell him about Nitadog and what she meant to me. How terrible I felt that I had to get rid of her, because she was all I had left.

Johan can't sit still any longer. He paces furiously up and down the room. He lets out a string of swearwords and says he's going to confront his father.

Priscilla tries to get him to calm down but I notice I'm feeling his fury wrap around me like a warm blanket. I tell him about my time in Den Bosch and how I met Peter, but nothing about the Church of Satan. I'm trying to give a good impression because I want to gain Johan's confidence.

Then he wants to know what my mother said about Diana and him. I tell him she really loved them and how sad she was that she was never allowed to have them with her again.

When he hears this and I show him the photos of his mother, Johan starts to cry. Peter fetches him a glass of water. I wonder if I ought to tell him any more, but he quickly gets over it. He tells me about the people he's met who used to live next door to her in Indonesia. They only had good things to say about my mother, too. He'd like to go and see them some time, together with me and Diana. Then maybe she'll believe it, too.

I'd really like to meet those people.

When they've gone, I start rejoicing. It's fantastic having spoken to Johan. At long last, justice for my mother. It wouldn't surprise me if he did something violent to his father.

Peter's less enthusiastic. He doesn't think Johan's in control of his emotions and that worries him. You shouldn't play on his feelings like that, he says.

I don't think that's a very nice remark. I go to bed cross. Peter's always so pessimistic and afraid things will go wrong. He hasn't got any idea what he's talking about.

In bed I secretly bathe in the memory of the evening. I promise my mother that Johan and I will take revenge on his father.

June 1991

Today we're going to see my mother's old neighbours. They live in Eindhoven. We're all going to meet up there. Diana and Dennis are coming, too.

Peter's borrowed a minibus from work. Halfway there, the kids are terribly sick. They're not used to being in a car. I've brought flowers and a cake with me. After all, we're descending on these people with an enormous family.

We're greeted by an old Indonesian man and his wife. *Selamat datang.* They're friendly and unassuming and speak *petjo* even more than my mother.

Johan and Priscilla are already there. Now we just have to wait for Diana and Dennis.

While Johan's little boy plays with my kids, the man tells us about his own children, who are grown up now, and his grandchildren. It sounds as if they all turned out well. He's obviously a proud father and grandad. His wife brings in some Indonesian snacks and keeps urging us to eat them. The children stuff themselves full.

When Diana and Dennis arrive, Johan takes the lead. He's spoken to these people before and he seems to feel responsible for the success of this visit. He gives the man a kind of awkward order to tell us what a good mother we had.

With an opening like this, the man only confirms what Johan wants to hear and doesn't get round to his own story. Diana evidently feels uneasy. I ask the man how long he lived next door to my mother and where it was.

He does remember a couple of things, he says. They had a tiger in the house at my mother's. The whole neighbourhood was scared of it.

I sit up with a start. I know this story but I always wondered if it was really true.

My mother used to tell me about the tiger, I say.

The former neighbour doesn't remember much more than what he's just told us.

I tell them what happened to the tiger: how the authorities made them take it to a zoo because, as an adult, it was a danger to the community; that my mother and grandad continued to visit the tiger regularly but that the tiger pined away shut up in its cage and finally died.

I'm so glad this man remembers the tiger. I always thought it was such a lovely story.

It seems they lived next door to each other until the war broke out. Their children often played at my mother's house. She was a decorous, gentle woman, says the man.

The conversation is interrupted repeatedly by Johan. You see? What did I tell you? He keeps trying to convince Diana.

The silences become longer and more frequent. After an hour, Diana has clammed up. Priscilla, who is irritated to death by Johan, has gone outside, as has Peter. Dennis lets out a noise now and again. Johan tries to salvage what he can from the situation.

The woman comes in with sour apples and sweet soya sauce. We often used to eat that at home, too. I'd completely forgotten. I haven't eaten it since my mother died.

I tell Diana and Johan that this is typically something our mother used to make for us. I do my utmost to call my mother our mother.

Johan gets really enthusiastic. He recognises the taste, he says, dipping the pieces of apple into the sauce bowl one after another. I'm sure he'd start remembering more about his mother if I served him the dishes we used to eat. That's what happened with me when I started cooking Indonesian food. The scents and the flavours bring back the memories.

The woman is pleased that her snacks are providing a happy ending to this rather awkward gathering.

When we leave, we thank her and her husband profusely for their hospitality and Peter takes a couple of pictures. It's the first time we've all been together in a photograph.

September 1991
Since the visit to my mother's old neighbours, Diana hasn't been feeling well. She has bad migraines and cries a lot. Unlike Johan, who

keeps remembering snatches, she can't recall a single thing about her mother.

When Johan was a child, for example, he once cut a leaf off a plant. He doesn't remember why. He only knows that his father punished him severely for it and remembers vaguely that it had something to do with his mother. Now I'm able to tell him that my mother always cut the leaves off the aloe vera. They're thick, fleshy leaves with a lot of juice in. She used to squeeze out the juice and rub it into my scalp, to make my hair grow long and strong. She must have done the same to Johan and Diana when they were little, too.

Johan keeps calling me with new questions. I dig into my memory, looking for answers. Now I've let him taste the kind of food we used to eat, maybe he'll remember even more. I think it's great that he wants to know so much about his mother.

I think Diana's jealous of the way Johan and I get on. She just can't remember her mother. She can only recall the nasty things that were said about her, and the cruel punishments our father gave them. She told me that he once made her clean her teeth with Vim as a punishment. It's an abrasive powder my mother used to use for cleaning and I remember the chemical smell well. What a bastard! She wasn't allowed to rinse the taste away with water. She had to drink rainwater out of a puddle to get rid of the taste.

Diana often felt humiliated. She can't connect anything positive with my mother. Sometimes it seems as if she actually resents the fact that I had a nice mother.

I count my blessings.

One day when I go round to her place, I take all the pictures I've got of my mother for her to see. I've got some duplicates that Auntie Bea and Auntie Lucia sent me. She can have those. After all, I've got my memories. Diana hasn't got anything. No memories and no pictures. When I visit her, she's still afraid the neighbours will guess that we're sisters. She doesn't dare talk to anybody. Dennis can only listen. He cries a lot, too.

October 1991

Johan has come up with a plan to confront his father with the good stories about our mother. Now Diana's angry with her father, too. She wants to tell him and his new wife that she and Johan are back in contact with me. And that they know their mother was a kind woman.

The woman he's married to doesn't even know I exist. She lives under the misapprehension that she's married to a widower with two children. Apparently she doesn't have anything to do with her own family any more, because of my father. He's abusing her kindness, Diana and Johan feel. They want him to stop all his lies. They want to prevent him from claiming any more victims.

They've decided to give him one more chance. If he apologises for the lies he spread about my mother and me, they'll forgive him. Otherwise they'll break off all contact. I've made it clear to them that I'll never be able to forgive him for what he did to my mother, me and my dog. I don't want to see him ever again. They understand.

I'm not sure that what they're planning to do is wise. Diana's such an unstable person, and Johan too, when it comes to it. Before you know it, there's going to be an accident. To be on the safe side I call Johan. I beg him to control himself if his father doesn't react in the way he hopes. It's not worth going back inside for something like that.

Think about Priscilla, I tell him. Think about your son.

He promises me he'll walk out if he's feels he's starting to get aggressive.

Just before the visit, I call Diana and Johan to wish them luck. I get Priscilla on the line. She's nervous. She thinks no good will come of any of this. When Johan comes to the phone I can hear how emotional he is.

He's surprised at himself, he says. He keeps having to throw up.

That's the frustration from all those years coming out, I tell him. I can't stop myself from asking him if he'll ask my father why I had to get rid of Nitadog. I want to confront him with it through Johan. Once more I urge him not to do anything to harm his father, whatever awful things he might say.

It's easy for me to hate my father. I've got nothing to lose.

Late in the evening Priscilla calls. In tears, she starts to tell me how it went.

My father remained seated in his chair like a dictator all evening. Every time Johan or Diana accused him of something, he waved it away. He denies everything, except making us kneel on the coconut mat. According to him, he gave us the punishments we deserved. He wasn't going to apologise for anything.

His wife, who couldn't believe her ears, walked out of the house halfway through the evening. Dennis just sat there crying.

Diana told him that she never wants to see him again.

When Johan said he didn't want to either, my father said he couldn't care less. He'd always thought he was a bad lot.

Priscilla had thought Johan would get aggressive, but he didn't. He cried like a child all the way home in the car. And now he's lost his voice. Priscilla's never seen him so upset.

I ask her if they asked about my dog.

The only thing my father said about Nitadog was that the animal had to be got rid of because it had mange.

I'm furious.

Spring 1992

Neither Johan nor Diana has made contact with my father for months now. He hasn't tried getting in touch with them, either.

I've hardly spoken to Johan and Priscilla since the whole incident. Johan's very tied up with his business, says Priscilla. She's pregnant with their second baby. I've noticed she's distant with me on the phone so I decide to drop it.

In the meantime, Diana's going from one depression to another. She's having therapy. She finds the contact with me difficult.

Diana would love to have children but that's impossible with Dennis. She thinks she might like to get back in touch with her father, but she's not sure if it's the right thing to do. She doesn't really dare talk to me about it. I've told her she should do what she feels is right. I can quite understand that our father has a different significance for her than he does for me.

I hear from Diana that Johan's back in prison. Priscilla obviously found it too painful to tell me.

I don't bother getting in touch with either of them again.

8

America

March 1996
I've had a letter from Auntie Lucia with sad news. She's ill. Her cancer is at an advanced stage and there's no point in having any more treatment. She would really like to see me one more time and invites me to go over to America with the whole family.

Right now, we haven't got a cent. There's no chance of the six of us making the trip. But I'd really like to see her, too.

Peter suggests I could go in April, when the child benefit comes in.

I decide to go for a week and write back to Auntie Lucia and Auntie Bea to tell them I'm coming. I just hope I'll be in time to see Auntie Lucia.

I feel nervous about making such a long trip on my own. I've never spent a day without the children since they were born. If anything happens to them, I won't be there. Peter's promised to take that week off work to look after them.

4 April 1996
Today I'm flying to Los Angeles where I'll be staying for exactly a week. I couldn't book anything shorter. Peter and the children wave me off at Schiphol Airport and I promise to bring them some presents from far-off America.

I find the flight terrifying. I keep listening to see if the engines stutter and keep a sharp eye on the stewardesses. I can't afford to crash. My children can't do without their mother, not yet. I'm relieved when we finally land.

Auntie Bea and her husband Gerrit are picking me up from the airport. I can see my aunt waiting in the arrivals hall. I recognise her from the photos. She's smaller than I'd thought.

We kiss. When she starts talking, I recognise my mother's voice. Auntie Bea's voice has the same melody. She pronounces her welcome, *selamat datang*, with a strong American accent. She hugs me and smiles a lot.

We drive to their place. On the way, we go through Beverly Hills and Hollywood. Uncle Gerrit shows me the celebrities' houses. He's obviously proud of America. There's not much left of his Dutch. There's so much to see.

Their house is in a suburb of Los Angeles. It's small and has a Spanish look. Behind the house is a garden with a pool. All the houses here have got pools. There are heavy bars across the doors and windows. When I comment on them, Uncle Gerrit says the place has really changed over the past few years. It used to be such a respectable neighbourhood, he says, but now it's all Mexicans living here. Luckily it's not as bad as further up, where the blacks live. You can't stop the car there, otherwise you get mugged. I can hear the bitterness in his voice.

Auntie Bea takes me into the kitchen. She's cooked a special meal for me. Over dinner, the conversation is peppered with familiar Indonesian words such as *masmira*, *adu* and *kassian*. I love it. It sounds so homely.

There's a garage in the garden where apparently their son lives. Auntie Bea explains that she can't call him in to join us. No one can talk to him. He came back crazy from the Vietnam War. One day, when the war was still in full swing, a taxi stopped in front of the house. It dropped him off at the door with a letter from the army. He hasn't spoken since. He lives in the dark in the garage. He's painted everything black and he sleeps in a crate. He only ever comes into the house for a little while to eat. A couple of times a week he gets picked up by a bus for therapy.

He knew my mother well, says Auntie Bea. He often played at her house when they still lived in Indonesia.

I can't get to sleep that night. I can feel the beginning of the jet lag and I miss my children. I hope they can sleep without the stories I usually tell them at bedtime. The youngest always wants me to sing her to sleep and kiss her goodnight loads of times. Peter must be

rushed off his feet there now that he has to do everything himself.
The bars in front of the windows make me feel insecure. Uncle
Gerrit's even got a gun by the bed. The thought of my cousin, who
I haven't seen yet, doesn't help to make me feel any safer, either. I
wonder how mad he actually is.

5 April 1996
This morning we're going to visit Auntie Lucia. She lives half an
hour's drive from Auntie Bea, in a suburb at the foot of the hills. It's
warm out, but in the house and car the air conditioning makes it feel
almost cold.

We've arranged for me to spend a couple of days with Auntie
Lucia because she's got a lot to tell me about my mother. Where she
lives is clearly more luxurious than Auntie Bea's neighbourhood. I
can see large houses with wide drives and a lot of well-kept gardens
with pools. There aren't any bars in front of the windows here.

The gardener lets us in. Auntie Lucia is sitting in a chair with her
legs up on a pouffe. She's got silver-grey hair and, for an Indonesian,
unusually light, green eyes. She looks less like my mother than Auntie
Bea does.

She gives me a big hug, holding me tight for a long time.

You look like your mother, she says.

That does me good.

Then the gardener comes in with some drinks and *lempers*. He got
them specially from the *toko* for me. Auntie Lucia tells me there are
lots of Indo-Europeans here. They came to California in the 1960s
and are all living next to each other in this neighbourhood.

It's almost an Indonesian ghetto, she jokes.

From the look in her eyes and the way she talks I can tell she's a
wise woman with a good sense of humour. She uses fewer Indonesian
expressions than Auntie Bea. Actually, she sounds really American.

I'm glad I came here.

After we've had something to eat and drink, Auntie Bea clears
away. Auntie Lucia can hardly do anything any more because of her
illness. She asks Uncle Gerrit to fetch a box containing all kinds of
pictures and letters from my mother that she's sorted out for me.
Then she starts to talk. About her work as a real estate agent. About

her husband, who she loved very much and who died a couple of years ago. About Indonesia. About the period just after they came out of the Japanese camp. For some time my mother and she lived in the same house.

Auntie Lucia talks and talks. Now and again I recognise snatches of the stories my mother told so often.

Then it's my turn. She asks about me and my family. She asks about Diana and Johan.

She can't help crying when she hears the lonely way my mother died. Auntie Bea cries, too, and even Uncle Gerrit has tears in his eyes.

I try to comfort them. Somehow, their grief isn't infectious. It makes me feel calm.

When Auntie Bea and Uncle Gerrit have left, Auntie Lucia suggests having a little lie-down. Her illness means she's in a lot of pain. I help her to her bedroom and cover her up.

Then I flop down on the bed in the spare room. I'm really tired from everything I've seen and heard. But I'm delighted with Auntie Lucia. She's a woman after my own heart and I'm sure she'll tell me a lot about my mother over the next few days.

In the evening we unpack the box of photos and papers. Auntie Lucia has written who's who on the back of all the photos for me. She shows me some pictures of her father and mother. My grandma and grandad. I've never seen them before. My grandad looks really Chinese. He was half Chinese and half German, Auntie Lucia tells me. He was called Carl August Christiaan Ludwig Gerke and he was a senior police officer. After the war, he stayed on in Indonesia. My grandma was called Christina Pauline Lucardie. She was half Italian and half Javanese and does, indeed, look like an Italian with some Asian features.

For the first time I make the connection with my second name, Christina. I must have been named after her.

Auntie Lucia has kept three letters from my mother. I recognise her handwriting and the scrap paper she wrote the letters on. She says I can have them. I decide to read them another time.

My mother obviously sent her photos of me. I see a picture of my first communion. I can't remember anything about it. There's also a picture of me holding a tame pigeon and a photo of my mother that I remember taking. There's a wedding picture of my parents and some lovely ones from Indonesia. My mother was a really pretty young woman.

Auntie Lucia has even got pictures of me as a baby, with my brother and sister. I've never seen those before.

At the end of the evening, Auntie Lucia tells me she hasn't got long to live.

I ask her if she's scared of dying.

Well, I've had a good, full life, she says. Anyway, since her husband died she doesn't see much point in living any longer. They didn't have any children. Auntie Lucia is spending her remaining days on a chair in front of the television and is tempted more and more often to buy things she sees advertised on TV that she doesn't need.

We need few words to understand each other. We make bizarre jokes, which she laughs heartily at. I can see from the way she talks about when she was young that she must always have been a liberated woman.

I tell her about my eventful past. I don't say anything about the Church of Satan but I do talk about my struggle to adjust and toe the line.

She confides in me that she loves gambling and would do anything to spend the last of her money in Las Vegas.

What's stopping you? I ask.

She bursts out laughing. Someone else who enjoys it, too, she says. She has trouble walking and needs help with the gambling.

I blurt out that I'd love to go with her and fulfil her wish. Actually I love gambling, too. I admit that I sometimes sneakily go to an amusement arcade in Amsterdam or have a sly go on the one-armed bandit in the snack bar or at the tobacconist's.

Gosh, *adu*, I hear her cry. It's the first time I've caught Auntie Lucia using an Indonesian expression.

I've got no idea how far Las Vegas is from here. Auntie Lucia says it's an eight-hour journey. I can't drive.

Right, then she'll ask Bea. She calls straight away. I can hear her tempting her sister over the phone. She offers her and Uncle Gerrit a few nights in a hotel if they'll take us. Auntie Bea discusses it with Uncle Gerrit. Auntie Lucia winks at me.

Uncle Gerrit will agree to anything if I'm treating them, she whispers to me. He's been bored out of his mind since he retired.

A few moments later, Auntie Bea says it's okay.

Auntie Lucia books a hotel for four days. Her eyes are shining at some private joke.

There's a surprise waiting for me in Las Vegas, she says.

6 April 1996
We take a long road through the desert. Uncle Gerrit is driving, singing along at the top of his voice with Frank Sinatra on the radio. He's trying to keep up our morale.

Auntie Lucia reclines in silence in the seat next to him. She's tired and her tummy's hurting. Auntie Bea's put a cool box full of food and drinks between us on the back seat and keeps offering me tasty snacks. It almost gets irritating.

The landscape looks just like the set of a cowboy film, exactly the kind of scenery I've seen so often on the television. Huge trucks with enormous, shiny, silver exhausts alongside the driver's cab thunder past us. Used car tyres lie by the side of the road. I wonder briefly how on earth you get help here if the car breaks down or you have an accident. There are no houses to be seen anywhere, just arid rocks and vast plains. I hope Uncle Gerrit will manage to get us safely to Las Vegas.

Finally, a restaurant looms up alongside the apparently endless road. We get out to freshen up.

Auntie Lucia doesn't look well. I help her to the toilet.

It's already dark by the time we drive into Las Vegas. This is another image I've often seen in films. Flickering lights and billboards everywhere. Couples in bridal attire queuing for the little wedding chapels standing between the gigantic illuminated advertisements that adorn the gambling joints. Fabulous façades have been built for the hotels. It looks as if every hotel has its own theme. There are castles, ships and waterfalls. A roller-coaster shoots out of the top floor of a tall hotel building with people hurtling through the air in little carriages down into another hotel. I feel really small and feast my eyes on all of it.

Auntie Lucia perks right up. She points out all kinds of places where she's had big winnings in the past.

At the end of The Strip, as they call the main street in Las Vegas, is a big hotel with CIRCUS CIRCUS on the sign.

Look, Karina, we're going to stay at the Circus. Auntie Lucia grins at me. She booked the hotel specially for me, after hearing what a good time I'd had in the circus as a child. The hotel is enormous. The foyer is crammed with slot machines. It's packed. Everything is decorated like in the circus. All the hotel staff are wearing circus costumes. Above my head real trapeze artistes fly through the air and everywhere you look circus performers are putting on their acts. At the same time, you can hear the tinkle of one-armed bandits. It sounds as if someone's winning the jackpot at every machine.

We check in and go to our rooms. Auntie Lucia is sharing a room with me. Auntie Bea and Uncle Gerrit are in the room next to us.

We agree that they'll go their own way for the next few days. Auntie Lucia and I are sticking together. I spot her slipping Auntie Bea some money with a mischievous look.

Don't say anything to Gerrit, she whispers. Auntie Bea quickly stashes the money away.

Later, Auntie Lucia explains that Bea also likes gambling but Uncle Gerrit thinks it's a waste of money. Now she can have a little flutter. She tells me she once slipped Auntie Bea some money and Bea suddenly won fifty thousand dollars when she was pretending to be in the toilet. Since then, she always slips her some money for luck.

I love that story. It goes along with gambling. It seems to be an unwritten rule that you never talk about your losses, but every gambler remembers the machine or the game where he won. It's only fun gambling with someone if you don't make a fuss about what you lose and know how to enjoy the moment you win, no matter how small the amount.

Auntie Lucia and I understand each other. Arm in arm, we walk through the hotel, looking for a machine that takes our fancy. We play for the rest of the evening. Tired from all the impressions and the excitement, we're in bed by about twelve. Auntie Lucia is exhausted and in pain, but she's enjoyed it thoroughly.

We can't get to sleep. In the dark, Auntie Lucia starts telling me about Indonesia. It reminds me of the past, when I used to lie in bed with my mother and she told me endless stories about the country she was so homesick for. But I soon discover a big difference between Auntie Lucia and my mother.

Auntie Lucia isn't homesick and says she never has been. Indonesia brings back other memories for her. She gets irritated by Indonesian people who tell romantic tales. She explains that the country was ruined by the colonial society.

As a child it was drummed into her that you belonged to a particular race. You weren't allowed to play with the native children, even if they lived in the same house as you, because their mother was a *babu* and cooked for you. At school, the Europeans and Indo-European children with mixed blood sat at desks, while the native children had their lessons squatting on the ground or went to separate little *dessa* schools.

Auntie Lucia always considered that unfair. Later, when she was older, she rebelled against the racial way of thinking and the class differences that prevailed there. She tells me you were categorised wherever you went. You were native, Chinese, an Arab or an Indo-European, not to be confused with an Indian or a European. The darker the colour of your skin, the lower your social position. Even in their own family it was a problem. She had green eyes and reddish hair and was therefore more highly regarded than my mother, with her Chinese looks, who was often discriminated against at school and later at work.

Auntie Lucia says my grandad fought against racism all his life. He too had problems with his Chinese appearance when he was young. After the war, he was forced by the government to choose what he wanted to be, Indonesian or Indo-European. If he chose to be an Indonesian, he would lose his job because he worked as a senior police officer in the service of the government. If he chose to be Indo-European, then he'd have to go to Holland. My grandad refused to choose and stayed on in Jakarta. In the end he was fired.

My grandma didn't dare choose to be an Indonesian. She looked European. She suffered terribly in the Jap camp and even after the war, during the Bersiap period, because of her light skin. A lot of white women were raped and mutilated or even murdered at that time. My grandma made the choice she did for her own safety and that of her daughters. With my mother, Auntie Bea and Auntie Lucia she left for the Netherlands, where she died within two years from homesickness and grief.

As a young girl, my mother always did what was expected of her, says Auntie Lucia. She was kind and caring, as befits a good Indonesian girl. Auntie Bea is like my mother. If she disagrees with something she keeps quiet. She'll never voice her own opinion, except when it comes to food. Then she knows exactly what's good and what isn't.

Be yourself, Auntie Lucia impresses on me. She says she can see a lot of herself in me. She'd already seen it when I was still a little girl.

Amazed, I ask her what she can remember about me.

She says she knew me until the age of four. She emigrated to America in 1964. Just long enough to know enough about you, she says lovingly.

I search my memory for images of Auntie Lucia and the only thing I can recall is her saying goodbye to my mother.

I can see her driving off in a car and ask if that's correct.

She confirms that she did, indeed, have a car, a gold Simca, really modern at that time. She remembers the parting very well.

I'm delighted with this shared memory. I don't know anyone else who can tell me anything about my childhood and I ask her what else she can remember about me.

She laughs and tells me that on my fourth birthday I went off to the primary school and sat down at an empty desk in the classroom because I'd heard that you could go to school when you were four. Of course I was not supposed to start school until after the summer holidays. When a teacher asked me what I was doing there, I told her that it was because I was four. Apparently I was really cross when the teacher and my mother explained that I could not start school until after the holidays.

The incident worried my mother. She was scared that I'd turn into a cheeky little girl, says Auntie Lucia, an attitude that was typical of your mother. Auntie Lucia had told her she thought what I'd done was good and made it clear that my mother should be proud of having such a daughter.

All the talking is wearing her out. We say goodnight.

I'm so glad I've met her just in time.

7 April 1996

The next morning we have breakfast in the hotel with Auntie Bea and Uncle Gerrit. Even that early in the morning they serve you in sequinned suits. The show must go on. I stare in amazement at the enormous breakfasts the Americans around me are putting away. I've never seen so many fat people together at one time. And it doesn't seem to bother them. Both men and women are wearing tight-fitting tracksuits that leave the fat free to roll. They don't make any attempt to hide the size of their bodies but wear their T-shirts tucked into their trousers instead of hanging outside them. I might be a couple of pounds overweight, but here I feel sylphlike.

Auntie Bea is going shopping with Uncle Gerrit in Las Vegas. Auntie Lucia and I didn't win anything last night and we're going to try our luck again today.

That night, lying in bed after a long day's gambling, with Auntie Lucia's dollars somewhat depleted, I ask about my mother and father's marriage. It's something that's been bothering me for years. How could my mother have lived with my father? I just can't imagine there having been anything between them, but there must have been.

Auntie Lucia says that, as young girls, they hung around a lot with the soldiers who were stationed all over Indonesia. First it was only the English and Canadians and, in fact, my mother was going to marry a Canadian. Auntie Lucia still remembers his name, Tommy O'Connor. They were engaged but then he had to go back to Canada so they got married by proxy, as a lot of girls did with soldiers from overseas. After that, my mother never heard from Tommy again.

One day, some Dutch soldiers arrived. One of them was my father. Auntie Lucia never liked him, she says, because he often behaved aggressively, but he could be really charming, too. My mother was seduced by his charm. But he mistreated her on a regular basis. That's why Auntie Lucia wouldn't have him in her house for some time.

I ask if she knew he'd been in prison.

Oh yes, she says, he was always getting arrested because he was often involved in fights. But as a senior police officer my grandad always managed to get him out one way or another. My grandma was very unhappy about my mother's choice, because she was afraid he would get her husband in trouble. They objected to the marriage for a long time but finally consented.

My mother and father were married in 1948. In 1956 they went to the Netherlands with the family. Only my grandad stayed behind. The parting was heartbreaking.

Auntie Lucia can still remember the voyage clearly. My grandma spent the whole trip crying in her cabin. In the meantime, her daughters amused themselves on board. It was a big steamship and there was dancing in the evenings. That's where Auntie Bea, who already had two children by an English soldier who died in the war, met Uncle Gerrit. He was working on the ship.

When they got to Holland it was snowing. They'd never seen snow before and they weren't dressed for it. On arrival woollen clothing was given out, which they had to pay through the nose for. You had no choice but to accept the accommodation you were allocated.

Auntie Lucia went with Auntie Bea and my grandma to a boarding house in Hilversum where they had to hand over almost all their money to the landlord. Auntie Lucia felt like a prisoner. You weren't allowed to do anything, not even work. Everything was decided for you, even how often you were allowed to take a shower. That was once a week, while she was used to bathing twice a day. She finally found a job and somewhere to live in Rotterdam. She got a loan for the things she needed to furnish the place, which took her years to pay off.

Auntie Lucia thought that was unreasonable. They had suffered so much in the Japanese camps and afterwards and when they got to Holland they weren't welcome. Nobody understood what it had been like in Indonesia. People only talked about the war against the Germans. The Indonesian people kept quiet about it. Auntie Lucia hated that attitude.

My mother went to live with my father's parents. That was on a farm, somewhere in the woods by the Belgian border. She was terribly homesick. She was expected to help with the work on the farm. Auntie Lucia can remember my mother writing to her once that she had to pick sprouts in the freezing cold and that everyone found her strange and made fun of her. They'd never seen an Indonesian before.

A year later, they got their own place in Leiden, where my father went to work in a canning factory. It was during those years that we were born. When my mother was pregnant with me, Auntie Lucia stayed with her a lot. My father had already gone off with another woman. He came home occasionally and argued with my mother. Auntie Lucia tells me she was there once when my father kicked her swollen belly, with me inside. My mother lost a lot of blood after that and was scared she would lose me.

The day I was born my father left for good and Auntie Lucia moved in to look after us. When I was about one, he came and demanded custody of all three children. Auntie Lucia still can't understand why. He was so heartless.

He married the other woman and managed to get custody of the two older children. How he managed that, Auntie Lucia doesn't know. They argued a lot and it's possible he went telling tales to the court. She can remember nasty stories being spread about my mother. I was still being breast-fed; that's probably why they let me stay with her.

He kept trying to take me away from my mother until I was about eight. Likewise, my mother tried to regain custody of Johan and Diana, but couldn't. A woman on her own on benefit wasn't a good basis for bringing up children, the court felt. My mother missed Johan and Diana so badly that all her hair fell out. She was bald for ages.

Just before Auntie Lucia left for America, they went secretly to take a look at Johan and Diana in the school playground in The Hague, where my father was then living. My mother didn't dare call them over. She just watched them playing and cried.

It hurts to hear how much grief my mother suffered, but what Auntie Lucia's telling me about her does me good, too. Now I can understand better why she was so scared of losing me.

My father I understand less and less. Why did he put so much effort into getting us away from my mother when he treated us so badly? I feel a deep hatred towards him that I don't think I will ever lose.

Auntie Lucia thought it was awful in Holland. She found it a narrow-minded, cold country. She felt very lonely there. She worked hard but she was looked down on because Indonesian people had the reputation of being lazy and unreliable.

In the early days she tried to explain who she was and where she came from and what work she could do. Time after time she tried to point out the difference between Indo-Europeans and Indonesians, until she grew tired of it and noticed she could only feel happy with other Indo-Europeans. When she realised how quiet she had become, she knew she had to get out of Holland.

She couldn't go back to Indonesia, but with government support it was possible for Indo-Europeans to emigrate to Los Angeles. Together with Auntie Bea, who couldn't get used to the Dutch ways either, that's what she did.

9 April 1996
Three days of non-stop gambling is beginning to take its toll. We haven't been out of the hotel and I haven't seen sunlight since we arrived. I'm cold all the time and tired. My biorhythm is completely disturbed. Auntie Lucia is exhausted and in a lot of pain, but there's no stopping her.

We don't win anything much. Now and then a hundred dollars, which we immediately bet again. At the end of the afternoon it's getting almost embarrassing. I'm sitting next to Auntie Lucia, supporting her body with my left arm. She can't sit upright any longer by herself. With my right hand I hold her arm so she can still throw the last few dollars into the slot in the machine herself.

Then we call it a day. She stumbles back to our room with me, I help her into bed and she falls asleep almost at once. I lie down myself; I'm worn out. I listen to the muffled sounds from the hotel. In the background I can hear marching music. It's just the kind of music we used to play during the circus performances, with drum-rolls while the excitement builds. I can hear the ringmaster far away continually announcing the next number and it brings back memories of Rob and my mother.

I wonder what kind of woman my mother really was. Auntie Lucia sees her as someone who was always accommodating others, someone who resigned herself to her fate. I remember another woman. I knew her in the happy times with Rob, kissing and cuddling passionately. She was definitely a caring and loving person, but she was creative as well. She could draw and paint beautifully. Maybe it's true what Auntie Lucia says, that she withdrew from the world, but she also went her own way and did her own thing.

She was proud, too. She never wanted to accept anything from anybody. Not from Rob and not from the church, either. I can remember someone from the church bringing round a basket of fruit every Christmas until I was about ten and she refused to accept it. I thought it was a shame because I could see all kinds of fresh and tinned fruit under the cellophane. But my mother didn't want to be provided for by charitable organisations. She considered it humiliating that the church gave out fruit baskets to poor people.

She wasn't poor, she always told me, they'd be better off giving those things to someone who really needed them.

But however proud she might have been, she didn't hesitate to rescue things from other people's rubbish so that she could make something new out of them with me at home. Old pram wheels became carts, and we built dens out of pieces of old furniture in the back room, sometimes with more than one storey.

If I imagine her more as a woman than as a mother, which I've actually never done before, I realise that we shared an unusual amount of intimacy. I knew exactly when she was overwhelmed with longing for Rob. We made ourselves beautiful together when he was coming to see us. And I can remember the times we lay in bed together when Rob wasn't there. Sometimes we masturbated. We called it fondling. We agreed not to look if we noticed the other was fondling. That was something private.

I still remember the shock it gave me when were told in sex education that fondling was the same as masturbating. I thought everyone did that with their mother and everybody called it fondling. It was also at school that I learnt that the nice feeling you get with fondling was called an orgasm. Masturbating, we were told, was something it was better not to do.

Apart from a great deal of intimacy, my mother also gave me an extraordinary amount of respect. She never forbade me to enjoy my own body and she never neglected to enjoy her own. She let me see her tremendous feelings of love for Rob and shared them with me, but never confronted me with their sexuality. I never saw them actually making love, except that one time I sneaked a look through the gap in the curtains. It was such a bewildering sight that I never peeped again. The strange thing is that now, as a grown woman, if I find myself in a similar situation, it really turns me on. Obviously the image of Rob holding my mother's bare buttocks under the dress he had lifted hasn't affected my sensuality.

In the background the ringmaster continues to introduce one act after another. Who was my mother really, apart from a mother? What was she interested in, apart from drawing? We didn't have any books at home. She did tell me once that they had a piano in Indonesia, which she often played. I don't know what kind of music she liked because we always tuned the radio to the music I liked.

She always wanted to listen to the news, though. She liked to read the papers, too, I remember, and took an interest in politics. She admired Marga Klompé, the first right-wing lady minister, but voted for the Pacifist Socialist Party.

I delve into my memories, searching for a woman I will never know, searching for my mother, who I realise was an extraordinary woman.

Auntie Lucia groans. She turns over. It seems that even sleeping hurts. I look at her dishevelled silver-grey hair and find myself chuckling at her, none the less. She's totally exhausted. We really did knock ourselves out today.

10 April 1996
We set off from Las Vegas in the early morning. Auntie Lucia sleeps throughout the journey.

Back in Los Angeles we take her home. Her gardener is already waiting for us. We have something to drink, but then we can't put off saying goodbye any longer.

Auntie Lucia gets up out of her chair with difficulty. We hug and I thank her for everything, the photographs, the letters, her stories, Las Vegas and the hotel she so thoughtfully booked.

It's all right, girl, she says, it's all right.

We end our hug in silence. Auntie Lucia doesn't walk with us to the car. It's better that way.

We drive to Auntie Bea and Uncle Gerrit's. Tomorrow I'm going back to Holland so they want to take me out to dinner.

Their son from the garage is coming, too.

He's quite a bit shorter than me and dark. Really looks like an Indonesian. A *katjong*, my mother would say. He doesn't look strange, or mad, but his clothes are dirty and he smells. He walks to the car with us in silence.

In the car Auntie Bea rattles away. She's evidently having difficulty with the fact that we'll soon have to say goodbye and is being extra cheerful. I let her get on with it, she's doing it for my sake. Auntie Bea talks about my mother and about Indonesia. They're stories of homesickness and longing. The only thing missing is the *kroncong* music.

This is Auntie Nita's daughter, she says to her son.

Then very quietly, but still understandably, he mumbles two words. *Kazan. Kazan*, he says.

Auntie Bea falls silent, all the colour draining from her face.

I ask her what he said.

'Did you hear that, Gerrit? He said something,' she stammers. She tries to get him to say more but he stares into the middle distance in silence.

I ask Auntie Bea what *kazan* means. Maybe he means *kassian*?

Then Auntie Bea, who still hasn't got the colour back in her cheeks, tells me that Kazan was the name of the dog my mother had in Indonesia. She was his favourite aunt.

We have dinner on my last evening in America at the Thai restaurant where Auntie Bea and Uncle Gerrit often eat. The atmosphere is a lot like McDonald's. Everything is served in disposable cartons, which you can take home. The choice is limited and it's just enough but it tastes good. Of course it's easier for Auntie Bea to come here instead of standing for hours in the kitchen. Uncle Gerrit probably makes high demands on her cooking skills. Good thinking on Auntie Bea's part, actually.

Auntie Bea and Uncle Gerrit have gone quiet. Their son, too, has reverted to absolute silence. Nobody feels like a lavish meal any more. We choose something simple. Auntie Bea fishes out the strings of rice vermicelli from her soup with disposable chopsticks. Uncle Gerrit completely forgets to argue about the difference between real Indonesian food and what you get at the Thai restaurant.

5 May 1996

Auntie Bea has just called to say that Auntie Lucia's died. She passed away peacefully, she says.

Liberation Day. What a good day to die. It doesn't feel solemn or sad, but I want to be alone for a while. Peter understands and takes the kids to the Liberation Day street market in Vondelpark. I go and sit in the garden and take out my folder, which now also contains the letters and photographs I got from Auntie Lucia in America.

I look at the photo of her when she was young. A pretty, clever, smart woman.

It's all right, girl, it's all right, I can still hear her saying when we parted. No matter how American she might have wanted to be, she pronounced that word 'girl' with a hell of an Indonesian accent. Some things never wear off.

The visit to America has brought me a lot of peace. It's important to know where you come from, what your history is. It's great if someone can tell you about your childhood, when someone knows what kind of child you were. Shared memories are vital. Now I'm far less introspective than I was. I can understand my sensitivities better. I have something to share.

I still get worked up when I hear anything about racial violence, but now I can see it's always been there and always will be. It's a great comfort to know that it wasn't only my mother who was discriminated against. If I'm really honest, she was prejudiced, too, and now and again I catch myself at it.

Auntie Lucia's criticism of the colonial system in the country she came from has made me look at my own history in a different way. The stories my mother told me were lovely, and I wouldn't want to have missed them as a child, but they were full of homesickness, of passively submitting to your fate. My mother made her past sound nicer than it really was. Perhaps that was her way of surviving.

Auntie Lucia, on the other hand, saw through the system and resisted the nice stories because they justified what happened later. She was never able to reconcile herself to it.

I hold a picture of my mother next to the photo of Auntie Lucia. They were both young and pretty and grew up in a well-to-do family. But they were very different, nevertheless. It wasn't just the colour of their eyes and skin that determined their futures, as Auntie Lucia would have had me believe; it was also their characters. My mother was loving and caring, Auntie Lucia clever and bold.

Even so, it's not as simple as all that. Since meeting Auntie Lucia I've started to look more critically at my mother and no longer see her only as caring and loving. She is no longer quite the ideal mother.

In Leiden, when she fell ill, whichever way I look at it, she let me down. I was a child. She knew I wasn't being looked after at home. She saw the mess the flat was in. She knew there often wasn't anything to eat.

For years, I made all kinds of excuses for her. She was ill. She was frightened. More than anything, she didn't want them to take me away from her and send me to live with my father. She knew I'd be worse off with him.

But she was a grown woman. She was my mother. She should have organised help for me. That would have really been caring. I was a child. I didn't know any better; things were just the way they were.

What stopped her? Was it perhaps, if only subconsciously, because of an unresolved feud with my father? She probably knew I'd end up with him. It must have been unthinkable for her to lose her last child to him. But then it was about a struggle between them, of which I became the victim. If only I could have talked to her about these things just one more time. That's probably the most unbearable part of her being dead, that so many questions will remain forever unanswered.

Maybe the feud between my parents was the reason my father had me to live with him. It had nothing to do with my well-being, any more than with Johan and Diana's well-being. But it would have meant that he'd won.

Auntie Lucia has made my own story more complete, in any case. I don't blame my mother. And I can't tell whether I would have been less lonely if there had been the help I needed. Losing your mother too young is simply painful. Damned painful.

I do blame my father, though, but that's probably because I've never loved him. He should have been a real father and loved me, but he couldn't. I still don't want to know why.

It would have done my brother and sister so much good to have had the love my mother could have given them – until she died, in any event. She might not have had so much to offer as my father from a material point of view but it's love that makes you strong, not expensive things. My father's incapacity to love has had a debilitating effect on all of us.

His way of bringing up children was based on intimidation and punishment. I can still remember how it felt the first time he hit me. I've forgotten why he hit me, I've forgotten the physical pain too, but the indignation, the impotent, furious feeling of injustice have remained with me. I didn't gain any insight from it, as my father possibly hoped I would. It didn't contribute to the development of my conscience; it hasn't made me see the consequences of my actions. It didn't achieve anything, except to humiliate me.

My mother set me a good example and I'm eternally grateful to her for that. She never hit me. She discussed the whys and wherefores of certain things with me and that enabled me to judge better next time whether it was a good idea to do something or not. She let me make my own decisions. She gave me responsibility, but she trusted me, too.

It hasn't saved me from making the wrong decisions sometimes. I was fully aware of what I was doing when I went to work at the Church of Satan, but it was my choice and it was I who finally decided it wasn't right. Perhaps my time at the Church of Satan left such a bad taste in my mouth because I did it of my own free will. Would the taste have been less bitter if someone had forced me to work there? Then at least I would have had an excuse.

The feeling that I sold myself cheaply goes deep. So deep that I can't sleep in the nude any more. A couple of times a night I get fully dressed while I'm half asleep, panicking that everyone can see me naked. Just when I've got all my clothes on I wake up.

When I look at the photographs that Auntie Lucia gave me I remember an unusual but, despite everything, good childhood, even though I had never looked at it like that before.

My mother understood the importance of play. Maybe she taught me the most by setting no limits to my play. Playing with rubbish was normal for me, but now I can see the real value of our back room. Here I could build and fantasise endlessly and keep trying to do things better. I lived in many houses in my own home.

Something else I've only just come to realise is how much I learned from the circus. Everyone's got a talent. Everything and everyone was useful and useable. You were appreciated for what you were good at and that was often more than one thing. No matter how much pain your act involved, you continued smiling during the performance. After the curtains closed, you could curse everything and everybody, but during the performance everyone acted out his role. The circus was based on cooperation and trust.

You had to perform your act well. If anything went wrong, you had to do it again. That's an old circus law. The audience often wasn't aware of it and thought they were being treated to three *saltos mortale*, while we knew that the first two hadn't gone right.

I still occasionally miss the freedom I felt as a child in the circus.

The sun is shining. Now and again a little cloud passes. Planes draw white stripes across the sky.

It's lovely and peaceful in the garden. My bleached blond Amsterdam neighbour, the kind of woman my mother was scared of, is going indoors with a screaming child under her arm.

I don't want you to turn out like that, my mother often said. On one occasion she really meant it. That was the moment when she closed the curtains for good. She should never have done so, no matter how hard the ice ball hit her in the eye. Neither should she have said that I wasn't to turn out like other children. There was nothing I would rather have been than like other children. I wanted to belong.

I often think about Auntie Lucia. I hope she just passed away in her sleep. I didn't think of asking Auntie Bea how she died. The prospect of dying didn't bother Auntie Lucia, or at least that's what she said. I think it made a difference that she didn't have any children.

I try to imagine what it was like for my mother in her final hours. Why did she have to die on the one day I wasn't there? On the one day when I went to a party instead of visiting her, she slipped away. Was that her way of leaving quietly? Maybe dying takes a lot out of you and the last thing you need is a child around. If that's the way it was, I can accept it. I'm glad I was able to say goodbye to Auntie Lucia, anyway.

It's all right, girl. My mother would have said it just like that.

I search amongst the papers in my folder for the letter Auntie Lucia gave me. It's a letter my mother wrote her when I was seven or eight. The curtains are still open. It's not dated.

Dear Lucia,
How are you all? It's Boxing Day and I'm sitting here all by myself writing this letter. I drew the curtains wide to watch the falling snow.

Karina is getting big. I can hear Christmas music coming through the walls from everywhere. Karina was chosen to play Mary yesterday. She really did her best. The mayor shook her hand and paid her a compliment. It was in the church with real, live animals. She had to ride a donkey and was dressed as Mary. At the altar there was a newborn baby in the crib. The church was packed. They filmed it and took photographs.

Karina is a real beauty. The bigger she gets, the prettier she gets, too. Her hair is down to her waist now. Luckily she's not vain, that's what I teach her, to be as modest as possible. They get conceited so young here, if they're just a little bit pretty, particularly those Indonesian girls. Luckily Karina's not like that.

She's been in the paper quite a few times already. That time with her communion and at the priest's party. Now she'll be in the Leiden paper. They've filmed her lots of times already. She's so natural. She can skate well, too. Everybody enjoys that child. She looks so sweet on her white figure skates.

I get a lot of pleasure from her, too, she's really sweet to me and obedient. That's lucky, isn't it? Let's hope it stays that way. Well, Lucia, that's about it. Write back quickly, too, won't you? Karina is really longing for a letter from you.

Lots of love,
Karina and Nita

I don't remember the communion, shaking hands with the mayor or playing Mary in the Nativity play. I do remember longing for a letter from America because it always had dollars in it. We bought those skates with the dollars Auntie Lucia sent us. I was crazy about the ice. I loved skating fast and turning pirouettes until I got dizzy.

My mother was always scared I'd have an accident and one day I skated on to thin ice and went through. Somehow I got myself out but my clothes were soaking wet and white smoke was coming off me. I can still clearly remember going home with my trousers frozen stiff. My mother rubbed me warm with coconut oil, so hard that I was red all over. She kept telling me that I was *tolol*, a silly twit. She was really cross with me for not being careful enough.

From the letter, I can sense that she was lonely and proud of her daughter. She hadn't met Rob yet, then. She never told Auntie Lucia about him or the circus either. I wonder why? I'll never know. My mother keeps her secrets.

My thoughts wander all over the place. Suddenly, I remember a maxim from the time of the domestic science school in Den Bosch. *A clever girl is always prepared for her future.* There was a poster of that in every classroom. What would I have done if I'd had more education, if my life had been less turbulent? I think I'd have gone on to university. Maybe I'd have become a journalist or a lawyer. Wanting to expose injustice was something I was keen on from an early age.

I hardly remember anything from primary school. I've forgotten even the spelling rules and the times tables they drummed into our heads, while I remember everything I learned at home and at the circus.

Looking back, I think the domestic science school in Leiden has a lot to answer for. They must have known I was living alone. They knew, in any case, that I was neglected because I was dirty and must have stunk. They should have intervened. And why did I get sent to a domestic science school anyway? I didn't learn anything there. I think I could have done much better. Didn't anybody see that? The domestic science school in Den Bosch also taught me little but they did offer the help and care I needed at the right time.

When Peter and the children come home, I put away my photographs and letters. The children are exhilarated. They've got balloons and have had ice-creams and now they're hungry. I put my folder in its usual place and go and cook the dinner.

I'm so glad I was able to get to know Auntie Lucia. Four days of Las Vegas was long enough. She helped me just by being who she was.

I don't want to be my mother's daughter any longer.

I'm a mother myself now. I'm a grown woman with four children and I'm responsible for equipping them for society.

One day my children will have to get to know me as a woman, too. How do I explain to them that, as a woman, I'm different from the mother they know?

I can't make the story any nicer. It's my story.

It's the story of a child who became a mother.

Afterword

In the autumn of 2003, I put the finishing touches to this book. The folder I brought from Leiden has now grown into more than thirty ring binders and these have formed the basis of the book. They contain documents, letters and photographs of all kinds of people from my past.

Diana last contacted me in September 2003 after a gap of several years. She told me that Dennis had been dead for three years already and that she was getting married again, this time to a Belgian. They now live in a village in Belgium. Diana's a housewife and doesn't work. She is still struggling to come to terms with her past.

I asked how Johan was. I haven't spoken to him for years. Neither has she, says Diana. All she can tell me is that he's back in prison, for five years this time. She no longer has any contact with his wife Priscilla and their children.

Diana sees our father regularly; according to her, he hasn't changed a bit.

I still don't want to see him.

In 1998, I visited San's mother in my old street in Leiden. Her husband had been killed in a car accident. San is married and has two children. Her nan and grandpa are dead.

I kept all the letters from Rob Roberti. In the summer of 2003 I tried to track him down but the telephone number he gave in his last letter was unobtainable and the winter quarters of the circus have been abandoned. The town hall in Aalsmeer was able to tell me that he died in 1999.

I've been back in contact with former artistes Tony Wilson and Olga Schelfhout, now Andreas's widow, since the autumn of 2003.

Olga turned out still to have a lot of pictures from my time in the circus. She sent them to me.

I see Marian at least once a year. She has several grandchildren by now and still lives with her husband at the same address.

Wim and Joop from De Druif I've never seen again. John died when he crashed his motorbike into the law court in Den Bosch.

Pim de la Parra now lives in Suriname and has stopped making films.

For years I used to bump into Herman Brood regularly in the street and we chatted and caught up with each other's news. From the moment he started going around with a parrot on his head, letting the creature shit all over his still luxuriant hair, he stopped recognising me when he passed. Then I knew the alcohol and drugs had done their destructive work. It took longer than I expected because he was tough as old boots, but I wasn't surprised when he finally jumped off the roof of the Hilton.

The day he was cremated or, as his fans would rather have it, flambéed, the funeral procession happened to pass just as I was coming out of a shop. Like so many other people lining the road, I stood still, watching. Just as the hearse drew up to where I was standing, it broke down. It was a while before the procession could continue. A crowd gathered around the cortège, with everyone cheering and clapping, but it was just as if Herman and I observed a moment's silence together.

It was a wonderful moment. I couldn't have wished for a better way to say goodbye to him. We met by chance and it was by chance that we were able to bid each other farewell.

The Church of Satan in Amsterdam doesn't exist any more. In 1988, the court in Amsterdam convicted Maarten, the ex-boss, of tax evasion running into several millions. He went abroad and now lives in a castle in France.

The Church of Satan does still exist in America and a number of other countries within and outside Europe. Anton Szandor La Vey, at that time head of the whole organisation, died in 1997.

Elvira married a client. I still bump into her now and again.

After the Church of Satan closed down, Nancy started her own club.

I haven't seen Afa, Eve or Ann since.

I do come across ex-clients regularly.

Yvette is still my best friend. Now she's got two children. After she finished her studies, she opened what has become a busy sandwich bar. Her mother wandered the streets for a long time and finally died.

In 1996, I took the Municipality of Amsterdam to court. I had, naturally, entrusted my children to the local school which, unfortunately, turned out to be a bad school. It took a court case to identify just who, exactly, was responsible for the poor quality of the education at my children's school.

In going to court over this issue, I had set the cat among the pigeons. Partly due to my own history, I have been convinced that a good education should never depend on the parents' attentiveness or the depth of their pockets; it is every child's right.

Through this court case, which, including the appeal, ran until 1999, I often came into contact with politicians. I won the case, became a member of a political party, specialised in educational matters and took part in many debates throughout the Netherlands. In 2000 I published *School Fight*, in which I reported on the Dutch government's policy on education. In that book I wanted to show how deep the cleft is between political propaganda and harsh, everyday reality.

In 2002 I stood as a candidate for the local elections and was elected as a counsellor.

My work as a counsellor suits me down to the ground. I'm the spokesperson for Education and I serve on the Social Services, Education, Youth and Diversity Committee. The ideal portfolio for me.

When I noticed that my turbulent past was starting to undermine my political credibility, I decided to write this book. At that point I had been confronted a couple of times with my past, for instance when I came across ex-client Menno at a political meeting. Our eyes met. I saw that he recognised me and I didn't like the look he gave me.

I started to wonder increasingly whether it was sensible to remain politically active. I'm scared of something about my past in the Church of Satan getting into the newspapers. A story like that, taken out of context, could cause problems for my children.

In my role as a politician I'm often approached by journalists, wanting to ask me ordinary questions about my background and what drives me, but I've had too disrupted a youth to be able to answer ordinary questions.

What brought you to Amsterdam?

What kind of family did you grow up in?

What kind of education have you had?

Every answer I give will prompt further questions.

In December 2002 I told my colleague Rob Oudkerk what had happened. Apart from being my party leader, he was also a general practitioner. I trusted him with my past. As an experienced politician, he knows, more than anybody, what representation in the media can do to you.

Should I remain active in politics or not? He was able to support and advise me at just the right moment in this difficult process of deliberation.

You've got a full past, he said, but you've got a future, too.

Burn those devils.

Time after time he held a mirror to my face. It helped me to make a well-considered decision. I decided to stay. I wasn't going to let them walk all over me.

It does mean, however, that I've had to come out with my story. If I want to continue in politics, I can't avoid publicising my past. I looked through my binders to sort out all the material that could be used against me and, in doing so, mapped out my life during the summer holidays of 2003.

Gradually, my story took on the contours of this book.